M000201023

Perfect Season Project

An Uncommon Arrangement of
Cleveland Indians History

Alex Harnocz

Copyright © 2020 Alex Harnocz

All rights reserved. No part of this book may be reproduced or
transmitted in any form or by any means, electronic or mechanical,
including photocopying, recording, or by any information storage
and retrieval system without the written permission of the author,
except for the use of brief quotations in a book review.

First Edition 2020

ISBN: 978-0-5786835-0-8

Ludicrum Press
Cleveland, Ohio

Cover Design, Casey Fritz

For Felix and Ezra

May you always be brave enough to try something new.

"People ask me what I do in winter when there's no baseball. I'll tell you what I do. I stare out the window and wait for spring."

- *Rogers Hornsby*

An Explanation of the Rules

Like chess, jazz, and the rest of humanity's most interesting inventions, baseball is a source of boundless variety. Baseball is brilliant because there are an infinite number of outcomes possible in every pitch, every play, every game. Every moment spent following baseball has the potential to reveal something baffling, amazing, or never before seen. That variety was my inspiration for the Perfect Season Project.

Baseball does not obey the clock. It takes its own time. Unlike other professional sports, baseball is only loosely tied to the calendar. Travel days, rainouts, double-headers, labor strikes, and natural disasters can and do alter the baseball calendar. The season plays out game by game, independent of time constraints. Perfect Season Project was created to explore the most noteworthy game in Indians history for each *game* in the baseball calendar.

Perfect Season Project covers the franchise now known as the Cleveland Indians. The team was a charter member of the American League when it was established in 1901. Several professional ballclubs existed in Cleveland before 1901, but for consistency this project sticks to the Indians.

Perfect Season Project was laid out with two simple rules:

- **One entry for each game in the 162-game season**
- **The Indians must always win.**

It is not hard to find an "On This Day" accounting of baseball history. There are newspaper columns, blogs, and twitter accounts of all stripes that attract eyeballs by recounting what happened on the diamond on a particular date. However, as noted above, baseball does not follow the calendar.

That raised a question for me. Since 1901, have the Indians won each game, 1 through 162, at least once? A database search revealed that they had.

If so, what is the most memorable, unique or interesting Game 1, Game 2, Game 3 and so on…

It started with a spreadsheet. A simple grid with 162 rows for each game of the regular season. A few rows were filled in with the

1

hallmark games in franchise history: Perfect games, cycles, no-hitters and the like. Next up were the oddities: stealing home, immaculate innings, suicide squeeze plays. The spreadsheet was filled in further with record-setting performances and milestones. Walk-off wins and amazing pitching performances from all eras and decades colored in additional cells. Finally, games highlighting performances of Cleveland's most memorable and interesting players rounded out the Perfect Season.

However; according to Rule 2, amazing plays, record-breaking performances, and outstanding achievements cannot be included if they occurred in the course of a loss.

Lots of ink has been spilled about "the greatest games in Indians history." Some of the usual suspects will appear here, but many more unique and unusual games are highlighted. Perfect Season Project compresses 120 years of Cleveland baseball history, in all of its infinite variety and beauty, into 162 games where something incredible happens every day. In short, a *Perfect Season.*

Game 1
April 16, 1940
Bob Feller's Opening Day No-Hitter

The 1940 season began on a chilly day on the south side of Chicago. With a high temperature of 48 degrees, the bats were not expected to be hot. Blustery winds off Lake Michigan held the crowd down to just about 14,000. Few of those fans could have predicted that they would witness a piece of baseball history that has yet to be repeated.

In his fourth season in the League and second year as the Indians' Opening Day starter, Bob Feller was maturing into full dominance. Feller came to the Major Leagues directly from high school at age 17. His fastball was the stuff of legend. In the absence of radar gun technology, "Rapid Robert" once raced his fastball against a motorcycle in Chicago's Lincoln Park at the request of the MLB Commissioner.

Game 1 of the 1940 season would only further Feller's legendary status. Feller striking out the talented Luke Appling looking to begin the second inning. Then, Chicago outfielder Taffy Wright reached on an error by Roy Weatherly. Feller recorded another strikeout, but after several walks, the bases were loaded. Feller struck out rookie Bob Kennedy to quell the threat.

The Indians lone run came on an RBI triple from Rollie Helmsley in the top of the fourth inning. After settling in from some early walks, Feller was in the groove. He retired 20 straight Sox on the way to his greatest test of the game.

With two outs in the ninth, future Hall of Famer Luke Appling battled Feller for a 10-pitch at-bat. Appling fouled off four two-strike pitches and finally drawing a walk. With the tying run at first, Taffy Wright stepped in for Chicago. He smashed a hard-hit ball to the right side of the infield. Rookie second baseman Ray Mack made a diving stop and narrowly threw out Wright at first to seal the game and complete the first and still only Opening Day no-hitter.

"I think I've thrown faster several times," Feller said following the game. "Of course, the wind behind me helped make me faster. But I couldn't seem to throw a curve very well."

Randy Johnson was perhaps the closest to matching this feat. In the first Home Opener at Jacobs Field in 1994, Johnson took a no-hitter into the eighth inning.

Feller was in the press box at that game, pacing the aisles and urging the team to get a hit. Feller was visibly relieved when Sandy Alomar poked a single between first and second base in the bottom of the 8th to keep his 54-year-old feat unique in the history of the game. He celebrated with the rest of Cleveland when Wayne Kirby won the game for the Tribe with a single in bottom of the eleventh.

Game 2
April 4, 2001
455 Game Sellout Streak Ends

The period between June 12, 1995 (see page 83) and April 4, 2001 will always represent one of the great love affairs between a City and its team. In 1995, John Hart and Dick Jacobs had cultivated a team of home-grown talent that was coming into its prime. Cuyahoga County's smokers and drinkers had funded the beautiful new retro-modern Jacobs Field via the infamous "sin tax." Perhaps most importantly, the Browns had just moved to Baltimore. This left both civic affections and corporate season-ticket dollars adrift and looking for a new home. From 1995 onward, the Indians were a juggernaut, dominating public affection and water cooler talk in Cleveland.

Five years on, however, the shine on the new stadium had begun to wear off. The Browns had returned as an expansion team to a new--if hastily constructed--home on the lakefront, and much of the core of the late-90's team had departed for greener pastures and bigger contracts.

Kenny Lofton, Omar Vizquel, Jim Thome, Manny Ramirez, Sandy Alomar, Paul Shuey, and Chuck Nagy were the only veterans present throughout the entire 455 game sellout streak. The Indians were sellers at the trade deadline during the 2000 Season, moving promising outfielder Richie "Big Sexy" Sexson and veteran David Justice prior to the trade deadline.

After a long winter, Cleveland loves a reason to call off work and perhaps do some day drinking. Along with St. Patrick's Day and Dyngus Day, the Home Opener has long been an excuse to skip work or school and turn Downtown Cleveland into a party. That was the case on Monday April 2nd when 42,606 packed into the Jake to watch the Indians lose to the White Sox in Game 1.

Two days later on April 4th, Chuck Finley faced Cad Eldred in Game 2. After 11 years with the Indians, 2001 was catcher Sandy Alomar Jr.'s first year with the White Sox. In the top of the 2nd, Sandy launched a home run off Finley, scoring Herbert Perry (another former Indian).

5

In the bottom of the second, Eldred gave up a leadoff walk to Jim Thome and consecutive singles to Ellis Burks and Jacob Cruz. Russell Branyan struck out swinging with the bases loaded (this would become a familiar refrain in 2001). Ed Taubensee, Alomar's replacement behind the plate was hit by the next pitch, forcing in Thome. Consecutive singles by Kenny Lofton, Omar Vizquel, and Sandy's younger brother Roberto Alomar gave the Tribe a 5-2 lead.

The Indians manufactured another run in the bottom of the fourth inning, and extended the lead via a Russel Branyan home run in the bottom of the fifth to cruise to an 8-4 victory.

The sellout streak ended with only 32,763 fans present for the first night game of the year. At the time, the stadium seemed empty. In fact, this would be a near-capacity crowd today as Progressive Field's seating has been reduced to 35,041 as a result of several renovations.

From 2003 to 2013, the Boston Red Sox sold out Fenway Park for 820 straight games, nearly doubling the Indians streak of the 1990's. However, the retired number 455 hanging in the stands at Progressive Field is a testament to the teams that reignited a passion for baseball in Cleveland.

Game 3
April 8, 1993
Carlos Baerga Switch-Hits Home Runs in the Same Inning

1993 started off with a disappointing 9-1 loss to the Yankees on Opening Day. The Indians bounced back in Game 2 for a 4-2 victory. The final game of the series fell on a surprisingly warm 71-degree early-April day and saw Mike Bielecki facing Sam Militello. The Indians 1993 lineup will be familiar to fans of the late-90's playoff run, since that was the year when many of the core players began to come into their own and attract national notoriety including Kenny Lofton, Albert Belle, and Sandy Alomar Jr.

The Indians jumped out to a 2-0 lead in the bottom of the first inning. The Yankees pulled Militello from the mound after the Tribe scored another three runs in the bottom of the third.

In the Yankees' half of the fourth inning, Paul O'Neill hit a solo home run off Bielecki to put the Yankees on the board.

In the bottom of the sixth inning, speedy Glenallen Hill had a leadoff triple. He was driven home by a Felix Fermin bunt.

The Yankees rallied in the bottom of the seventh, adding three runs. The Indians found themselves down by a run heading into the bottom of the seventh.

The Tribe answered with an offensive explosion that would be often imitated by the hard-hitting Jacobs Field teams of the later 90's. Alvaro Espinoza pinch hit for Jeff Treadway to lead off the inning with a single to right field. Carlos Baerga stepped in from the right side of the plate. On the 10th pitch of the at-bat, he launched a 380-foot home run to right-center. On the next pitch, Yankees reliever Steve Howe hit Albert Belle. Angry words were exchanged, and Howe was clearly rattled. He gave up three consecutive singles to Paul Sorrento, Reggie Jefferson, and Glenallen Hill.

Steve Farr was called in from the bullpen with two on and no outs. He immediately retired Sandy Alomar and Felix Fermin, but then lost his command. Kenny Lofton hit a single through the left side of the infield, scoring Jefferson. He worked Espinoza into a full count, but the crafty utility man took the next pitch into deep left field. With the bases clear and the Tribe up 14 to 5, Baerga stepped back to the plate.

Always a talented switch hitter, this time Baerga stepped in from the *left* side of the plate. He sent Steve Farr's 2-0 pitch into the bleachers and became the only player to ever homer from both sides of the plate in the same inning. Baerga's homer scored the 15th and final run of the game.

60 players have hit two home runs in the same inning in MLB history. Baerga's switch-hitting feat has since been matched twice, by Mark Bellhorn in 2002 and Kendrys Morales in 2012.

In my mind, this is a baseball anomaly that is heightened in stature because it is both an individual and a team accomplishment. Hitting two consecutive home runs is a notable individual feat--and a very good day for any ballplayer. Likewise, batting around in an inning is not an everyday occurrence and represents a very good day for a team. Hitting home runs from either side of the plate takes an exceptional switch-hitter. Combining all of this into one inning is truly a historic event.

Game 4
April 6, 2007
Home Opener Snowed Out, Played in Milwaukee

Indians starter Paul Byrd took the mound after a one-hour and ten-minute delay into a driving snowstorm. To the TV viewer's eye, there was little difference in the conditions during and after the delay. Evidently, the umpires thought that they saw some relief in the radar signature. Byrd was working on a no-hitter through four innings, certainly assisted by the falling snow.

With two outs and two strikes in the top of the fourth, Mariners manager Mike Hargrove exited the dugout to plead his case with the umpire crew. He urged that the game be delayed because his batters could not see the ball against the white background of swiftly-falling snow.

At this point--one strike away from being an official game--the game was delayed. The sell-out crowd remained in the stands building snowmen for another hour and seventeen minutes. With no improvement in the weather in sight, the game (and eventually the entire series) was called due to snow.

Progressive Field was buried in over a foot of snow. After the series with the Brewers, the Mariners were supposed to come to Cleveland. That series was rescheduled to various open dates in the calendar to give MLB time to figure things out. The 10-day forecast indicated that the April 10th game against the Angels was in jeopardy as well, and the League began looking for an alternate site for the opening series.

On April 10th, flatbed trucks were busy removing snow from Jacob's Field. 500 miles away in Milwaukee, over 19,000 fans came to Miller Park in Milwaukee for the Indians "Home Opener." The Tribe did all that they could to bring the home field advantage to Wisconsin: John Adams was in the crowd with his drum, the staff had loaded the Indians' hype videos and walkup music into Miller Park's systems, and Slider took a ride down Bernie Brewer's famous slide.

The game itself was a fairly standard affair. Kelly Shoppach hit a home run off Ervin Santana in the bottom of the second inning. The

9

Angels threatened several times, but CC Sabathia had a solid outing. He held the Angels to three runs through seven innings.

The Angels scored two runs in the eighth. Then the Halos pulled within one run of the lead when Casey Kochman scored Garrett Anderson on a two-out single in the bottom of the ninth against closer Joe Borowski. Eric Eybar came in as a pinch runner for Casey Kotchman who was on second. On a 1-1 pitch, Shoppach caught Eybar stealing to end the game.

After all of the drama of the last five days and a memorable win, all the Indians wanted to talk about in the post-game interviews was the Milwaukee crowd. "I thought it would be like five, maybe 500," Borowski said. "I thought it would be like an American Legion game. I mean, come on, less than 24 hours' notice? I didn't think anyone would be here."

Game 5
April 20, 1910
Addie Joss is the First to No-Hit the Same Team Twice

By most contemporary accounts, Addie Joss was an unusual athlete. Reporters referred to him as "The Human Hairpin" for his extremely long arms and unusual delivery style. Joss had a corkscrew delivery and turned his back entirely to the plate before using a sidearm motion. Despite this dramatic delivery and high leg-kick, he did not fall off the mound in the way that some corkscrew pitchers do. He completed his motion and was ready to field anything that came back up the middle.

Joss' fielding was a crucial factor in his Game 5 no-hitter. He recorded assists on 10 of the 27 outs, mostly on ground balls. Joss threw only two strikeouts in the entire no-hit performance.

However, the day was not without controversy. In the second inning, White Sox shortstop Freddie Parent hit a weak topper to third base. Bill Bradley juggled the ball and the throw to first was late. The play was initially ruled a base hit, but the official scorer later changed it to a fielding error on Bradley.

Second baseman Terry Turner had the Naps' lone RBI on the day with a double in the top of the sixth inning. Joss already had a Perfect Game against the White Sox in Game 152 of the 1908 season (see page 292). Joss became the first pitcher to ever no-hit the same team twice. This record would stand for 104 years, until Tim Lincecum no-hit the San Diego Padres for the second time in 2014.

Joss played for only nine seasons before he lost his life in April 1911 to tuberculosis meningitis. In 1977, the Hall of Fame's Board of Directors voted to waive the 10-year tenure rule in Joss' case and make him eligible to the Hall of Fame. He was inducted by the Veterans Committee in 1978.

Game 6
April 7, 2013
Masterson Defeats Both Cy Young Winners to Open the Season

In Game 1 of 2013, Justin Masterson and the Indians defeated the Blue Jays behind NL Cy Young winner R.A. Dickey, who had been traded from the Mets to the Jays in the offseason.

The Indians sat at 2-3 on the season coming into Game 6 against the Rays. David Price was scheduled to pitch this Sunday afternoon game. It seemed like a cruel twist of fate that Masterson would be matched up with both of the previous year's Cy Young winners in the first week of the young campaign.

Michael Bourn led off the game with a double and then stole third, but the Indians were retired without scoring. In the top of the second inning, Drew Stubbs drove in Mike Aviles to put the Tribe on the board.

In the top of the third inning, Price walked Asdrubal Cabrera and Ryan Raburn. After a lineout by Nick Swisher, Mark Reynolds socked a home run to deep center field. After that, the rout was on. Lonnie Chisenhall, and Michael Bourn notched their first home runs of the season. Carlos Santana had an incredible day with 5 hits in 5 appearances, including a line drive home run off the right field foul pole to add an exclamation point to the 13-0 game.

Masterson pitched a gem of a game. He went seven innings, recorded eight strikeouts, and gave up only three walks. Masterson faced a bases-loaded threat only once in the bottom of the first inning. With Ben Zobrist on third, Evan Longoria on second, and James Loney on first, Masterson struck out Rays shortstop Yunel Escobar on three straight pitches to escape the jam.

After the game, Masterson demurred with some solid pitcher platitudes, "The boys came out and they just bamboozled, just started hitting some balls. It was pretty cool to see. That's pretty much the testament. They played good defense, made some good plays out there, and they were just crushing balls. And they were putting runs on the board, and it makes the job on the pitcher a lot easier."

In 1989 Bruce Hurst and the San Diego Padres defeated Orel Hershiser with the Dodgers and Frank Viola after Viola was traded from the Twins to the Mets at the trade deadline in 1989. Pitching for the Braves in 2003, Shane Reynolds defeated Randy Johnson with the Diamondbacks and Barry Zito with the Athletics in an interleague game. However, Masterson is the only pitcher to have accomplished this unlikely feat, dueling with the reigning Cy Young winners in *consecutive* starts and coming out on top.

Game 7
April 12, 1999
Travis Fryman Walk-off Home Run in Home Opener

During the 1998 American League Championship Series, Travis Fryman batted only .167. He had no RBIs and committed one fielding error. The Indians were ousted by the Yankees in six games, ending their hopes for a repeat World-Series appearance and leaving Fryman with a disappointing end to his own first post-season.

After a winter of sports talk radio griping about his playoff performance, Fryman was back at third base for the Tribe in 1999. After losing Game 1 of the 1999 campaign in Anaheim, the Indians won five straight on the road against the Angels and Twins and were finally home to face the Royals in Game 7.

Dave Burba was matched up against Jose Rosado in front of 42,798 of the Jacobs Field faithful for the Home Opener of the 1999 season.

In the top of the third inning, Burba walked Carlos Febles. Joe Randa advanced Febles to third with a line drive over second base. With runners at the corners, Johnny Damon slapped one through the right side of the infield. Febles came around to score and put the Royals up by a run.

Jermaine Dye extended the Royals lead in the top of the fourth when he smashed one down the right field line for a solo home run. The two starters battled through the middle innings, as the Tribe could not get any offense going against Rosado.

In the top of the seventh inning, with Royals on first and third, Burba was pulled in favor of reliever Mark Langston. Langston got Carlos Beltran to ground into an inning-ending double play.

Travis Fryman and Richie Sexson chased Rosado from the game in the Indians' half of the seventh inning with consecutive singles. Scott Service replaced Rosado on the mound and got Sandy Alomar to ground into a very similar inning ending double-play.

14

Joe Randa led off for the Royals in the eighth inning. He hit a triple to center field on Langston's third pitch. Johnny Damon followed, hitting a fly ball to deep left center. Kenny Lofton ran it down and threw Randa out at the plate for the dramatic outfield double play.

The turning point in the game was in the bottom of the eighth, when Enrique Wilson hit a line-drive home run down the right field line, scoring Kenny Lofton and tying the game at two runs apiece.

Paul Shuey replaced Langston and made the final out of the eighth inning. In 2⅓ innings of work, Shuey recorded four through the bottom of the Royals lineup, holding on to the 2-2 tie.

With the score still tied in the bottom of the ninth inning, Travis Fryman led off with a single to left. Richie Sexson lined out to center. Sandy Alomar grounded to short, sending Fryman to second base. With first base open, Royals reliever Jose Santiago intentionally walked Kenny Lofton. Then, Santiago walked Enrique Wilson on six pitches to load the bases. The Indians seemed poised for some of the 9th inning magic that was so common in the late 1990's. Robbie Alomar grounded out to second and send the game into extra innings.

Paul Shuey returned to the mound to pitch the tenth inning. He struck out Rey Sanchez and Carlos Febles. Carlos Beltran dribbled a weak hit back to the mound. Shuey fielded it and flipped it to Thome at first to end the inning.

After a Manny Ramirez ground-out to lead off the bottom of the tenth, Santiago walked Jim Thome. Wil Cordero singled to left. Travis Fryman stepped in with one out and two runners aboard. He sent Santiago's 0-1 pitch over the wall in right-center and sent the Home Opener crowd home happy.

Game 8
April 10, 1998
Jim Thome Walks Off the Home Opener

One of the latest Home Openers in Indians history occurred after a seven-game west coast trip in 1998. The Tribe opened the season at a blistering pace, defeating Seattle in the first two games, sweeping a weekend series in Anaheim, and then splitting 1-1 with Oakland before returning to Cleveland on April 10, 1998.

With the near-miss disappointment of the 1997 World Series still stinging, the 1998 campaign began with great hope. After a week of watching the Tribe chew through west coast opponents late at night, the sold-out crowd at Jacobs Field was electric.

Bartolo Colon matched up with Allen Watson in this contest. The Indians got on the board early when Kenny Lofton hit a leadoff double, stole third base, and was driven home by Shawon Dunston's sacrifice fly. Later in the inning, Travis Fryman doubled, scoring David Justice. The Tribe had an early 2-0 lead after the first inning.

Bartolo issued a five-pitch walk to Jim Edmunds to lead off the bottom of the second. Cecil Fielder struck out swinging, but then consecutive singles by Garret Anderson and Norberto Martin pushed Edmunds across to put the Angels on the board. Colon found his command and struck out Matt Walbeck and Carlos Garcia to end the inning.

Indians' left fielder Geronimo Berroa led off the bottom of the fourth with a line drive past the shortstop. Travis Fryman hit a grounder and Berroa was forced out at second, but Fryman was safe at first. Jim Thome shot a double down the right field line that put Fryman on third. After Sandy Alomar struck out on three pitches, Omar Vizquel came through with a two-out line-drive single to center field. Fryman and Thome came around to score and put the Tribe up 4-1.

Colon began to lose his command in the fifth inning. After a fly-ball out to Darin Erstad, and consecutive singles by Dave Hollins and Tim Salmon. Jim Edmunds punched a ball between second and short, scoring Hollins. Salmon rounded third and a rare throwing

16

error by Kenny Lofton allowed him to score. Cecil Fielder slapped a double into right field, plating Edmunds. Paul Shuey replaced Colon and was able to end the inning with no further damage. The score was tied at 4-4.

The game remained locked in a 4-4 tie until the bottom of the seventh inning, when David Justice hit a line drive single into short right field, scoring Omar Vizquel.

In the top of the ninth inning, Indians' closer Michael Jackson hit Dave Hollins with an 0-2 pitch to lead off the inning. Jim Edmunds put Hollins on third base with a double. Cecil Fielder grounded one back to the pitcher. Edmunds was caught in a rundown. Damon Mashore came in to pinch run for Fielder at third. Garrett Anderson poked a single through the right side of the infield to tie the game at five runs apiece.

Eric Plunk retired the Angels in order in the tenth inning. Angels closer Troy Percival came back out to pitch the bottom of the tenth. Percival gave up a single to Manny Ramirez and then walked Brian Giles. Jim Thome stepped in and clubbed Percival's 1-1 pitch onto the home run porch in left field for the first walk-off win of the young season.

Thome would go on to be the Indians all-time home run leader with 317, and would finish his Hall of Fame career with an MLB record 13 walk-off home runs (9 with the Indians).

The 1998 Indians would go on to lead the Central Division wire-to-wire. This is the first and only time in franchise history that the Tribe has been atop the standings for the duration of the season.

Game 9
April 16, 2016
Couple Having Sex in Upper Deck Goes Viral

It was a perfect fifty-four degrees and sunny on this Saturday afternoon of early-season baseball. One amorous couple in the cheap seats temporarily stole the show from the big-leaguers.

In an odd April interleague matchup, the New York Mets came to Cleveland for a weekend series. The announced crowd of 20,165 was solid for an early Spring weekend, but several of the outfield upper-deck sections were closed.

Josh Tomlin gave up a home run on the third pitch of the game to Curtis Granderson, but then gained his composure. Mets' ace Matt Harvey struck out the side in the bottom of the first inning. Both offenses struggled in the early going.

Around the middle of the 4th inning, Twitter user @savannah3marie posted a photo of a couple in the very top row of a closed seating section in right field with the caption "S/O [shoutout] to the people having sex at the Indians game!"

While the lusty occasion went largely unnoticed in the ballpark (except for the lone security guard in the photo), it lit up the internet. Headlines making the most of middle-school metaphors appeared across the web such as "Couple Photographed Scoring Home Run in Nosebleed Seats", "Couple Covered All the Bases in the Middle of an Indians Game", and "Fans Ignore Game, Have Sex in Stands Instead."

In the bottom of the fifth inning, the Indians took a 2-0 lead on a double by Jose Ramirez and a single by Juan Uribe. The Tribe manufactured another three runs in the bottom of the sixth off the bats of Jason Kipnis, Mike Napoli, and Yan Gomes.

Rafael Mantero replaced Harvey on the mound and secured the final out of the sixth inning. He returned to pitch the seventh. The Tribe stretched the lead to 7-1 when they scored two more runs on hits by Francisco Lindor and Mike Napoli.

18

Brian Shaw came in to pitch the top of the eighth inning. He allowed the Mets back into the game, giving up a three-run home run to Yoenis Cespedes and a solo homer to Neil Walker.

Shaw was pulled in favor of closer Cody Allen who recorded the last four outs of the game and sealed the Indians victory.

News Channel 5 later followed up with Cleveland Police. No one was cited for indecent exposure or anything else related to the incident. So, it is unclear whether Granderson, Cespides, and Walker had the only home runs in the ballpark that day or not.

Game 10
April 16, 2009
Indians Spoil Opening of New Yankee Stadium

Pomp and circumstance were the order of the day at the opening of New Yankee Stadium in 2009. Yogi Berra threw out a ceremonial first pitch. Hall of Famers patrolled the pre-game warmups in letterman jackets. Finally, Babe Ruth's bat was laid across the plate as Derek Jeter approached the batter's box to lead off the bottom of the first.

After being traded by the Indians to the Brewers in July 2008, CC Sabathia signed with the Yankees in the off-season and became their Opening Day starter for 2009. CC came into this game already 1-1 on the season. He delivered the first pitch in the new ballpark to his former teammate Grady Sizemore.

In the top of the third inning, Grady Sizemore and Mark DeRosa were on first and second after consecutive walks. Victor Martinez popped a ball into short left. DeRosa mis-judged the hit and took off for third as Derek Jeter backpedaled into the outfield. Jeter made the catch and DeRosa was easily thrown out in an inning-ending double play.

Jhonny Peralta led off the fourth inning with a line drive double down the right field line. Shin Soo Choo grounded one to second and was put out, while Peralta advanced to third. Peralta was tagged out at the plate when Ben Francisco hit into a fielder's choice. Kelly Shoppach stepped in with two outs and smashed a double off the top of the wall. Francisco raced around from first to score the game's first run.

Cliff Lee struck out the first two batters in the bottom of the fifth inning, but gave up the historic first home run in the stadium to Jorge Posada.

Joe Veres came in to relieve CC in the top of the seventh inning. Veres issued a walk to DeRosa, and gave up consecutive doubles to Victor Martinez and Jhonny Peralta. Facing a 3-1 deficit, the Yankees called on Damaso Marte to replace Veres.

Marte fared even worse. He hit Shin-Soo Choo with his second pitch. Ben Francisco moved Peralta to third and Choo to second with a sacrifice bunt. Kelly Shoppach knocked a single into right field which scored Peralta and loaded the bases. Tony Graffanino popped out weakly to first, but the bases remained loaded. Demaso walked Trevor Crowe on five pitches to force in a run.

On the third pitch of his at-bat, Grady Sizemore sent a home run over the iconic W.B. Mason sign in right-field, putting the game entirely out of reach and recording the first grand-slam in the new ballpark. Victor Martinez would homer two batters later to put the icing on this 9-run inning.

Robinson Cano had a two-out RBI single in the bottom of the seventh, but the Yankee offense failed to seriously threaten against Rafael Perez and Rafael Betancourt. The Yankees were a dismal 1 for 11 with runners in scoring position, resulting in audible boos from the Opening Day crowd by the later innings.

Although they played the spoiler on Opening Day, the Indians have had a fairly dismal record at New Yankee Stadium. Factoring in the playoffs, especially the ALCS collapse of 2017, maybe all of that superstition did work for the pinstripes after all.

Game 11
April 17, 1992
Charles Nagy Complete Game Win

The first inning was a rough one, with two hits, a walk and a wild pitch putting the Indians in the hole by a run to start the game. However, the first would be the only multi-hit inning of the game and the only walk recorded.

He would record seven strikeouts--rather high for Nagy, who usually relied on his sinker to force ground ball outs--and scatter 5 additional hits over a complete game.

The Indians offense that evening would prefigure some of the offensive explosions the team was famous for in subsequent years. The five-hit, five-run fourth inning featured a towering two-run home run by Albert Belle and a three-run home run by "Hard Hittin" Mark Whiten.

Carlos Baerga homered in the top of the 5th, followed by Sandy Alomar in the top of the 6th. Ultimately delivering an 11-1 win in Yankee Stadium.

Although he is remembered best for his efforts with the championship teams of the mid-90's, 1992 was perhaps Nagy's best year in the majors. He had a 17-10 record (.630), far outpacing the Indians overall winning percentage of .469.

This performance, along with other gems in the first half of 1992 earned Nagy a spot in the 1992 All-Star Game. After pitching the bottom of the 7th for the AL, he batted in the 8th because there were no players left to pinch-hit. Nagy wore a Texas Rangers batting helmet and hit an infield single. He is very likely to be the last pitcher ever to get a hit in an All-Star Game, since the designated hitter has been used in all All-Star Games since 2011.

Game 12
April 29, 1931
Wes Farrell Throws No-Hitter and Hits Home Run

Wes Ferrell is regarded by many baseball historians as the greatest hitting pitcher who remained a pitcher throughout his career (therefore, excluding one Babe Ruth). He was often used as a pinch-hitter in clutch situations. In 1931, only Earl Averill and Ed Morgan outpaced him in home runs on the team.

On a Wednesday afternoon at League Park, Jim Levey led off for the Saint Louis Browns. Levey reached first on a booted ground ball by Bruce Hunnefield at shortstop. Ferrell's superb pitching would hold the Browns scoreless despite two errors by Hunnefield.

Ferrell recorded eight strikeouts in the course of the no-hitter, scattering only three walks. In the top of the seventh inning, the Indians were already up 4-0 when Ferrell helped out his own cause. He hit a two-run home run into the League Park stands to extend the lead to 6-0.

In an odd twist, Wes was facing his own brother. Hall of Fame catcher Rick Ferrell grounded out in the third, and sixth innings. In the eighth, Rick had the opportunity to break up his brother's no-hitter. "I didn't want a base hit, but I had to get up there," Rick said.

Rick hit a line drive down the third-base line. Browns third baseman Johnny Burnett dove to make the catch, but came up without the ball. The hapless Hunnefield backed him up, retrieved the ball, and threw to first base for a bang-bang play.

Rick Farrell was initially called safe at first. Then, the official scorer ruled that Hunnefield's throw pulled first baseman Lew Fonseca away from the bag—a throwing error. The no-hitter was preserved, but not without controversy.

Despite the recent ascendancy of hitting pitchers like Madison Bumgardner and Shohei Ohtani, Wes Ferrell's 37 home runs as a pitcher are likely to stand as an enduring record in MLB history.

Game 13
April 29, 1952
Al Rosen 3 Home Runs, Jim Fridley 6 for 6

Only 7,858 fans came out to Shibe Park in Philadelphia to see their woeful Athletics on a Tuesday afternoon. The A's had dropped seven of their first eight games to start off the 1952 season.

The prospect of facing Bob Feller likely did not inspire too much confidence in the anemic A's offense. The Indians offense, on the other hand, posted some stat lines in this game that would remain unchallenged for the next half-century.

The Indians sent ten men to the plate in the top of the first inning. They notched six runs on five hits including the first by Fridley: a two-run single.

Elmer Valo tripled for the A's in the bottom of the first. Gus Zernial's grounder to second base eluded Mike Avila, and Valo was able to score on the error and make it 6-1 Indians.

Al Rosen led off the top of the second inning with his first home run of the day. It was followed by another Fridley single. Fridley came around to score on a Bob Kennedy double. Kennedy advanced to third on the throw to the plate. The throw was wide, allowing Kennedy to score as well. Jim Hegan popped out and the inning ended with the Tribe up 9-1.

In the top of the third inning, Al Rosen hit his second home run of the game, a three-run shot off of Harry Byrd, who had been sent in to relieve the scuffling Alex Kellner. The final out of the inning came with Fridley at the plate when Dale Mitchell was caught stealing.

Fridley recorded his third hit to lead off the fourth inning. Another blunder by the A's allowed him to reach second base. He eventually came around to score on a single by Harry Simpson. The Indians were up 14-2.

Fridley hit another two-out single in the top of the fifth, but was stranded at first when Bob Kennedy grounded out.

In the eighth inning, Fridley once again dropped a single into left field. Backup catcher Berdie Tibbetts drove him in with a three-run homer. With two outs and runners on first and second, Al Rosen jacked his third home run of the day. This three-run bomb put the Indians up 21-6. Jim Fridley came up again as the 11th batter of the inning. He knocked yet another single into left field for his sixth hit in six at-bats.

Although Bob Feller gave up seven earned runs on eighteen hits, the Indians offense more than picked him up. The Tribe recorded 25 hits on the way to posting 21 runs. The teams shared one of the more outlandish combined stat lines in history: Cleveland 21, Philadelphia 9 on 43 hits and 7 errors.

Fifty-seven years later, Shin-Soo Choo would match Rosen's four hits and seven RBI in a 15-3 win over the same Athletics (now in Oakland) in Game 81 of the 2009 season (see page 156).

Fridley's six-hit performance has only been replicated twice in Tribe history: by Jorge Orta in Game 56 of 1980 and Omar Vizquel in Game 133 of 2004 (see page 254).

Game 14
May 4, 1966
Wagner and Brown Collide on Pop Fly

The Indians started the 1966 campaign red hot. They were riding an 11-1 record into a mid-week series with the Yankees. With Sam McDowell, Sonny Siebert, and Luis Tiant in the rotation and hitters like Rocky Colavito, Leon Wagner, and Fred Whitfield, the 1966 Indians were one of the more promising Cleveland teams in a decade. Luis Tiant threw a four-hit shutout against the Yankees Tuesday night, setting up this Wednesday evening showdown in the Bronx.

Leon Wagner was one of baseball's most endearing characters in the 1960's. The muscular, always affable Wagner was the first star of the expansion California Angels. After two All-Star performances and some disputes with management, "Big Daddy Wags" was traded to the Indians in 1964.

Sonny Siebert and Mel Stottlemyre were matched up for this contest. Both pitchers came out firing. The Tribe recorded only one hit through the first three innings. Likewise, Siebert retired the first eleven Yankees in order.

With two outs in the bottom of the fourth inning, Roger Maris popped a fly into short left field. Shortstop Larry Brown raced into the outfield, as Leon Wagner charged in from left. There was a spectacular head-on collision in short left field. Both players lay motionless near the field foul line for several minutes. Some sources indicate that Brown swallowed his tongue and nearly died in Yankee Stadium. Brown credited trainer Wally Bock with carrying him off the field and saving his life.

Wagner had a concussion and a broken nose, but returned to the field only a few days later. Brown fared far worse. He suffered multiple skull fractures, a broken nose, and broken eye sockets.

Indians third baseman Max Alvis said "I've played college football, and I've seen split lips, smashed noses, cut faces, and earlobes torn off. But this was the worst I've ever seen."

Brown spent 18 days in the hospital in New York, and did not return to the field for six weeks. He lost 10 pounds while in the hospital, and was out of condition when he returned. His batting average dropped 24 points from the .253 he posted in 1965.

Dick Howser replaced Brown at short and Chuck Hinton replaced Wagner in left field. Siebert and Stottlemeyer continued their pitching duel until Sonny Siebert led off the top of the eighth inning with a bunt single. Vic Davalillo grounded to short and Siebert was thrown out at second. Davalillo stole second. When Chuck Hinton hit one back at Stottlemyre, his throw to first missed the mark. Davalillo came home on the error and broke the scoreless tie.

In the bottom of the eighth, the Yankees manufactured one run when Lou Clinton came in to pinch hit for Stottlemyre and knocked an RBI single into center field.

Steve Hamilton replaced Stottlemyre on the mound in the top of the ninth and gave up a leadoff home run to Indians first baseman Fred Whitfield. Hamilton would be pulled in favor of reliever Pedro Ramos in short order, but the damage was done.

Siebert would go on to record the complete game win, and moved the Indians to 13-1 for the season.

1964 turned out to be Leon Wagner's most productive year with the Tribe. He totaled 100 RBI with 31 home runs, and 14 stolen bases. As productive as he was on offense, Wagner was sometimes comically bad in left field. When asked why he caught fly balls with only his glove hand he once quipped, "I've found that I field better if I catch the ball with only one hand. When you use two hands, the other one just gets in the way."

Game 15
April 17, 2018
Lindor Homers in Puerto Rico

San Juan, Puerto Rico has history as an MLB venue, but rarely has there been more hype on the island than the April 2018 series between the Indians and Twins.

San Juan's Estadio Hiram Bithorn is named after the first Puerto Rican to play in the majors—Cubs pitcher Hiram Bithorn. It served as a second home stadium for the Montreal Expos for 22 games in the 2002 and 2003 campaigns. The dimensions of the stadium were expanded in 2002 to match Stade Olympique in Montreal due to an MLB rule that a team's home stadium dimensions must remain the same throughout the season (thank you, Bill Veeck and the 1947 Indians).

Although the Twins were technically the home team for the series, Francisco Lindor was by far the hometown favorite. After an emotional introduction in front of his family, Lindor led off the game with a long fly-out to the warning track. After this initial scare, Jake Odorizzi settled in for the Twins. He held the Indians scoreless until the top of the fifth inning.

Minnesota left-fielder Eddie Rosario–also a Puerto Rican native with family in the stands–led off the Twins half of the fourth inning with a single off Corey Kluber. However, Rosario was left on base and the game remained scoreless into the top of the fifth.

After striking out Yan Gomes and Tyler Naquin, Odorizzi was set to face Bradley Zimmer. The rookie center fielder drove a line drive into deep right field and ended up on second base. Odorizzi's 0-2 pitch to Lindor escaped the glove of Twins catcher Jason Castro and Zimmer advanced to third on the passed ball.

Lindor worked himself into a full count, and on the sixth pitch of the at-bat launched a homer to deep right field. The shortstop known for his smile and enthusiasm was in his element. Lindor rounded the bases waving to the crowd and was promptly summoned from the dugout for a curtain call.

Francisco later described the trip around the bases, "Unreal. Unreal. It's a dream...definitely a dream playing in front of the crowd. How the crowd got up. The home run...it was special. Something I will never forget."

After another quick-work inning by Corey Kluber, Jose Ramirez and Michael Brantley led off the top of the sixth inning with back-to-back home runs.

Brian Dozier drove in Max Kepler to get the Twins on the board in the bottom of the seventh inning. Andrew Miller replaced Kluber on the mound and recorded two strikeouts in 1⅓ innings of work.

Yonder Alonso added to the Tribe lead in the top of the eighth inning, making it a 6-1 game. Cody Allen walked Max Kepler to lead off the ninth, but secured the final three outs to give the Tribe their first win outside of the lower 48 states.

Game 16
April 20, 2013
Tribe Scores 14 Runs in First 2 Innings

The Indians were in Houston to face Phil Humber nearly one year removed from his Perfect Game (April 21, 2012). Humber had struggled early in 2013 since signing with the Astros and was 0-2 on the young season.

For the Tribe, Scott Kazmir was pitching in the MLB for the first time since being released by the Angels after just one inning of work in 2011. Kazmir spent 2012 with the Independent Atlantic League's Sugarland Skeeters trying to regain his pitching touch.

After a pop fly out by Michael Brantley to lead off the game, the Indians batted around. The cavalcade of offense included singles by Jason Kipnis, Asdrubal Cabrera, and Drew Stubbs; doubles by Nick Swisher and Jason Giambi and Michael Brantley; and a three-run home run by Mark Reynolds. Overall, the Indians plated 8 runs on 8 hits, chasing Humber from the game after the tenth batter.

In the bottom of the first, Mike Aviles replaced Asdrubal Cabrera in the lineup. Cabrera had injured his wrist falling down the dugout stairs immediately before the game.

In the second inning, Dallas Keuchel did not fare any better against the Indians lineup. The Tribe plated six more runs on five hits.

Travis Blackley replaced Keuchel on the mound to start the fourth inning. Mike Aviles drew a walk on a nine-pitch at-bat. Nick Swisher doubled into left field, advancing Aviles to third. On a 0-1 pitch, Jason Giambi launched a homerun to deep right-center. This was his 421st career home run. It brought him into a tie with Cal Ripken Jr. as #42 on the all-time home run list.

Coming into the game, Giambi was batting .083 on the season, and his 'veteran leadership' qualities were being questioned in light of his abysmal hitting in the DH role. In retrospect, this 5-RBI game was something of a turning point for Giambi and the Indians in 2013. Although his batting average would rise only to .183 for the season, Jason would account for some of the most memorable and inspiring moments of the 2013 campaign and the team coalesced around him on a run to an appearance in the Wild Card Game.

Nick Swisher also had a career day with four hits, including three of the Indian's seven doubles.

Terry Francona commented on the turnaround, "I think it helps guys feel better about themselves. I thought they did a good job of that going into the game, but I do think it helps guys loosen up a little bit."

Game 17
May 7, 1957
Herb Score Injured by Line Drive

By the beginning of 1957, many baseball writers considered Herb Score to be the left-handed second coming of Bob Feller. Score had been discovered and signed by Cy Slapnicka, the same scout who signed Feller. Score was a flamethrowing young pitcher with endless potential. Prior to the 1957 season the Red Sox offered the Indians a million dollars for Score--an astronomical amount at the time--but were rebuffed by Indians GM Hank Greenburg.

Building off his Rookie of the Year campaign in 1955 and All Star 20-win season in 1956, Score had started 1957 strong.

This Tuesday night game against the Yankees was his fifth pitching appearance of the year. After Yankees right fielder Hank Bauer grounded out to lead off the game, Gil McDougald stepped to the plate.

McDougald drove a low pitch straight up the middle and struck Score directly in the eye. Blood streamed from his eye, mouth and nose. Third baseman Al Smith played the ball off Score and threw to Vic Wertz at first for the out while catcher Jim Hegan rushed to the mound.

Score never lost consciousness, but suffered severe hemorrhaging of his eye. He spent several weeks in the hospital, and his vision did not recover enough to let him pitch for the rest of the season.

Bob Lemon came in to pitch in Score's stead. Over the remaining 8 ⅓ innings he allowed only one run on six hits.

In the bottom of the eighth inning, Gene Woodling singled to center field. He advanced to third when Hank Bauer misplayed an Al Smith fly ball to right. Yankees pitcher Tom Sturdivant intentionally walked Vic Wertz to load the bases. Sturdivant struck out Indians rookie Roger Maris. Then, Score's best friend and road-trip roommate Rocky Colavito stepped to the plate.

Rocky drew a walk which forced in Wertz. This turned out to be the game-winning run, as this 2-1 score would hold up. Lemon retired the Yankee side in order in the ninth.

After the game, McDougald was distraught. "If Herb loses the sight in his eye, I'm going to quit this game," he said in the locker room.

McDougald knew the pain of a line-drive injury first hand. Two years prior, he was hit in the head during batting practice. After a few days out with a concussion, he returned to baseball, but would eventually lose his hearing as a result.

Score attempted a return to baseball in 1958, but was only marginally successful. He recorded only 17 more wins from 1958 to 1962. Bob Lemon later said, "He became mechanical. He wasn't bringing it like he used to, not holding anything back."

Most Indians fans of my generation remember Herb Score only as the humorous and sometimes contradictory radio announcer. Herb called Tribe games from 1968 to 1997. Some announcers are known for the vivid picture that they paint with their words or for famous catch phrases. Listening to Herb was more like watching baseball with an older uncle. It was pleasant and comfortable, if not always accurate.

He could go innings--sometimes it seemed like days--without giving an update on the score. In his defense, for most of his tenure the Indians were usually losing. Repeated phrases turned into a kind of shorthand. A pitch in the dirt was mumbled "downtoolow" in a certain cadence that confused my mother. Once she asked me how long Don Cheelow played for the Indians, since she heard his name so much.

The most famous Score-ism captures the almost meditative quality of listening to a Herb Score broadcast: "It's a long drive. Is it fair? Is it foul? It is!"

Game 18
May 1, 1968
Sam McDowell 16K Complete Game

1968 is often referred to as the "Year of the Pitcher." The strike zone had been expanded after 1961, and ERAs fell throughout the mid-1960's. 1968 was the last season before the mound was lowered from 15 inches to 10. Twenty-two pitchers had sub-2.00 ERAs. Red Sox outfielder Carl Yastrzemski won the 1968 batting title with a mark of .301. He was the only player to bat over .300 that year.

Enter Sam McDowell in the Year of the Pitcher. The A's, (just recently moved to Oakland) had travelled cross-country for a Wednesday night matchup in Cleveland. Sudden Sam was scheduled to face off against Blue Moon Odom. McDowell was a fastball pitcher with a wild streak. His lack of command could be an issue at times, but he could usually overpower hitters with pure speed.

True to form, McDowell hit Ted Kubiak with a pitch to lead off the game. He then retired Reggie Jackson and Sal Bando on strikeouts. Danny Cater singled to left field, advancing Kubiak to second. But John Donaldson was cut down by McDowell's fastball to end the inning.

McDowell recorded two more strikeouts in the top of the second inning. In the A's half of the third, Reggie Jackson tripled to left field. Sal Bando popped one to right field. Vic Davalillo made the catch and fired toward home. Duke Sims mis-handled the catch and allowed Jackson to score. The A's were ahead 1-0 in the early going.

McDowell and Odom continued to duel through the middle innings. Neither pitcher allowed a hit from this point through the top of the sixth inning.

In the Cleveland half of the sixth, the Indians offense finally showed some life. Chico Salmon led off with a single, then stole second. Salmon advanced to third on a groundout by Larry Brown. Then McDowell helped out his own cause, dropping a single into center field which scored Salmon to tie the game at one run apiece.

34

McDowell retired the side in the seventh inning, recording two more strikeouts against John Donaldson and Rene Lachmann.

Leon Wagner led off the bottom of the seventh with a strikeout. Then, Tony Horton knocked a single into left field. Duke Sims followed with a single into right field, sending Horton to third base. Horton scored the go-ahead run on a passed ball with Chico Salmon at the plate. Then Salmon poked a single to right field, scoring Sims. This put the Tribe up 3-1.

McDowell recorded another three strikeouts in the eighth and ninth. His final stat line was a three-hit complete game, no walks, sixteen strikeouts. This game exemplifies McDowell's most enduring quote, "It's no fun throwing fastballs to guys who can't hit them. The real challenge is getting them out on the stuff they can hit."

Game 19
May 8, 1920
Tris Speaker Platoons the Tribe to the Championship

Tris Speaker is regarded as one of the best hitters of the first half of the 20th century, and an exceptional center fielder as well. Speaker spent his first nine seasons with the Red Sox, including an MVP season in 1912. After the 1915 season, he got into a salary dispute with Red Sox owner Joseph Lannin who wanted Tris to take a pay cut from $15,000 to $9,000. Speaker balked at the offer. He was soon traded to the Indians.

Speaker showed up in Cleveland and instantly became the on-the-field leader. He was effectively an assistant to manager Lee Fohl from day one. In the middle of the 1919 season, Fohl resigned from his post as manager after particularly bad beat by Boston and Babe Ruth. Speaker officially became player-manager of the club.

On the field, Speaker was spectacular. Despite the 460-foot distance to center field at League Park, he was known to play so shallow in center that he could catch a fly ball and make the tag at second. The records show six unassisted double plays from center field. The Press dubbed him the "grey eagle" for his early-greying hair and his ability to cover the expansive outfields of the day.

As manager, "Spoke" had an almost instinctive ability to get the best out of his players. Many of the members of the 1920 Indians were on second—or last—chances in the league. At the time, lineups were not established based on matchups. Tris developed the 'platoon' system and put players into games and situations where they were most likely to be successful. He took the opposing pitcher, the park, and all other factors into the mix when filling out the lineup card.

On this Saturday, the Indians were in Chicago. Elmer Myers was set to face off with Red Faber and the White Sox. Prior to the start of the 1919 season, Speaker had urged the Cleveland club to trade temperamental outfielder Braggo Roth. Myers came to the Indians in that trade, along with third baseman Larry Gardner and pitcher turned outfielder Charlie Jamieson.

Jack Graney led off the game with a single past first base. Ray Chapman followed with another single down the right field line. Speaker himself stepped in and dropped a sacrifice bunt that advanced both runners. Elmer Smith flied out to center. Then Larry Gardner plated both of the runners with a well-placed double into right field.

The Sox got one run back in the bottom of the second inning. Happy Felsch dropped a single into left field. Myers got a little wild, and Happy went to second on a passed ball. Swede Risberg drove him in with a ground ball scorched into center field.

Speaker doubled into center field to lead off the top of the fifth inning. He came around to score on Larry Gardner's single into right field which made the score 4-1, Cleveland.

The Tribe extended the lead in the top of the sixth. Elmer Myers drove in Bill Wambsganss with a sacrifice fly.

Tris drew a walk to get the bottom of the seventh started. Smoky Joe Wood drew a second walk-off Sox reliever Dickey Kerr. Wood was a former teammate of Speaker's in Boston. Wood was a pitcher in Boston, but his skills were declining precipitously. At Speaker's urging, Tribe owner James Dunn paid Boston $15,000 for the rights to Smoky Joe, but by 1917 it was clear his arm was shot. His old friend Tris coached him into playing outfield. In 1920 he hit .270 while appearing in 61 games, mostly against left-handed pitchers. Some historians have suggested that Speaker adopted outfield platooning primarily to find a place for his old friend Smoky Joe.

Larry Gardner beat out a bunt down the first base line to load the bases. Wambsganss squibbed one back to the pitcher, and Speaker was forced out at the plate. Doc Johnston knocked a two-run single into center field that plated Wood and Gardner. Johnston's batting average had been in decline for several seasons. In 1918, he hit .227. Under Speaker's tutelage, he hit .305 in 1919 and would finish with a .292 average in 1920.

Catcher Steve O'Neill was up next. He sent a long fly ball into left field that dropped for a two-run double. O'Neill was a middling hitter who stayed on the roster because of his proficient defense behind the plate.

As manager, Speaker gave O'Neill three simple rules for hitting:
1. Go to the plate thinking you'll get a hit.
2. Outthink the pitcher.
3. Don't swing at bad balls.
O'Neil hit .321 during the 1920 season. The inning ended with the Tribe up 9 runs to 1.

The White Sox tacked on two runs in the bottom of the seventh, and Speaker called to the bullpen for reliever Dick Niehaus. Niehaus got the final out of the inning when Eddie Collins popped out to Chapman at shortstop.

Niehaus retired the heart of the Sox' lineup in order in the bottom of the eighth. Ray Chapman singled in Doc Johnston in the top of the ninth to give Niehaus a seven-run cushion heading into the bottom half of the ninth inning.

The Sox put together a comeback rally. Swede Risberg kicked it off with a single into center. Niehaus got two quick outs on pop flies by Schalk and Shano Collins. Then, a passed ball advanced Risberg to second. Fred McMullin slapped a single which sent him around to score. Buck Weaver drew a walk. Ray Chapman extended the inning when he muffed a grounder off the bat of Eddie Collins. One run came in to score on the error. Shoeless Joe Jackson singled into right and drove in Weaver. Finally, Happy Felsch sent a liner directly at Wambsganss at second base. It stuck in his glove and sealed the 10-6 victory for Cleveland.

At the time, some around baseball not only questioned the platoon strategy, but considered it a moral failing. John B. Sheridan of *The Sporting News* wrote: "The specialist in baseball is no good and won't go very far...The whole effect of the system will be to make the players affected half men... It destroys young ball players by destroying their most precious quality— confidence in their ability to hit any pitcher, left or right, alive, dead, or waiting to be born."

Under Spoke's innovative management, the Indians would go on to a 98-56 record in 1920. They finished two games ahead of the White Sox to take the American League Pennant. They defeated the Brooklyn Robins five games to two to take the World Series, proving that, under a competent leader, the platoon system can be a winner.

Game 20
May 4, 1975
Walk-off Win in Baseball's Worst Uniforms

The Indians unveiled a new set of uniforms at the beginning of 1975 that are infamous as one of the worst outfits in baseball history.

The double-knit polyester pullovers featured a pseudo-Greek script that came to be known as the "Caveman font." "Sans-a-Belt" elastic waistbands replaced traditional belts. The road red-on-red uniforms were particularly hideous, although the mono-color mix-and-match nature of the uniforms were pretty bad in any combination.

I reached out to Paul Lukas of the venerable Uni-Watch for his take on the 1975 set. Paul and the Uni-Watch team have written about Caveman uniforms several times, but he was kind enough to comment on this look, "Ah, the blood clot uni -- a true '70s classic. One of those uniforms that would look absurd if you brought it back today but somehow felt Just Right for its era."

Game 20 of the 1975 campaign was the second half of a true Sunday afternoon double-header. The Tribe had dropped the first game 1-11 after beating the Orioles both Friday and Saturday night.

Don Baylor got the Orioles on the board in the top of the first inning with a two-run RBI double off Indians starter Don Hood.

In the bottom of the second inning, the beloved Oscar Gamble hit a solo home run. The Tribe manufactured two additional runs in the bottom of the fourth when Buddy Bell hit a single, stole second, and was driven in by catcher Alan Ashby's single to left field. John Lowenstein bunted to move Ashby over to third base. With Tommy McCraw at the plate, Ashby stole home to put the Tribe up 3-2. Lowenstein advanced to second. McCraw eventually drew a walk, but was stranded when George Hendrick flied out.

The big day for catchers continued. Orioles catcher Dave Duncan touched up Indians starter Don Hood for a solo home run in the top of the seventh which evened the game at three runs apiece. Two batters later, Dennis Eckersley entered the game in relief and struck out Paul Blair to end the inning.

39

Eckersley retired the side in the top of the eighth inning. In the top of the ninth, Eck got in some trouble when he gave up a hit to Doug DeCinces and walked Jim Northrup and Ken Singleton. With the bases loaded, he got Al Bumbry to ground out weakly back to the mound.

The Indians would get runners on base in both the ninth and tenth innings, but were unable to bring them home. In the bottom of the eleventh, with runners on first and third, George Hendrick hit a single off Orioles reliever Jesse Jefferson to score Frank Duffy and end the game.

The 1975 jersey has become an (ironic?) fan favorite. You can always spot at least one 1975 jersey in the stands, whether the Indians are home or away. However, I have to agree with Paul Lukas. It has not aged well when it is worn by actual ballplayers. Changes in fabric and cut are not kind to the looks of the 1970's when they are reproduced for throwback day.

Game 21
May 11, 1930
Blue Laws Force Series Shift to League Park

In 1930, the Indians were scheduled to play a Friday to Monday wrap-around series against the Athletics in Philadelphia. Playing Professional sports on Sunday was banned in Pennsylvania. Pennsylvania was founded by the Quakers, who considered any form of paid work on Sunday to be immoral. In 1794, the state Assembly passed "an Act for the prevention of vice and immorality, and of unlawful gaming, and to restrain disorderly sports and dissipation."

In the late 1920's and early 1930's, several other states and municipalities relaxed their blue laws to allow Sunday baseball. Apparently in this confusing environment of referendums, court cases, and changing social mores, the American League had slipped up and scheduled a Sunday game in Philadelphia.

During the prior season, the Pennsylvania attorney general brought suit against the A's for violating the prohibition of Sunday baseball. In early 1927 the Pennsylvania Supreme Court ruled, by a vote of 7 to 2, that Sunday Baseball was both "unholy" and "worldly employment".

The Court also threatened the A's, that if they continued to play on Sunday, the team's incorporation would be revoked. Therefore, to avoid any additional trouble, the A's and Indians boarded a train after Saturday afternoon's contest and took an overnight trip to Cleveland where Sunday baseball had been legalized in 1918.

The A's were reigning World Series Champions. They had been rebuilt throughout the 1920's by legendary manager Connie Mack. An overflow crowd of over 28,000 came to League Park to see the A's and their star players. When the grandstands were full, people were seated on the field down the foul lines. Manager Roger Peckinpaugh, seeing the unique conditions, directed the Indians to try to push balls down the foul line. Fair balls that bounced into the crowd just outside the lines would go as ground-rule doubles.

The Indians delivered. Earl Averill hit the first ground-rule double of the day in the bottom of the first. He came around to score on a single to left by second baseman Johnny Hodapp. Luke Sewell added another ground-rule double before the inning came to an end with the Indians up three runs on five hits.

A's starter Roy Mahaffey walked Wes Ferrell to kick off the bottom of the second inning. Averill drove him in with his second ground-rule double of the day. The Tribe were up 6-0 at the end of the second.

Wes Ferrell retired the A's in order in the top of the third. Bibb Falk led off the Indians half of the inning with another ground-rule double as the ball disappeared into the crowd. Charlie Jamieson pushed Falk across the plate to tack on an additional run for the Tribe.

The Indians batted around in the bottom of the fourth inning. They took advantage of two Philadelphia errors to add another seven runs and extend the lead to 14-0.

The A's finally got on the board in the top of the fifth inning thanks to two fielding errors by Hodapp at second. Philly closed the lead to 14-4.

Another two runs came the Indians' way in the bottom of the fifth, as Jonah Goldman had a sacrifice fly and Wes Ferrell had an RBI ground-rule double.

The A's added a run in the top of the sixth after their first ground-rule double of the day by second baseman Dib Williams.

Cleveland pushed the lead to 22-5 in the bottom of the sixth by batting around the order once again. The Tribe touched up Al Mahon for six runs on seven hits including another ground-rule double by Bibb Falk. After rookie pitcher Al Mahon gave up eight runs in these two innings, he never pitched in the majors again.

Sal Gialito came on to replace Farrell in the top of the seventh inning. Despite working with a huge lead, Gialito got off to a rocky start. After giving up a single to Spence Harris and striking out Jimmie Foxx, he put Harris on third base by committing two consecutive balks. Then he walked Wally Schang. Eric McNair cleared the bases with a two-run single into left. The score was 22-7.

Glenn Liebert came on to pitch for the A's and gave up a leadoff single to Ed Morgan. Then Hodapp and Falk bounced consecutive ground-rule doubles into the crowd outside the foul lines. The Indians added their final runs of the game, which wrapped up an absurd Cleveland 25 Philadelphia 7.

The four combined errors and three balks probably highlight the fatigue of an all-night train trip to evade the blue laws. However, Bibb Falk had one of the Indians all-time stat lines. He went five-for-five at the plate including three ground-rule doubles, scored five runs, and had five RBI on the day.

Game 22
April 24, 2014
Corey Kluber Arrives

The Indians were wrapping up an early-season homestand with a Thursday 12:05 businessman's special against the Royals.

After going 11 and 5 in the 2013 season, Corey Kluber was a rising star among the Indians pitching staff. However, he was still second in the rotation to Justin Masterson.

Kluber worked through the Royals order with Maddux-like efficiency. He faced only three batters in the first, second, fourth, sixth, eighth, and ninth innings.

Royal's starter Bruce Chen also cruised through the first four innings. In the bottom of the fifth, Carlos Santana led off with a double to center field. Michael Brantley poked the very next pitch into center field, scoring Santana. Chen then walked Ryan Raburn. Yan Gomes singled through the hole on the left side of the Infield, advancing the runners to second and third.

With the bases loaded, David Murphy hit a ground ball single into left field, scoring Brantley and Raburn. Mike Aviles laid down a sacrifice bunt, advancing Gomes and Murphy into scoring position. Asdrubal Cabrera stepped in and hit a line drive double to left field scoring Gomes and Murphy.

Bruce Chen was pulled in favor of Michael Mariot after giving up five runs on five hits in the inning. This was all the offense the Tribe would need with Kluber mowing through Royals batters.

In the top of the seventh inning with two outs, after a left-field single by Omar Infante, Nick Swisher made a half-hearted effort on a Mike Moustakis grounder. It rolled all the way to the right-field wall and allowed Infante to score from first base. Kluber then got Alcides Escobar to strike out swinging and end the threat.

Kluber was already known as a ground-ball pitcher, who relied on his sinker to get batters out. In this case, eleven ground outs were matched with eleven strikeouts and no walks. This was Kluber's first complete-game win, and he accomplished it using only 101 pitches.

After watching Kluber's game mature, fans recognize this as Corey performing at the top of his game. However, in 2014 this was one of the first indications that Kluber would surpass Justin Masterson as the ace of the staff. The game took only two hours and fifteen minutes, leaving many fans wondering what to do with the rest of their afternoon.

Game 23
May 12, 1914
Terry Turner 13th Sacrifice Hit of Season

Terry "Cotton Top" Turner is one of the all-time great Indians whose memory is being lost to the fog of history.

In 1914, Turner led the league in sacrifice hits. This skill made him an indispensable part of the early Indians/Naps teams along with Shoeless Joe Jackson and Lajoie himself. Terry Turner was a fearless baserunner who pioneered the use of the head-first slide, because traditional feet-first sliding aggravated his achy ankles.

On this early-season Tuesday against the Athletics, Turner went on a tear with three hits, two runs scored, and a walk in five plate appearances. He notched his sixth stolen base of the season, and his sacrifice hit was his thirteenth of the young season.

For comparison, in 2018, Julio Tehran and Delino DeShields led the MLB in sacrifice hits with 12. For the season. Turner was averaging a sacrifice hit nearly every other game.

Turner's solid day, along with four hits by Shoeless Joe Jackson, helped propel the Naps to a 12-4 victory in Shibe Park.

Terry Turner had a 15-year career with the Indians playing shortstop and third base. He is still the team leader in putouts with 4,603. His career mark of 254 stolen bases stood as a franchise record for seventy-seven years until it was broken by Kenny Lofton in 1996.

Game 24
May 15, 1981
Len Barker's Perfect Game

If you start a conversation about Indians history–at a barbeque, a bar, a birthday party–someone will tell you they were at Len Barker's perfect game. The odds of this being the truth are exceptionally low, given that only 7,290 fans were in attendance for this Friday night contest against the expansion Blue Jays.

I have a friend who was there. The ticket stubs and scorecard hanging in his home were one of the inspirations for this project. I asked Neil to tell me about the game from a fan's perspective. His description is included in the game narrative below.

I invited my girlfriend of 2 months (we just celebrated our 37th wedding anniversary) to go to the game with me. We drove up from Warren where we lived at the time. It was a cool misty night. I bought two general reserved seats along the first baseline figuring we would be able to move up close to the field, which is exactly what we did, as there were very few fans there due to the inclement weather. I bought a program and a pencil to keep score, which my wife found interesting not being all that much of a baseball fan.

Nine days earlier, Bert Blyleven and the Indians took a no-hitter into the ninth inning against the Blue Jays in Toronto's Exhibition Stadium.

The newly-formed Blue Jays had a team batting average of .218 heading into this Friday night game. Temperatures dipped into the 40s, and a misty rain was blowing in off Lake Erie.

On the first play of the game Alfredo Griffin hit a slow roller behind the mound. Shortstop Tom Veryzer fielded it and threw to first for one of the toughest outs of the game.

In the bottom of the first, Rick Manning led off with a single to left field. Jorge Orta flied out to shortstop. Mike Hargrove got on board due to an error by the first baseman, advancing Manning to third. Andre Thornton's sacrifice fly to center scored Manning and sent

47

Hargrove to second. Catcher Ron Hassey stepped in next, pushing Hargrove across the plate with a single into right field.

Although he was known as the American League's premier fastball pitcher (after the departure of Nolan Ryan to the Astros in 1980), Barker did not record a strikeout until the 10th batter he faced. From the top of the fourth inning on, Barker struck out eleven batters swinging. His curveball was so dominant that a Blue Jay hitter never faced a three-ball count at any point in the game.

"Along with having uncommon control, Barker's curveball was really breaking sharply that night and the Expansion Blue Jays were overmatched. Celtics GM Danny Ainge played second for them that night which was kind of interesting as he was also attending Brigham Young at the time and was eventually named the college basketball player of the year."

Barker threw 103 pitches, and 74 were strikes. He threw only 17 fastballs after the fourth inning. Ron Hassey later remarked on the dominance of Lenny's curveball, "By the ninth inning we decided if there was going to be a base hit, it would have to come off a breaking pitch."

Lenny later remarked on how the inclement weather worked to his advantage. "I'm always wetting the ball and rubbing it up to get a better grip. The mist just gave me more moisture to work with."

Jorge Ortega hit a solo home run to lead off the bottom of the eighth inning. Long-time fans may remember that the Muni stadium scoreboard always displayed a trivia question, usually in the later innings. These questions were chosen earlier in the day by team staff and programmed into the display board.

That day's trivia question was "Which two teams have never been involved in a no-hitter." The answer was Toronto and the Seattle Mariners. Some players in the dugout feared that the stadium itself had invoked the jinx that comes with talking about a no-hitter.

"As the game wore on and Barker showed no signs of tiring, other fans lined up behind us to copy our scorecard."

Barker was well aware that he was on the cusp of something special as he headed to the mound to begin the ninth inning. Lenny later recounted, "I was so nervous at the end that I dropped the ball on the mound one time. My stomach was a wreck." Rick Bosetti led off the top of the ninth. He fouled off one of Barker's only poorly-located pitches of the night. He was then retired on a pop foul to the third base side. Al Woods pinch hit for Danny Ainge and struck out swinging.

The 27th batter was Ernie Whitt, another pinch hitter who entered the game with a .188 batting average. Whitt lofted a fly ball into center field. Rick Manning caught the popup and a raucous celebration began.

"Many years later I took my son to an autograph show to get Lenny to sign the scorecard and stubs. He couldn't have been nicer and spent a bit of time looking at the scorecard before signing it."

Perhaps the reason so many people claim to have been at the game was because so many more people saw on television than normally would have in 1981. The game happened to be broadcast over the air on WUAB Channel 43. Bruce Drennan and Joe Tait were the broadcast team. One week later, a compressed-game recap was aired with Drennan and Tait providing further commentary.

Game 25
May 10, 1977
Larvell Banks Ends Pitching Duel with a Walk-off

Pitcher Jim Bibby had been brought to the Indians in a trade for Gaylord Perry. Both were talented pitchers of the era, and both had pitched no-hitters (Perry for the Giants in 1968 and Bibby in 1973 for the Cardinals against the defending champion A's.)

However, Perry had a long-stewing feud with player-manager Frank Robinson. In 1974 Robinson was claimed off waivers. At that point, Perry was the indisputable leader of the clubhouse--or at least the white portion clubhouse. Off the field, the team was largely divided along racial lines. There was a well-publicized locker room blowup when Robinson caught word that Perry intended to demand "the same salary, plus a dollar more" than what Robinson was making.

When Frank Robinson became player-manager of the Tribe in 1975–the first black manager in baseball–Perry undermined his authority in the clubhouse on everything from the conditioning regimen during Spring Training to whether pitchers could take infield practice. By late June, GM Phil Seghi was forced to trade both of the Perry brothers in an attempt to bring peace to the locker room.

Game 25 of the 1977 season was postponed from Monday night due to the cold. The resulting double-header began at 2:00 p.m. on Tuesday. Jim Bibby would face off with Jim Slaton of the Brewers in what would become a great pitcher's duel.

Bibby cruised through the beginning of the game, retiring the Brewers 1-2-3 in the first, third, fourth, fifth, and eighth innings. He issued only one walk in the top of the sixth.

Slaton was less efficient, scattering five hits and issuing five walks. Both teams struggled offensively. The Indians left seven men stranded on base.

Bibby was tested in the sixth, seventh, and ninth innings, but he was able to get out of each jam. The Brewers were 0 for 5 with runners in scoring position.

In the bottom of the ninth, after a groundout by John Lowenstein, shortstop Larvell Blanks stepped to the plate. By the middle of 1977, Blanks was having his own issues with Frank Robinson. In 1976 he batted .280 while appearing in 104 games for the Tribe. Larvell felt that he ought to be starting over Frank Duffy. Duffy was a better defensive shortstop, but he hit a paltry .212 the previous year.

Blanks stepped in and launched a home run into the cold Muni Stadium afternoon. The walk-off homer sealed a complete game shutout for Jim Bibby, spoiled a potential complete game for Slaton, and furthered Blanks' case for the starting shortstop position. Discontent in the clubhouse continued to grow over playing time and personnel issues, and Frank Robinson was let go after Game 77 of the 1977 season. Larvell Blanks would see more playing time under the new manager Jeff Torborg, but would later be traded to the Rangers in a deal for Len Barker.

Game 26
May 14, 1961
Indians Give Up 13 Hits, Win 1-0

This Sunday afternoon contest from 1961 features one of the most unlikely box scores ever recorded. The two teams combined for twenty-three hits, and the final score was 1-0.

In the bottom of the second, the Indians threatened when Johnny Temple and Jim Piersall led off the inning with consecutive singles. Tito Francona (father of Indians manager Terry Francona) grounded to third and Temple was forced out. Chuck Essigien popped out to center field, and the Orioles' Billy Hoeft walked Vic Power to load the bases. Catcher John Romano popped out to right to end the inning.

This kind of frustration would be the order of the day. The Indians stranded runners in scoring position in the second, fifth, sixth, eighth, tenth, and twelfth innings.

Across the diamond, the Orioles faced similar frustration. Jim Perry pitched the first eight innings of the game for the Tribe, scattering nine hits and only one walk. Frank Funk pitched the final seven innings of the game, issuing four hits and no walks.

The Orioles staff of Hoeft, Hoyt Wilhelm, and Jack Fisher combined to give up ten hits and nine walks.

With both offenses refusing to score, the game could only end on a mistake. In the bottom of the fifteenth inning, John Romano drew a walk to lead things off. Woodie Held struck out. Bubba Phillips knocked a single into right field, bringing Romano to second. Bob Hale (who had spent most of his career with the Orioles) was brought in to pinch hit for Funk.

Hale grounded to Jerry Adair, the Orioles shortstop. Adair got the force out at second, but botched the throw to first to complete the double play. This allowed Romano to score on the walk-off error.

Overall, the Orioles left 11 men on base, while the Indians stranded 18. Even for an extra innings game, this game is outstanding for its futility.

The game took three hours and thirty-one minutes to play, which does not seem too bad by modern standards. However, the teams returned to the field shortly for the second game of the Sunday double header. The Tribe won that one as well, 6 to 4.

The 1961 Indians were in the midst of a winning month, and hopes were high in Cleveland. In June, this team spent fifteen days in first place in the American League. But it would not last. They collapsed after the All-Star break to finish 30½ games out.

Game 27
May 3, 1997
Sandy Alomar Walk-off Hit

Although Indians fans often soured on players from the 90's who left for greener pastures and bigger paychecks, Sandy Alomar is one of the most universally beloved figures from the mid-90's dynasty.

He was often sidelined with injuries, overshadowed by his Hall of Fame brother, or edged out for awards in favor of fellow Puerto-Rican catcher Pudge Rodriguez. Along with his Rookie of the Year 1991 season, 1997 was the year that everything came together for Santos.

Sandy was once again behind the plate as Chad Ogea faced off against the Tiger's Brian Moehler in this Saturday afternoon contest. The field was soaked after a rainy morning, but the sold-out crowd was in place for this division tilt.

Omar Vizquel walked to lead off the game. Tony Fernandez and Jim Thome moved Vizquel over with consecutive ground outs. Matt Williams knocked a single past the first baseman to bring Omar home and get the Tribe on the board.

In the top of the third, the Tigers sent nine batters to the plate. With the bases loaded, Travis Fryman hit a line-drive two-run single. Next up, Tony Clark scorched a three-run home run to deep right center that put the Tigers up by four runs.

Tony Fernandez led off the bottom of the third with a home run. Later in the inning Julio Franco drove in Matt Williams to bring the score to 5-3.

Julio Franco drew a walk to lead off the bottom of the eighth inning. Brian Giles poked a single into short left field to move Julio into scoring position. Sandy Alomar laid down a perfect sacrifice bunt up the first base line to advance the runners. Omar Vizquel tied the game when he dropped a two-run double into left field off Detroit reliever Dan Miceli.

Eric Plunk made quick work of the Tigers in the eighth inning and returned to pitch the ninth. He started off by issuing a walk to Brian Johnson. The speedy Omar Olivares was sent in to pinch run for Johnson. A wild pitch by Plunk sent Olivares to second. Jody Reed was retired on a fly ball to right, but with two outs on a 0-1 pitch, Brian Hunter knocked a single through the gap between second and short. Olivares scored from second, putting the Tigers up 6-5.

Matt Williams led off the bottom of the ninth with a single over second base. A wild pitch by Tiger's closer Doug Brocail advanced him to second base. Backup catcher Raul Cassanova lost track of the 2-0 pitch to David Justice, and Williams reached third on the passed ball.

David Justice sent a fly ball into center field which allowed Williams to tag up and tie the game on the sacrifice. Next up, Manny Ramirez would reach on a line drive to short center field. Brocail issued a walk to Julio Franco, sending Manny to second. Chad Curtis was sent in to pinch run. Brian Giles grounded to third, and the runners advanced. But the Indians were down to their last out.

On a 1-0 pitch, Sandy drove a fly ball to deep right field. It stayed in the park, but easily scored Curtis for the walk-off RBI. This was the first of five walk-off wins in the 1997 campaign.

Later in the month, during Game 50. Sandy would record the only hit of the game, breaking up Mike Mussina's bid for a Perfect Game. In July of 1997, Sandy was selected to the All-Star team. The All-Star game was being hosted in Cleveland for the fifth time, and the first time at Jacobs Field. In front of the home crowd, Sandy hit the go-ahead home run in the seventh inning of the midsummer classic. He was the first player ever to be selected as the All-Star MVP in his home stadium.

Game 28
May 7, 1999
Tribe Completes Comeback with Huge 7th and 8th Innings

On a warm Friday evening at Jacob's Field, a steady wind was blowing directly out to center. Dwight Gooden was matched up with Rays starter Bobby Witt.

The Rays struck first when Enrique Wilson mishandled a routine ground ball, putting Fred McGriff on first. John Flaherty laced a single down the right field line, allowing McGriff to come around and score from first.

Tampa Bay added another three runs in the top of the third. The first run came via an RBI single by former Indian Herbert Perry. That was followed by a two-run homer by McGriff.

Kenny Lofton drew a walk in the bottom of the third. Enrique Wilson shot a double into right field that moved Lofton to third. Robbie Alomar hit a sharp grounder to second that allowed Lofton to score. The Rays were up 4-1.

Gooden lost his command in the fourth inning. He gave up a single to Kevin Stocker who then advanced to second on a wild pitch. He intentionally walked Dave Martinez to get to Herbert Perry, who drove a single down the left field line which scored Stocker and put Tampa ahead 5-1.

Gooden's day ended early, and Paul Wagner came in from the bullpen. The Rays scored another four runs as Wagner struggled to find his footing.

David Justice blasted a solo homer to deep right center in the Indians' half of the fourth inning, but that barely closed the gap. The score sat at 9-2 in favor of the Rays.

Former Indian Paul Sorrento lined an RBI single through the right side of the infield. This drove in Herbert Perry and extended the Tampa Bay lead to 10-2.

56

The Indians' comeback began in the bottom of the sixth inning. Robbie Alomar led things off with a triple. Manny Ramirez hit a liner into left field which scored Alomar. After a Travis Fryman strikeout, Wil Cordero slapped a single into left that put Manny on second base. David Justice stepped in and smashed a three-run homer into the bleachers. The Rays brought Rick White into the game in relief. White got the final two outs of the inning, but not before the Indians closed the deficit to four runs.

The Tribe sent 13 batters to the plate in the bottom of the seventh inning. Travis Hafner hit a three-run bomb, and was followed immediately by a solo shot from Wil Cordero. Cleveland took the lead on a two-run single off the bat of Enrique Wilson. Reliever Jim Mecir walked in another run. After seven runs on six hits in the inning, the Tribe were up 13-11.

Reliever Steve Reed sat the Rays down in order in the top of the eighth inning. Eddie Galliard came on to pitch for the Rays and the offensive onslaught continued. The Indians batted around once again. The inning saw another seven runs on six hits including Robbie Alomar's majestic grand slam into the right field seats.

The Indians were down eight runs after six innings. The Win Expectancy at this point was 99% in favor of the Rays. The Tribe hit 8 for 16 with runners in scoring position and ended up winning the game 20 to 11.

Game 29
May 2, 2018
Three Home Runs from Encarnacion

This game is the first in the series that I saw in person. Driving home from a late day at work Tuesday night, Tom Hamilton was previewing the next day's game. "Wednesday afternoon. Beautiful Spring weather. Corey Kluber on the mound. Be here if you can find a way." I couldn't agree more. In my estimation, one of the best feelings in the world is standing at the bus stop with a half day of work behind you and half a day of baseball ahead of you.

The previous evening, the Rangers topped the Indians 8-6 in twelve innings and appeared to be eager to get back to Texas. It was a perfect early May day with temperatures in the 80s, abundant sunshine, and a stiff breeze out to right field that would certainly come into play.

Kluber came out firing, retiring the Rangers in order with strikeouts against Delino DeShields and Jurickson Profar.

Rajai Davis grounded out to lead off the game, but the Indians' office got spun up quickly. Jason Kipnis lofted a double down the left field line. Francisco Lindor shot a grounder through the right side of the infield, advancing Kipnis to third. Michael Brantley scored Kipnis on another ground ball single. Edwin Encarnacion stepped in and rocked a three-run home run halfway up the bleachers. Yonder Alonso and Brandon Guyer both lined out to end the inning.

My cousin and I often text each other during ballgames to alert the other that exciting things are happening. He was a huge Encarnacion fan during Eddie's tenure in Cleveland. A single-character message--the bird emoji--had become our shorthand for an Encarnacion home run, in reference to his "parrot ride" gesture. I quickly fired off a message between innings to my cousin who was still at work.

Kluber would rarely miss today, but in the top of the second, Nomar Mazara caught hold of the 2-1 pitch, driving a homer to right center and making it a 4-1 game.

In the bottom of the second, Erik Gonzalez and Rajai Davis got aboard with one out. Jason Kipnis launched a home run over the right field wall for the Tribe's second three-run home run of the game. With two outs and Lindor on second, Encarnacion sent Matt Moore's first pitch over the right field wall in front of the bullpens. At the end of the inning I picked up my phone. BIRD BIRD was already in my inbox.

In the top of the third, Kluber once again gave up a leadoff home run--this time to Juan Centeno. The Rangers would eventually get runners to first and second, but Kluber would work his way out of the threat with the score 9-2.

Kluber retired the Rangers in order in the fourth, fifth, and sixth innings. In the seventh, he gave up yet another leadoff home run to Joey Gallo. He would retire the next three Rangers and finish the day giving up 6 hits, three runs, and recording six strikeouts.

Dan Otero took the mound in the 8th and gave up the only run the Rangers scored by way other than the longball. Former Indian Shin-Soo Choo drove in Drew Robinson with a sharp single up the middle.

In the bottom of the eighth, Francisco Lindor would tee off into the wind, sending a home run into the bullpen. Two batters later, with two outs in the eighth, Encarnacion ripped a third homer, once again into the bleachers.

I didn't wait for the end of the inning this time:
BIRD BIRD BIRD.

Quickly a reply came in: AGAIN? I should have taken off work.

Reliever Ben Taylor came on to pitch the bottom of the ninth. He walked Nomar Mazara to lead off the inning, but was able to seal the 12-4 victory.

Game 30
May 15, 1977
Indians Win Despite Rick Manning's Platinum Sombrero

In 1858 British cricketer H. H. Stephenson took three consecutive wickets on three balls for the All-England Eleven. A collection was taken up in the stands, and Stephenson was presented with a new hat. Since then, positive things happening in sports–and arriving in threes–are referred to as a hat trick.

In the first half of the 1900's, baseball writers would occasionally refer ironically to a player who struck out three times in a game as having "completed the hat trick."

If three strikeouts is a (negative) hat-trick, then what embarrassment would four strikeouts in a single game bring? Carmelo Martinez of the Padres coined the term "Golden Sombrero" in the 1980's. And for the rare five-strikeout feat? The Platinum Sombrero, of course.

Sixty-four players have worn the Platinum Sombrero in MLB history. Only three Indians have recorded five-strikeout games in nine-inning contests. Interestingly, they are all household names. Even more curiously, the Indians have won every game in which a single player has recorded five strikeouts. Larry Doby wore his in Game 4 of 1948 and went on to win the World Series. Jim Thome wore his in Game 6 of 2000 and would go on to be the Indians all-time home run leader. Rick Manning's platinum sombrero came in May 1977.

On a Sunday afternoon on the south side of Chicago, Dennis Eckersley was set to face off with Francisco Barrios of the White Sox. Batting third in the lineup, Manning struck out swinging in the top of the first.

In the second inning, the Indians manufactured three runs on three hits, including an RBI single by Jim Norris. In the top of the third, Barrios got Manning to strike out swinging again for the first out.

In the bottom of the fourth, Ritchie Zisk hit an RBI triple to left field bringing the score to 3-1.

Manning struck out swinging in the top of the fifth inning once again. In the Chicago half of the inning, the White Sox drew to within one run on an RBI single by Jorge Orta.

Barrios faced only three batters in the top of the seventh, including a fourth swinging strikeout for Manning.

Buddy Bell extended the Indians lead to 4-2 in the bottom of the eighth inning. He pushed Paul Dade across the plate with a single to left field.

The Sox answered in the bottom half of the eighth with a solo home run by Lamar Johnson off Indians reliever Don Hood. Reliever Jim Kern came on to pitch and got the final out of the inning.

Rick Manning recorded the Indian's 27th out, when Sox reliever Dave Hamilton got him to strike out looking to end the top of the ninth inning. Despite issuing a walk to Royle Stillman in the bottom of the ninth, Kern was able to close out the 4-3 victory for Cleveland.

While there is no special term for a Platinum Sombrero in only 5 plate appearances, this certainly puts Manning's performance at the forefront of futility even among Sombrero-wearers.

Of course, this single game is not reflective of Rick Manning's career. He was enshrined as one of the Top 100 Indians of the Century by the team in 2000. Manning was a career .257 hitter, a prolific base stealer, a Gold Glove winner in 1976, and of course caught the final out of a Perfect Game in Game 24 (see page 47). He is now the longest-tenured Indians broadcaster.

Game 31
May 28, 1934
Earl Averill Walk-off Double

Connie Mack's Athletics were wrapping up a weekend series at League Park on this Monday afternoon. The A's had some outstanding athletes on the roster in 1934 and some even more outstanding old-timey baseball names such as Doc Cramer, Pinky Higgins, and Rabbit Warstler.

Warstler led off the game with a single. Warstler caught Indians starter Oral Hildebrand napping and quickly stole second. He was driven home when Jimmie Foxx sent Hildebrand's first pitch over the League Park wall and put the A's up 2-0 early.

With two outs in the bottom of the first, Earl Averill answered with a home run of his own. In the bottom of the second, Hal Trosky tied the game at two runs apiece with an RBI double.

The A's pulled ahead again in the top of the third inning. Rabbit Warstler once again led off with a double. Jimmie Foxx drove him in with an inside-the-park home run.

Indians right fielder Bob Seeds walked to lead off the bottom of the third. Bill Knickerbocker moved Seeds over with a single into right field. Averill grounded to short, scoring Seeds while Knickerbocker was forced out at second. Joe Vosmik and Odell Hale got aboard to load the bases, and then A's pitcher Johnny Marcum hit Frankie Pytlak, forcing Averill home. This tied the game at four.

Hildebrand would not give up another hit through the seventh inning. In the bottom of the seventh, Odell Hale led off by dropping a double into center field. Hal Trosky grounded one slowly to the second baseman, allowing Hale to advance to third. Frankie Pytlak grounded one to the shortstop. Hale was tagged out at home on a fielder's choice. The A's intentionally walked Willie Kamm to get to the pitcher Hildebrand with two outs. The pitcher stepped in and slapped a single into center and put the Tribe up 5-4.

Monte Pearson replaced Hildebrand on the mound for the Tribe in the ninth inning. With two outs, Pearson walked Foxx and then gave up the tying run when A's shortstop Eric McNair knocked a triple into the spacious League Park outfield. Pearson got Lou Finney to ground out to end the inning with the game tied at five runs apiece.

The Tribe were unable to score in the bottom of the ninth. They stranded Frankie Pytlak on third and headed into extra innings. Pinky Higgins led off the A's half of the tenth inning with a double, but Pearson was able to retire the next three A's without incident.

In the bottom of the 10th, Bill Knickerbocker poked a single into center field. Then, Earl Averill stepped in and knocked a double into left. Knickerbocker hustled around to score from first and end the game. Averill's three hits, three RBI, and one intentional walk were key in securing the extra-inning win and the series sweep of the A's.

Averill was one of the more prolific hitters of early Indians history. His career total of 226 homers was a franchise record for 55 years. That mark has only been surpassed by Jim Thome (337), Albert Belle (242), and Manny Ramirez (236).

Averill's natural hitting prowess would be tested during the next season. Just before Fourth of July 1935, Averill was lighting fireworks with his children and one exploded while he was holding it. He suffered burns to his face, chest, and hands. Despite the injury, he still hit .288 for the season and made the All-Star team.

Game 32
May 13, 2015
Kluber Shaves Beard, Strikes out Eighteen in Eight Innings

The start of the 2015 season had been rough on Corey Kluber. After winning the AL Cy Young award in 2014, he lost his first five decisions of the 2015 campaign. Of his eight starts so far in 2015, the Indians had lost seven. By mid-May many fans and commentators were worried about their presumed ace pitcher.

The Cardinals were in Cleveland for an interleague series and sent veteran pitcher John Lackey to the mound for this Wednesday evening contest against the normally hirsute Kluber. When Corey came to the mound clean-shaven, fans assumed that, in a fit of baseball superstition, he was trying to change his luck.

Kluber got leadoff hitter Kolten Wong to strike out swinging on five pitches to start the game. Matt Carpenter flied out to center. Kluber hit left fielder Matt Holliday with the first pitch of his at-bat. It was perhaps his only major lapse in control. Former Indian Jhonny Peralta struck out swinging to end the inning.

Lackey got off to a rough start. He walked Jason Kipnis on four pitches right out of the gate. This was followed by a six-pitch walk to Carlos Santana. After a Michael Brantley strikeout, right fielder Brandon Moss hit a liner down the right field line which allowed Kipnis to score from second. David Murphy knocked a ground ball single to right, bringing Santana home.

With a 2-0 lead established, the rest of the night was the Corey Kluber show. He racked up a franchise-record eighteen strikeouts in eight innings of work. He recorded at least one strikeout in each inning pitched.

He took a no-hitter into the top of the seventh inning, when former Indian Jhonny Peralta poked a single into center field.

He threw 113 pitches in the game, 74 of them were strikes. With his pitch count climbing, the no-hitter broken up, and Cody Allen ready to slam the door, Kluber did not return to the mound for the top of the ninth inning. Cody Allen retired the side in order on 11 pitches and earned the save.

In Indians history, only Bob Feller had eighteen strikeouts in a nine-inning game (Game 152 of 1938, which was a 4-1 loss to the Tigers!). Luis Tiant holds the single-game strikeout record for the Tribe, but his 19 Ks came in a 10-inning victory over the Twins (see page 158).

Kluber would go on to put together one of the most amazing months of pitching in Indians history, with 60 strikeouts in the month of May. Sam McDowell holds the record for most strikeouts in a calendar month with 76. However, McDowell pitched in a four-man rotation prior to the institution of the designated hitter. Normalized for innings pitched, Kluber recorded 12.56 strikeouts per nine innings in May 2014. McDowell's best month was 12.35 K/9 in September of 1966.

When asked in a post-game interview if he shaved his beard to change his luck, Corey stated, "I did it for Mother's Day."

Game 33
May 14, 1994
Paul Shuey Strikes Our Four in the Ninth Inning

The Indians selected Paul Shuey as the second overall pick in the 1992 amateur draft. He was projected to be Cleveland's closer as the 1990's dynasty began to gel together.

About a month after moving into Jacob's Field, the Indians had a 16-17 record and were facing the Tigers in a weekend divisional series. Jack Morris started for the Tribe against Bill Gullickson.

Eddie Murray put the Indians in the lead in the bottom of the first inning with a line drive triple which bounced around the right field corner. Murray's triple sent Carlos Baerga and Albert Belle around to score.

With two outs in the bottom of the fifth inning, Manny Ramirez launched a three-run bomb run to deep right field. The Indians would continue to cruise through the rest of the game. They brought a 9-3 lead into the top of the ninth.

Paul Shuey came on to replace setup man Jose Mesa who had given up one run on three hits in the seventh and eighth innings. Shuey got Chad Kreuter to strike out looking on six pitches. Next up was Chris Gomez, who struck out looking in a seven pitch at-bat. Then, Shuey issued two consecutive walks to Tony Philips and Milt Cuyler.

With two outs, Travis Fryman came to the plate. On the 0-2 pitch, Fryman struck out swinging, but the ball got away from Sandy Alomar. Fryman took first base on the wild pitch, and the other runners advanced to load the bases. Undeterred, Shuey headed back to the mound and struck out Cecil Fielder to end the game.

He became the 24th MLBer to record four strikeouts in an inning, and the *first* to do so in the ninth to end the game. Eighty-eight different pitchers have pitched four-strikeout innings to date.

Game 34
June 4, 1995
Paul Sorrento Completes Nine Run Comeback

The Blue Jays (still considered the defending Champions, since there were no playoffs in 1994) were wrapping up a weekend series in Cleveland. The pitching matchup did not set up favorably, with reigning Cy Young winner David Cone pitching for the Jays against Jason Grimsley. Grimsley was making his second start of the year in a role recently vacated by Mark Clark.

Grimsley got off to a dismal start by walking the first three batters he faced. Joe Carter then plated two runs with a single to left field and John Olerud knocked in another. Robbie Alomar bunted to advance the runners, and was followed by a three-run home run by Shawn Green. Grimsley walked Ed Sprague while Chad Ogea was getting warm in the bullpen.

Sprague scored on a Devon White sacrifice fly before Ogea was able to right the ship. At the end of the first, the Tribe found themselves in a 7-0 hole.

Cone mowed through the Indians, facing only seven batters in the first two innings. The Jays added an insurance run on a sacrifice hit by Devon White in the top of the third.

The Tribe began the long climb back from the eight-run deficit in the bottom of the third. Omar Vizquel scored Wayne Kirby on a two-out single into left field.

Ogea found his footing and retired the Jays in order in both the fourth and fifth innings.

Eddie Murray cut the lead to three with a two-run home run in the bottom of the fifth inning. After Albert Belle singled in backup catcher Eddie Tucker (in his 17-game cup of coffee with the Tribe) David Cone's day was done.

Jay's reliever Tony Castillo held on to the 8-6 lead until the bottom of the ninth inning. After Carlos Baerga was thrown out attempting to bunt, Castillo was pulled in favor of Darren Hall. Albert Belle dropped a single into short center field, starting the late-night rally. Eddie Murray singled into right, advancing Belle to third base. Alvaro Espinoza was brought in to pinch-run for Murray. Espinoza was forced out at second when Jim Thome grounded out to short. However, Belle scored on the groundout, cutting the Jay's lead to one run.

Paul Sorrento smashed the first pitch he faced to right field. A stiff breeze was blowing in, and appeared to knock it down a bit. However, it squeaked over the right field wall and set off the first walk-off celebration of the 1995 season.

In a post-game interview, Sorrento commented on the homer,
"The wind was blowing in. I got a good pitch and I just killed it. "I thought I may have celebrated too early because it barely went out—it was only like the first or second row. ...I just remember thinking, 'Please go out, because I'm going to look like an idiot if it doesn't.' It ended up just capping off a great team win. We never gave up."

Sorrento's contributions to the 1995 World Series run are often overlooked. Over the first six weeks of the season he slashed .303/.394/.775. In 104 appearances, he hit .235 with 25 home runs, providing solid protection for the likes of Jim Thome and Manny Ramirez hitting in the 5 and 6 holes.

Game 35
May 23, 1970
Jack Heidemann Walk-off in the 13th vs Yankees

Sometimes the most unremarkable teams and the most forgettable players end up being heroes for a day. The 1970 Indians were one of the most forgettable teams in Tribe history. They finished fifth in the AL East with a record of 76 and 86. Sam McDowell and Ray Fosse are probably the only 1970 teammates with name recognition beyond the most loyal fans.

Jack Heidemann was drafted 11th overall by the Indians in 1967. He made his Major League debut in May of 1969. He appeared in nine games during the 1969 season and ended up with a .000 batting average.

Just over 6,800 tickets were sold for the Saturday afternoon contest with the Yankees on the lakefront. The fans who actually attended got to see plenty of baseball, though. The Indians matched up starter Rich Hand (no relation to reliever Brad) with the Yankees Gary Waslewski.

Hand would scatter two runs on five hits over the first six innings. Waslewski lasted only four innings, giving up two runs on four hits, including a two-run home run by left fielder Duke Sims in the bottom of the fourth

The Yankees took a 3-2 lead in the bottom of the seventh inning on an RBI single by Frank Tepedino. The Tribe answered in the bottom of the eighth when Duke Sims teed off again, this time with a solo home run that tied the game at three runs apiece.

In extra innings, Indians reliever Phil Hennigan was brilliant, retiring 9 out of 10 Yankees in the eleventh, twelfth, and thirteenth innings. In the bottom of the thirteenth, Duke Sims trotted to first after being hit by a pitch. Backup third baseman Larry Brown sent Duke to third on a ground-rule double.

With runners on first and third, the Yankees brought in reliever Jack Aker and intentionally walked the dangerous rookie Ray Fosse (who would go on to hit .307 with 18 home runs for the season).

69

Jack Heidemann stepped in for his sixth plate appearance of the day. He was hitting just above .200 on the season. Heideman was six feet tall and only 178 pounds. At age 20, he was the ninth-youngest player in the league at the time. In other words, he looked like an easy out.

His only hit of the day was the game winner. Heidemann poked a single into left field. Sims came around to score and secure the win. Thirty-four players saw action in this extra-inning contest, which took nearly four hours to play.

Game 36
May 15, 2012
Derek Lowe Throws Complete Game Shutout with No Strikeouts

Derek Lowe had long been known as a ground-ball pitcher who relied on his strong sinker as his out pitch. That sinker carried him through a 16-year MLB career and ensured that he would never buy a drink in Boston after a 3-0 playoff record in the Red Sox's historic 2004 World Series run.

Game 36 of 2013 was perhaps the purest distillation of Lowe's style. Against a Twins team that was scuffling on offense and had been particularly inept against ground-ball pitchers, Lowe induced 20 ground-ball outs including four double-plays.

He was supported by RBI singles in the second and third innings by Casey Kotchman and Asdrubal Cabrera, respectively.

Things got out of hand for Twins starter Jason Marquis in the top of the fifth inning. He gave up solo home runs to Shin-Soo Choo, Asdrubal Cabrera, and Carlos Santana. The Indians had a 5-0 lead and Lowe was not about to look back.

Lowe cruised through the Twins lineup. In the fifth, sixth, and ninth innings all three outs came on ground balls. He threw 127 pitches, 76 of which were strikes.

In a post-game interview, a reporter observed that his season strikeout total (13) was nearly matched by his double-play count (10). Lowe quipped, "If all goes well, I should get to 40 [strikeouts] by the end of the year."

Later in the 2012 season, Lowe was designated for assignment in order to make a roster spot for a young ground-ball pitcher with a wicked sinker–Corey Kluber.

Game 37
May 25, 1926
George Uhle Walks Off His Own 11 Inning Complete Game

George "Bull" Uhle was the most dominant pitcher of 1926. Uhle was a native Clevelander and graduate of West High School. As a teenager, he played in the semi-pro industrial leagues around Cleveland, eventually landing a spot on the Standard Parts team, and a lucrative manufacturing job with Standard.

In 1919, Uhle reported to Indians Spring Training in New Orleans with a stipulation in his contract that he could not be sent to the minor leagues. He was resolved to return to Cleveland either on the roster or to his job. He later said. "If I wasn't good enough for the majors, I wanted my release. I figured I could do better working at Standard Parts."

Uhle earned a spot on the pitching staff, and developed his game throughout the 1920's, including pitching in the 1920 World Series. A ligament ailment set him back a bit in the early half of the decade, but by 1926 he was hitting his stride.

The St. Louis Browns were at League Park (then called Dunn Field after owner Sunny Jim Dunn) for a Tuesday afternoon contest. George Uhle was matched up with Tom Zachary of the Browns.

Harry Rice led off the game for St. Louis with a double into left field. After two outs, Ken Williams doubled into left. Rice scored easily and put the Browns up 1-0 in the early going.

In the bottom of the second inning, the Indians got on the board when George Burns dropped a double into right and then was driven in by a Homer Summa single to tie the game.

The starting pitchers battled through the first six innings, until the Tribe broke through against Zachary. In the bottom of the sixth Luke Sewell led off with a single into right field. Batting at the bottom of the order, Uhle singled to center, advancing Sewell to third base.

Charlie Jamieson and Freddy Spurgeon reached on consecutive errors by Browns second baseman Ski Mellilo. Tris Speaker scored

Uhle on a fielder's choice. Joe Sewell walked, and then Jamieson scored on a sacrifice fly by George Burns, bringing the score to 4-1 Indians.

In the top of the eighth inning, Pinky Hargrave knocked a two-run home run into the League Park seats, bringing the Browns within one run.

Gene Robertson pinch hit for Zachary in the top of the ninth inning. He drove a triple to the center field wall. Robertson scored on a throwing error to tie the game.

Win Ballou came in to pitch for the Browns in the bottom of the ninth. The Indians threatened, but left the bases loaded to send the game to extra frames.

Uhle only seemed to get stronger as the day went on. He retired the side in order in both the tenth and eleventh innings. Uhle achieved his season-high strikeout total with ten.

In the bottom of the eleventh, Homer Summa drew a walk to lead things off. Rube Lutzke dropped a bunt down the first base line which moved Summa over to second. Luke Sewell knocked a single into right field. Brown's outfielder Harry Rice fielded the ball and fired home. He gunned down Summa for the second out of the inning while Sewell advanced to second.

Uhle stepped to the plate looking to help out his own cause. The Bull blasted a Walk-off home run over the tall right field wall at League Park. He sealed the win for the Indians and the best outing of his career.

Solid hitting was not unusual for Uhle, whose .289 career batting average is the highest for any pitcher (playing only as a pitcher). After four years with the Tigers, Uhle spent a few years as a player-coach in various organizations. After baseball, he returned once again to the Cleveland area. He lived in Lakewood until he passed away in 1985.

Game 38
May 16, 2011
Vin Mazzaro Gives Up Most Earned Runs Since WWII

Josh Tomlin faced off with Kyle Davies to start off a weeknight series in Kansas City. The game started off inauspiciously for the Royals, as Davies walked three out of the first four batters and was pulled in favor of Nathan Adcock after recording only one out.

Coming in with the bases loaded, Adcock got Travis Hafner to strike out on three straight pitches. Orlando Cabrera recorded the Indians first two runs by singling in Asdrubal Cabrera and Shin-Soo Choo. Carlos Santana got caught in a run down, ending the inning, but not before the Tribe hung two runs on the board.

Adcock struggled through the second inning as well, giving up one run on two hits. After walking Carlos Santana to lead off the top of the third, Royals manager Ned Yost made the call to the bullpen for Vin Mazzaro.

Mazzaro had proven to be a serviceable starting pitcher with Oakland through the 2009 and 2010 seasons. On May 10th, the Royals called him up from the AAA Omaha Storm Chasers to fill the spot in the rotation vacated by the injured Bruce Chen. Rather than deplete his bullpen, Yost elected to bring in Mazzaro who was originally scheduled to start the next day.

Besides a wild pitch to Tribe left fielder Travis Buck, the third inning went by without incident for Mazzaro. What followed was a combination of bad command, good hitting, and old-fashioned luck. The stars aligned to bring about a stat line not seen since the World War II era.

In the top of the fourth inning, things began to unravel for Mazzaro. Matt LaPorta led off the inning with a line drive single to right. Asdrubal Cabrera drove in Jack Hannahan to push the lead to 4-0. In a normal situation, most managers would have pulled Mazzaro after Travis Hafner's three-run double. However, Ned Yost was already on his second starting pitcher. He decided to press on. Still with two outs, Orlando Cabrera drove in Hafner with a single down the right field line. Travis Buck singled, and then was driven in by a

Matt LaPorta double. Hannahan singled, and then Michael Brantley's three-run homer made the score 10-0. Asdrubal Cabrera, the fourteenth batter of the inning, brought the top of the fourth to a close with a strikeout.

Billy Butler got the Royals on the scoreboard in the bottom of the fourth inning, but the Royals could only manage one run.

Improbably, Mazzaro emerged from the Royals dugout to pitch the top of the fifth inning. Choo led off with a fly out to deep right. Carlos Santana hit a ground ball double into right field. Mazzaro walked Hafner, and Orlando Cabrera dribbled a weak ground ball to third to load the bases. Travis Buck poked a line drive single into left-center, scoring Santana.

Finally, Yost made the call for reliever Jeremy Jeffress. Jeffress entered the game facing a thirteen-run deficit. Matt LaPorta welcomed him to the game with a two-run double and Jack Hannahan drove in Travis Buck with a grounder. This pinned a total of fourteen earned runs on Mazzaro.

His ERA for 2⅓ innings of work was an astronomical 22.74. The last pitcher to give up 14 earned was the A's Mike Oquist who did so over five innings in a start in 1988. Even Bob Feller is on the list of 14-ers. He gave up fourteen runs over seven innings against the Yankees in 1938. However, Mazzaro was the first to give up 14 earned runs in relief since Les McCrab in 1942, and the *only* MLBer to do it in less than three innings pitched.

The Indians cruised to a 19-1 victory, and Mazzaro was promptly sent back to Omaha. At the time, many writers and fans speculated that this historic defeat would be the end of Vin's career. In fact, Mazzaro was called back to the Royals on June 7. He finished the season with a record of 4-3 in 18 mostly relief appearances.

Mazzaro was quoted in a post-game interview, "Some of the plays didn't go my way. It's a funny game. You've just got to keep battling and attack the zone."

Game 39
May 17, 1996
Manny Ramirez Pinch-Hits a Grand Slam

The Indians came into this weekend series with the Rangers riding a five-game winning streak. Orel Hershiser matched up with Kevin Gross in front of a sold-out Friday night crowd.

Eddie Murray punched a single through the right side of the infield to lead off the bottom of the second inning. After two outs, Sandy Alomar hit a dribbler up the third base line. Gross charged from the mound to field it, but botched the throw to first. Sandy was safe at first. Omar Vizquel took advantage of the extra out when he drove a single sharply into center field which allowed Murray and Alomar to score.

Hershiser gave up a lead-off home run to Kevin Elster in the top of the third, but retired the next three batters to keep the Tribe on top 2-1.

Things went sideways for Hershiser in the top of the fourth inning. Texas scored five runs on six straight hits, including four doubles. After Kevin Elster's double, Joe Roa was summoned from the bullpen. Roa gave up the sixth run of the inning on a line-drive single by Pudge Rodriguez, but otherwise was able to stop the bleeding.

In the top of the fifth inning, Roa walked Mark McLemore and then gave up back to back doubles to Kevin Elster and Darryl Hamilton. Alan Embree replaced Roa and secured the last out of the fifth. The Indians were now down 9 runs to 2. Fans were wondering if they would see some Jacobs Field comeback magic, or if they ought to beat traffic out of downtown Cleveland.

The Tribe began to close the gap in the bottom of the fifth inning. Sandy Alomar sent Gross' first pitch into left field for a single. Omar advanced Sandy to third with a line drive double into right field. A deep fly out by Kenny Lofton allowed Alomar to tag and score. Julio Franco drove a single into right field which brought Omar home, but the Indians were still behind 4 to 9.

Alan Embree battled through the top of the sixth inning, striking out the Rangers side in order on 19 total pitches.

Eddie Murray led off the bottom of the sixth with a solo home run. After the homer, the Rangers called to the bullpen for reliever Dennis Cook. Cook quickly struck out Jim Thome. Manny Ramirez was brought in to pinch hit for right fielder Jeromy Burnitz. Manny Ramirez and Sandy Alomar were retired in order, unable to build on the solid start to the inning.

Kevin Elster touched up Embree for a line-drive solo home run in the top of the seventh inning, extending the Rangers lead to 10-5.

With two outs in the bottom of the seventh and Kenny Lofton on first, Carlos Baerga hit a bloop single into short right field. Lofton reached third on a throwing error. With runners at the corners, Albert Belle singled to center, sending Lofton in to score. Next, Eddie Murray stepped in and knocked an almost identical single to center driving in Baerga.

Reliever Ed Vosburg came in to face Jim Thome, walking him to load the bases. Vosburg was promptly replaced by Gil Heredia. Heredia headed to the mound and immediately got behind in the count to Manny Ramirez.

Manny drove a laser shot into the bleachers. Manny's grand slam put the Tribe ahead 11-10. Albert Belle would later drive in Lofton for an insurance run. Jose Mesa secured the save, and the 1996 Indians kept on rolling toward a second-straight Division Championship.

Manny is regarded as one of the best clutch hitters of all time. He was masterful with runners on base. Ramirez hit thirteen grand slams over his eight-year career with the Indians. Over his entire career, he recorded twenty-one, which is third on the all-time list only behind Alex Rodriguez (25) and Lou Gehrig (23).

Game 40
May 14, 2014
Lonnie Chisenhall and David Murphy Combine for Ten Hits

Corey Kluber was matched up with Justin McGowan for this mid-week contest north of the border. It was a banner hitting day for the Indians offense, but particularly for David Murphy and Lonnie Chisenhall. Everyone in the batting order, except for first baseman Nick Swisher, had at least one hit, and even Swisher walked twice.

In the top of the second inning, David Murphy had an RBI single, sending Carlos Santana in to score. Lonnie Chisenhall singled to left field with two outs, but both Murphy and Chis were stranded on second base by a Mike Aviles pop-out.

Murphy led off the fourth with a double to right field. Chisenhall drove him in with an RBI single to right.

In the top of the fifth inning, Michael Brantley led off with a double into right field. Carlos Santana cranked a homer out to right-center to extend the Tribe lead to 4-0. Later in the inning, Murphy flied out to center, while Chisenhall beat out the throw on a dribbler in front of home plate, but both were stranded when Mike Aviles grounded out to end the inning.

Murphy drove home Asdrubal Cabrera in the top of the seventh, who had reached on a leadoff double. After a Yan Gomes ground out, Chisenhall reached on a single to left field.

By the end of the seventh inning, the score sat at 6-2 Indians. Corey Kluber had quietly pitched a very solid start, giving up two runs on four hits using only 108 pitches. Kluber retired the first 13 batters before giving up a hit, which was a double by Adam Lind.

With runners on first and second in the top of the eighth inning, Murphy smacked a line drive double into right field, scoring Carlos Santana and Asdrubal Cabrera. Lonnie Chisenhall ended the inning with a line-drive out to deep center field. Manager Terry Francona later said, "Lonnie probably could've had another one. His out was hard hit." The score sat at 9-2 Indians.

The Tribe sent ten batters to the plate in the top of the ninth inning. After an RBI triple by Michael Bourn, and an RBI single by Jose Ramirez, Murphy was up again. He sent a sharp liner down the right field line to score Ramirez. Yan Gomes battled through a twelve-pitch at-bat, finally rocking a line drive three-run home run into right field. After Gomes had cleared the bases, Jays backup infielder Steve Tolleson was brought in to pitch.

Chisenhall doubled down the right field line off one of Tolleson's knuckleballs for his fifth hit of the day. Tolleson got Mike Aviles to pop out to end the inning.

Carlos Carrasco pitched the ninth inning. He gave up two runs, but secured the Indians 15-4 victory.

Two Indians had not had five hits in the same nine-inning game since Johnny Hodapp and Luke Sewell had five each in Game 101 of 1928 against the Yankees (see page 191).

Game 41
May 30, 1977
Dennis Eckersley's Memorial Day No-hitter

On Memorial Day 1977, the Angels were in town and Cleveland had a young, brash pitcher on the mound. A still clean-shaven Dennis Eckersley was matched up with Angels ace Frank Tanana. In his previous start, Eckersley recorded a complete game and had held the Mariners hitless for the final 7⅔ innings.

Tommy Smith, a teammate of my father, shared a story with me about his experience of this game. His observations are interspersed with the game narrative.

"We had started the day finishing up in third place in a softball tournament. Our last game concluded about 1:00 p.m. Four of us, along with three of our wives decided to grab a bite to eat at the local tavern and make plans for the rest of the evening. The guys' intention was to go see the young phenom Dennis Eckersley pitch on a beautiful evening. We were vetoed when one of the wives decided she had seen enough baseball and softball. So, we asked what she wanted to do. She wanted us all to go see a movie. We let her have her way and went to see It's Alive."

Eckersley issued a walk to Tony Solaita in the top of the first inning, but otherwise made quick work of the Angels.

Rick Manning struck out to lead off the Indians' half of the first. Duane Kuiper hit a fly ball to center field. Gil Flores attempted a shoestring catch, but narrowly missed the ball. The hit rolled to the base of the wall, and Kuiper was aboard with a triple. Right fielder Jim Norris executed a suicide squeeze to bring Kuiper home. This first-inning run is the only support Eck would need.

"It was one of the worst movies I have ever seen in my life. We walked out of the theater about 9:15 and turned on the game as we headed out to dinner."

Eckersley mowed through the Angels lineup. The only other California baserunner was Bobby Bonds. Bonds struck out to lead off the eighth inning, but strike three bounced away from Tribe catcher Ray Fosse. Bonds made it safely to first base, and it was ruled a wild pitch.

"It was the top of the eighth inning, and Eckersley had not given up a hit. A no-no, and we were missing it! We got to the restaurant in the top of the ninth and the ladies walked in while the four guys stayed near the car to hear the end of the game."

With Bonds at first, Don Baylor bounced a grounder to the shortstop. To some, it appeared that Bond's beat the throw to second base. Umpire Dale Ford called him out. The 6-4-3 double play stood, despite Angel's manager Norm Sherry's argument.

"We turned the car radio up as loud as it would go, and none of us said a word, hoping not to jinx the moment."

California shortstop Grich led off the top of the ninth inning. He struck out for the second time of the evening. Next up was pinch hitter Willie Aiken. He lifted a short fly ball to left field for out number two. Everyone in the crowd of 13,400 was up on their feet as centerfielder Gil Flores came to the plate.

Flores took him time stepping into the batter's box. Eckersley shouted at Flores from the mound. He later recounted, "He was trying to psych me out. So, I yelled at to him to get up to the plate." Flores finally stepped in,

"Strike one was called and Flores was not happy. Ball one came and the crowd was anxious. The third pitch was fouled back and now the count was 1 - 2. You could hear a pin drop in the stadium, and in the parking lot, as the next pitch was delivered."

Flores swung and missed! Eckersley had completed the thirteenth no-hitter in Indians history. He also had a chance, in his next start, at Cy Young's record of 23 consecutive hitless innings.

"The four of us looked at each other and couldn't utter a word. Baseball history in our own backyard and we had missed it in

81

favor of It's Alive. *A game that goes down in Indians history...sure would have been nice to have been there.*"

Eckersley would go on to strike out over 191 batters in the 1977 season. He fell just short of Cy Young's streak when he gave up a homer in the fifth inning of his next start. He led the league with a 3.54 strikeout to walk ratio. He will appear again in the Project, pitching for his hometown Oakland A's in Game 71 (see page 139).

Game 42
June 12, 1995
The Sellout Streak Begins

The 1995 Indians would go on to win 100 games and fall just short in the World Series. General Manager John Hart's home-grown talent was finally bearing real fruit. The team featured All-Stars at nearly every position. Solid hitters who would have populated the heart of the order on lesser teams like Paul Sorrento and Manny Ramirez were often listed 7th or 8th behind mashers like Albert Belle and Jim Thome.

On a Monday night in June 1995, Jacobs Field sold out. In most cities, baseball attendance picks up when school is out for the summer and when folks begin to take vacations. So, this was not altogether surprising. What followed was exceptional.

The Indians would go on to win six straight division titles and treat the fans to 44 walk-off wins over the next six years. The sellouts would continue: 455 consecutive regular season home games. Until Game Two of the 2001 season (see Page 5), a ticket was not available at first pitch.

Throughout the streak, seats were consistently added to Jacobs Field, bringing it to a peak capacity of 45,569. Some readers may remember the "Auxiliary Bleachers" that sprouted beyond the former picnic patio in center field for a few years. Subsequent renovations have dialed back capacity significantly, with current seating listed at 34,788.

From 1996 to 2001 Tribe attendance totaled over 3 Million each season. Currently, there are eight major league teams that have never drawn 3 million fans in a single season.

So, what happened on June 12, 1995 to kick it all off? Chuck Nagy pitched a solid seven innings, giving up three runs, only one of which was earned. Omar Vizquel drove home Wayne Kirby with a sacrifice hit in the bottom of the third inning.

The Tribe pulled away in the bottom of the fourth with an RBI double by Eddie Murray, an RBI single by Wayne Kirby, and a walk by Omar Vizquel with the bases loaded to force in a run.

Paul Assenmacher and Jose Mesa each pitched 1-2-3 innings in the eighth and ninth to close out the contest. In short, it was the type of game that happened nearly every night for the 1995 squad.

In 2001, Jim Thome commented on the end of the streak, "We appreciate what our fans did to achieve that streak. There were lots of nights when they could have stayed home and watched the game on television, but they came out to the ballpark."

Game 43
May 23, 2012
Vinnie Pestano Strikes Out a Batter in 23 Straight Appearances

2012 was a tumultuous year for the Indians. In mid-May, you could say that the fanbase was divided. The Tribe was in first place in the Central Division, but dead last in attendance. Fans had not bought in to the team after their hot start and slow decline throughout 2011.

The previous Saturday closer Chris Perez was quoted in a post-game interview saying, "Guys don't want to come over here, and people wonder why. Why doesn't Carlos Beltran want to come over here? Well, because of that [poor attendance] That's part of it. It doesn't go unnoticed -- trust us. I'm not calling out the fans. It's just how it is. ...Nobody wants to play in front of 5,000 fans."

In fact, 22,000 filed into the ballpark for this Wednesday evening matchup with the Tigers. Both starters, Zach McAllister and the Tiger's Doug Fister pitched shutout baseball through the fifth inning.

In the top of the sixth inning, Tigers center fielder Quentin Berry led off with a double. Andy Dirks drove him in with a line drive double into right field. Dirks tagged up on a long fly out by Miguel Cabrera, and was driven in on a fielder's choice by Prince Fielder.

Jason Kipnis led off the bottom of the sixth with a line drive into short center field. Travis Hafner tied the game at 2-2 on a home run to deep right field.

McAllister began to struggle again in the top of the seventh inning. He gave up back to back singles to Ramon Santiago and Gerald Laird. Matchup pitching by bullpen arms Nick Hagadone and Joe Smith got the Tribe out of the seventh unscathed.

Prince Fielder reached on a Jason Kipnis throwing error to lead off the top of the eighth inning. Vinny Pestano was brought in from the bullpen. Pestano was quickly becoming a reliable setup man, but got into a bit of trouble early in this outing when he gave up consecutive singles to load the bases.

With the bases full of Tigers, Pestano got former Indian Jhonny Peralta to strike out swinging on three consecutive pitches. With this, Pestano made an obscure–but impressive–entry in the Indian's franchise record book. He recorded a strikeout in twenty-three consecutive appearances. Pestano got Ramon Santiago to ground out, and then struck out Alex Avila to end the inning.

The Indians manufactured two runs in the bottom of the eighth that would make the deadball era proud. Kipnis scored on a fielder's choice when Travis Hafner hit once sharply to first and Prince Fielder botched the throw to the plate. Carlos Santana pushed Asdrubal Cabrera across the plate with a sacrifice fly, bringing the score to 4-2.

Chris Perez retired the Tigers in order to get his 15th save of the season. He was cheered heartily by the 22,000 in the ballpark, but remained a controversial figure throughout his stay in Cleveland.

Although Pestano's mark is impressive, it falls far short of the MLB record for consecutive appearances with a strikeout. Indians' World Series nemesis Aroldis Chapman holds the all-time record. While pitching for the Reds, Chapman struck out at least one batter in forty-nine straight appearances.

Game 44
June 2, 1933 (Second Game)
Mel Harder Complete Game Shutout

Game 44 was the second half of a Friday double-header. Mel Harder was matched up with Bump Hadley of the St. Louis Browns.

For the Tribe, Dick Porter doubled into left field to lead off the game. After Bill Cissel was put out on a line drive to left, Johnny Burnett drove Porter home with another double. The Indians took an early 1-0 lead.

Harder and Hadley would continue to battle through the evening. Both pitchers put up impressive stat lines. Harder gave up six hits and struck out four with no walks.

The Browns threatened in the bottom of the seventh inning. With runners on the corners, Harder got Sam West to ground out to third and end the inning. In the end, Hadley gave up only four hits and two walks but the one run in the first was all that Harder needed to get the complete game win.

Mel Harder was known for command of his pitches and being strategic, rather than overpowering hitters with speed. Not unlike the Indians of the late 2010's, the pitching staff of the early 1930's was one of the best in the league, but the offense was sub-par. In 1933, Harder led the league with a 2.95 ERA, but finished 15-17 in the win-loss column. Poor defense was a factor, but this was mostly due to a lack of run support, (the Indians scored three runs or less in 20 of his 31 starts).

A year earlier in 1932, Mel Harder threw the first official pitch at Municipal Stadium. In 1993, he was honored to throw a ceremonial "last pitch" at the Stadium after the final home game of 1993. Harder pitched for 20 seasons with the Tribe 1928 to 1947, only Walter Johnson of the Senators pitched more consecutive seasons (21) for one team. He then served as the Indians' pitching coach from 1948 to 1963, revolutionizing the role of a pitching coach in the MLB by promoting the use of the sinker.

Game 45
May 19, 2019
Shane Bieber Complete Game, 10 Strikeouts

The Indians were 4½ games back of the division-leading Twins coming into this Sunday afternoon game. Shane Bieber was scheduled to start against Yefry Ramirez and the lowly Orioles.

Bieber started the 2018 season in Akron with the RubberDucks. He posted a 1.16 ERA through five starts in Double-A and was quickly promoted to the AAA Columbus Clippers. On May 25, 2018 he threw the eighth no-hitter in Clippers history. That caught the attention of the big-league club, and Shane was brought up to join the Indians on May 31, 2018. In the intervening year he had honed his craft and was quickly becoming a dominant strikeout pitcher.

Bieber opened the game by striking out Jonathan Villar and Dwight Smith, Jr. Trey Mancini grounded out to first to end the inning.

The Indians staked Bieber to an early lead. Francisco Lindor led off with a drive into the right field corner. Lindor thought about stretching the hit for a triple, but ended up safe on second base. Jason Kipnis dropped a bunt right in front of the plate. Lindor advanced to third while Kipnis beat the throw and was safe at first. Carlos Santana stepped in and dropped Rodriguez' third pitch into right field. Lindor scored easily. Carlos Gonzales smashed a fly ball into the right field gap. O's centerfielder Stevie Wilkerson raced in, jumped, and made the catch on the warning track. Jason Kipnis tagged and scored from third.

Working with a 2-0 lead, Bieber Struck out Chris Davis on four pitches to start the top of the second inning. He quickly dispatched with Stevie Wilkerson and Renato Nunez to retire the side.

Catcher Roberto Perez led off the bottom of the second with a single into left field. Back at the top of the order, Lindor hit a nearly identical line drive down the first base line into the corner. Perez motored to third. With Kipnis at bat, Baltimore catcher Austin Wynns mishandled a pitch in the dirt. It took off between his legs and rolled nearly to the backstop. Perez hustled home on the passed ball to put the Tribe up 3-0.

Rio Ruiz led off for the O's with a single into left center. Hanser Alberto hit one sharply to first base. Carlos Santana caught it on one hop and deftly backpedaled to the bag and then threw to Lindor for the double play. Bieber struck out Dwight Smith Jr. for the second time to end the inning.

Santana blasted a homer to right field to begin the Indians half of the third inning. Yefry Rodriguez was quickly losing his command. After two consecutive walks and a wild pitch, Roberto Perez grounded out to short, but scored Carlos Gonzales.

Bieber racked up another two strikeouts in the fourth inning, and again in the fifth. In the top of the sixth he punched out Dwight Smith Jr. for the third time with a filthy slider. Trey Mancini slammed his helmet to the dirt after a failed check-swing.

The Tribe added another three runs in the bottom of the sixth inning, as the Orioles pitching staff could not find a groove all day. Rookie Oscar Mercado got his first big-league RBI with a double into left that scored Leonys Martin.

Bieber notched another two strikeouts in the top of the seventh inning. In the bottom of the seventh, Leonys Martin and Oscar Mercado got aboard with consecutive singles off O's reliever Gabriel Ynoa. Mike Freeman lined one off the out of town scoreboard in left center and put the Tribe up 10-0.

Richard Martin struck out to end the Orioles half of the eighth. Bieber had thirteen strikes and looked to be going strong, but had already thrown 98 pitches. Pitching coach Carl Willis was concerned about pushing Bieber's arm too far. He had never pitched more than seven innings in a Major League game. Tito Francona told Willis to ask Bieber how much pitching the ninth would mean to him. "A lot," Bieber said.

Shane came out to pitch the top of the ninth. He hung the golden sombrero on Dwight Smith Jr. as he struck out for the fourth time. Joey Rickard swung at Bieber's first pitch and grounded out to third. Chris Davis tried to check his swing on another slider but was called out to end the game. It was Bieber's first complete game, and first shutout. He joined Luis Tiant as the only Indian ever to record 15 or more strikeouts and no walks. Tiant did it in Game 82 of 1968 (see page 158).

Bieber racked up another five wins in the few weeks before the All-Star break. He was a last-minute addition to the 2019 All-Star roster when he replaced Rangers pitcher Mike Minor. Shane was called on to pitch the fifth inning of the All-Star Game. In front of the home crowd, he struck out Willson Contreras, Ketel Marte and Ronald Acuna Jr. This was the first time that a pitcher ever struck out the side in an All-Star contest. Bieber was selected as the All-Star MVP, joining Sandy Alomar, Jr. as the only players to earn the All-Star MVP in their home ballpark.

Game 46
May 25, 2009
Memorial Day Miracle

The Indians came into Memorial Day 2009 with a disappointing 17-28 record in last place in the AL Central. The Rays were fresh off their surprise appearance in the 2008 World Series, but were also scuffling early in the season. They arrived in Cleveland playing exactly .500 baseball.

Although Progressive Field was customarily unkind to the Rays—they had lost 14 straight at the corner of Carnegie and Ontario—things seemed to be trending upward at the start. The Rays had recalled David Price, who had blossomed in the 2008 playoff run, from AAA Durham to match up with Fausto Carmona.

Fausto pitched a 1-2-3 inning to lead off the game, but lost his control in the second inning. He walked the first four batters he faced and forced in a run before finally striking out Dioner Navarro. Then he gave up consecutive RBI singles and walked Evan Longoria before Eric Wedge made the call to the bullpen.

Jensen Lewis took the mound with the bases loaded and got out of the jam, but not before the score sat at 5-0. The Rays would add on in the third inning with a two-run shot by Gabe Gross. Lewis' afternoon ended after he led off the top of the fourth with two consecutive walks and then gave up an RBI single to Carlos Pena. The Rays scored two more runs off Rich Rundles (in his only MLB appearance of 2009) bringing the score to 10-0 Rays.

The Indians began to chip away in the bottom of the fourth inning with a two-run home run by Ryan Garko. David Price was on a strict pitch count, and was pulled in favor of Lance Cormier partway through the bottom of the fourth. Reddit user /u/OhioIT shared with me, "If it wasn't for an Indians home run in the 4th inning to give me a little hope, I might have left the stadium after the seventh inning like many people did that day. In the eighth we finally started hitting and added a couple more runs to the board."

The Tribe scored two more runs in the bottom of the eighth inning, and entered the bottom of the ninth down 10-4. Grady Sizemore led off the inning with a walk. Victor Martinez popped out, and Jhonny Peralta got a base hit. Left-hander Randy Choate was summoned from the Rays bullpen to face Shin-Soo Choo.

Choo hit a double play ball to short that should have ended the game. However, rookie shortstop Reid Brignac threw the ball wide of second base. Sizemore scored, and everyone was safe on the basepaths.

Grant Balfour was brought in to replace Choate. Mark DeRosa lined out to third and the Indians were down to their last out.

Ryan Garko stepped in and launched his second home run of the evening into the left field bleachers. With the score now 8-10 It was at this point the fans felt the momentum shift, and somehow it seemed that the Indians had the upper hand, even being down by 5 runs!

Asdrubral Cabrera came on to pinch hit for Matt LaPorta and drew a walk on four straight pitches. With no further insurance, and perhaps some doubt creeping in, Rays manager Joe Maddon brought in closer Jason Isringhausen. In almost a mirror image on the beginning of the game, Isringhausen walked the first three batters he faced, forcing in Cabrera and cutting the Rays lead to one.

The eleventh batter of the inning was Victor Martinez, who was 0-5 so far on the day. On a 2-2 count, Martinez sent a ground ball back up the middle for the Tribe's second walk-off win of the season. The Indians scored their seven runs in the ninth inning on only three hits, but Victor certainly made his only hit of the day count. The Rays would go on to lose 18-straight games at Progressive Field, a streak that extended until Price finally defeated the Indians on July 24, 2010.

Game 47
May 21, 2014
Walk-Off Balk in the 13th Inning

The Indians were set to get out of Michigan and be home for dinner with a 12:05 start on this Wednesday afternoon in Detroit. Zach McAllister was matched up with Max Scherzer. The contest turned into a five-hour see-saw battle of a game.

McAllister got into trouble immediately. Rajai Davis led off with a line drive single into left field. Ian Kinsler grounded one to Lonnie Chisenhall at third, who sailed the throw to first. Davis ended up on third, with Kinsler on second after the error. Miguel Cabrera plated Rajai with a sacrifice fly to right field. Victor Martinez scorched a grounder through the right side of the infield which scored Kinsler. J.D. Martinez teed off on McAllister's second pitch, sending a two-run homer over the wall in center. The Indians were down 4-0 in the early going.

In the bottom of the first, Michael Bourn got aboard with a line drive double. Asdrubal Cabrera moved him over with a bloop single into center field. Bourn advanced to third on a wild pitch. He tagged and scored when David Murphy lofted a fly ball into left field which went for a sacrifice.

The Tigers had Ian Kinsler on second with the always-dangerous Miguel Cabrera at the plate. McAllister got Miggy to pop one into foul territory to end the inning.

After Carlos Santana flied out to lead off the Indians' half of the second inning, Lonnie Chisenhall and Mike Aviles hit consecutive doubles. Michael Bourn dropped a single in just over the shortstop's head. Asdrubal Cabrera grounded out, but Michael Brantley came through with a two-out single that plated Aviles and Bourn to tie the game at four runs apiece.

Brantley stole second base, and then scored the go-ahead run when David Murphy sent a double into deep left field. Nick Swisher lined one into short right field to put the Tribe up 6-4.

Victor Martinez touched up McAllister for a solo home run in the top of the third, but a greater threat did not materialize.

93

Lonnie Chisenhall led off the bottom of the third with a solo homer of his own. This made the score 7-5 in Detroit's favor.

Marc Rzepczynski replaced McAllister on the mound to start the fifth inning. He walked Miguel Cabrera on five pitches to start things off, then gave up a line drive double to Victor Martinez. Austin Jackson sent a fly ball deep to right field. David Murphy was able to track it down, but Cabrera tagged and scored. Nick Castellanos bounced one off the warning track in right-center for a ground rule double which tied the game at seven runs apiece.

Detroit pulled ahead in the top of the eighth inning. Ian Kinsler got to reliever John Axford with a single into center. Axford issued a walk to Don Kelly who had replaced Cabrera playing first for Detroit. Victor Martinez hit one sharply to second base for an apparent fielder's choice. Asdrubal Cabrera botched the catch. The error allowed Kinsler to score and everyone was safe. J.D. Martinez followed with a line drive RBI single that put the Tigers up 9-7.

David Murphy tied the game with a two-run home run in the bottom of the ninth off Tigers closer Joe Nathan. This was about the time that my wife and I picked up the keys to our first home. I had been following the game on the radio at work all afternoon. I kept it on in the car as we drove back to the new house.

In the top of the thirteenth, the Tigers took the lead when Alex Avila launched a home run on the first pitch he saw from Josh Tomlin. Tomlin was the ninth Indians pitcher to work that day.

In the bottom of the thirteenth, Michael Brantley tied the game with an RBI single to left field. David Murphy grounded out, and Al Albuquerque was brought in from the Tiger's bullpen. Albuquerque intentionally walked Yan Gomes to load the bases and pitch to Raburn.

On the way to the 1-0 pitch, Albuquerque started his throwing motion and stopped to reset. A slight twitch of the glove hand and notion of a turn were enough. Home plate umpire Craig Gibson immediately called the balk. This forced in Cabrera and ended the game in a most unlikely fashion.

I had just turned onto our new street when Raburn came to bat. When Tom Hamilton delivered the news, "and a BALK! Ballgame! HOW ABOUT THAT?"

I drove right past the house. I was so engrossed in the moment that I missed the driveway. Much to my wife's dismay, I had to circle the block while celebrating.

Honorable Mention
May 26, 1993 - Martinez Home Run off Canseco's Head

Carlos Martinez hit a long fly ball to the warning track in Municipal Stadium. It bounced off Jose Canseco's head and over the wall for a very unusual home run that will appear in every blooper reel until the end of time.

Game 48
May 28, 1989
Joe Carter Walk-off Bunt

The Indians came into this Sunday afternoon game on a five-game losing streak trying to avoid a sweep by the Orioles. Pitcher Greg Swindell later remarked to the media, "Everybody was feeling the pressure of the losing streak. The players were ducking their heads. They were walking on the field instead of running. I wanted to pump this team up."

On Swindell's superstitious suggestion, Cleveland switched bat boys in an attempt to break the losing streak. Matt Rowland, who usually worked the home dugout, was told to put on the visiting uniform.

Orioles' Bob Milacki was nearly unhittable through the first eight innings. Milacki struck out six, gave up only two hits and two walks.

Swindell, was used to putting the struggling Indians on his back. He held the Orioles hitless through six innings. He retired the Orioles in order in the first, second, fourth, and fifth innings. After 27 batters, he had used only 117 pitches, but the Indians offense had provided zero support.

Felix Fermin drew a walk-off Milacki to lead off the bottom of the ninth inning. When Milacki got behind 2-0 to Indians left fielder Oddibe McDowell, Baltimore made a move to the bullpen. Mark Williamson came into the game. McDowell moved Fermin over to second with a sacrifice bunt. Fermin reached third on an infield ground-out by Jerry Brown.

The powerful Joe Carter stepped to the plate with two outs. Indians' manager Doc Edwards signaled to third base coach Jim Davenport. Davenport relayed the message to Carter.

Carter laid the perfect bunt down the third base line. Fermin scored, and the Indians ended their losing streak on a 40-foot bunt off the bat of their most prolific power hitter.

Game 49
May 29, 2001
Jim Thome Becomes Indians All-Time Home Run Leader

In 1990, minor-league hitting coach Charlie Manuel instructed a young Jim Thome to relax and extend his bat toward center field at the beginning of each at-bat. That pose is now immortalized as a statue in the plaza beyond center field in Cleveland.

After breaking into the big-leagues full-time in 1994, Jim Thome became a powerful slugger who was sometimes overshadowed on teams full of power hitters with big personalities.

After Albert Belle and Manny Ramirez signed elsewhere as free agents, Thome continued on with the Tribe through the 2002 season, bringing continuity and production year upon year.

In the middle of a weekday series with Detroit, Thome was hitting fifth in the lineup when Dave Burba matched up with the Tiger's Victor Santos at Comerica Park.

Santos struck out Jacob Cruz and Omar Vizquel to start the game. Robbie Alomar tripled, and Santos walked Juan Gonzalez on five pitches. Thome kicked off the scoring with a line drive RBI double down the right field foul line.

The Tigers manufactured two runs off Burba in the bottom of the third inning, pulling into a 2-1 lead.

Leading off in the top of the fourth inning, Thome sent an opposite-field home run over the wall in left-center. This was his 243rd career home run, all with the Indians. He surpassed Albert Belle as the all-time franchise home run leader.

Marty Cordova followed with a home run of his own. His solo shot put the Indians ahead 3 runs to 2.

Damion Easley tied things up in the bottom of the fourth inning with a solo home run to right-center. Later in the inning, the Tigers had a threat brewing with runners on second and third, but Burba got Robert Fick to fly out to left field and end the inning.

Tony Clark led off the Tiger's half of the fifth inning with a line drive into the expansive Comerica Park outfield. By the time Jacob Cruz tracked it down, Clark was headed to third base. Burba walked Wendell Magee to put runners at the corners. Deivi Cruz plated Clark when he poked a single into center field for the go-ahead run.

Victor Santos walked Thome and Cordero to start the top of the sixth inning. Detroit made the call to the bullpen for Heath Murray. Murray gave up a game-tying double to Russell Branyan.

Robbie Alomar's two-run home run off Heath Murray in the top of the seventh would put the Tribe up for good. The Indians went on to a 6-4 victory.

The next year, Thome would break the single-season home-run mark of fifty, also set by Belle in 1995. He smacked fifty-two before departing for Philadelphia as a free agent in the off season.

Game 50
May 31, 1992
Nagy Win, Steve Olin Save

Before John Rocker played Twisted Sister, Chris Perez was the Firestarter, and Andrew Miller told hitters to "Beat it," there was the Yellow Submarine. The Municipal Stadium organist would pipe up with a few bars of the Beatles jaunty classic as Steve Olin made his way from the bullpen to the mound.

Much like hockey goalies, closers have always been a bit different. Closers must pitch with short memories. Many of them have more than a few eccentricities, probably because they only make the news when they fail.

Steve Olin came to the Indians in the sixteenth round of the 1987 amateur draft. Olin claimed that he developed his submarine delivery while skipping stones as a child. Since high school, various coaches tried to get him to change his delivery and focus on a more traditional pitching style. Olin insisted that he would make it big his unorthodox delivery, or he would not make it at all.

By 1992, Olin was effectively the Indians closer, although manager Mike Hargrove had reservations about using Olin against left-handed hitters.

Charles Nagy was matched up with Jim Abbott for this Sunday afternoon game in Anaheim. With the bases full of Angels in the bottom of the first inning, Rene Gonzales grounded one to second. Two runs scored to put the Tribe in an early hole.

Albert Belle drew a walk to lead off the top of the second inning. Mark Whiten lined one into the second baseman's glove. Carlos Martinez grounded one to California shortstop Gary Disarcina. Disarcina botched the throw to first, and Belle motored around to score. Brook Jacoby grounded one weakly toward third. Rene Gonzales fielded it and got Jacoby out at first, but Martinez was able to advance to third. Junior Ortiz dribbled one just to the right of the pitcher. Martinez raced home to score the tying run.

Both pitchers settled in after this point. Ultimately Nagy would go seven innings, giving up five hits, four walks, and only the two runs

99

noted above. Abbott pitched seven innings, giving up seven hits, while recording four strikeouts.

Carlos Baerga drove in the Indians' final two runs on a single in the top of the fifth inning and a fielder's choice in the top of the seventh.

Steve Olin was brought in to face Angel's catcher Lance Parrish with one out in the bottom of the ninth. Gary Gaetti was on first after he singled off Kevin Wickander. On his fourth pitch, Parrish grounded into a game-ending double play off one of Olin's submarine sliders. Olin got his tenth save of the season as the Tribe secured the 4-3 victory.

By season's end, Olin saved twenty-nine games out of thirty-six opportunities. He set a club record with seventy-two appearances by a right-handed pitcher while posting an ERA of 2.34. GM John Hart once remarked, "He had the heart of a lion, the guts of a burglar. He courageously threw that fringe stuff up there and got people out."

Prior to the 1993 season, the Indians had only one off-day built into their Spring Training schedule. On March 22, Olin, Bob Ojeda, and strength coach Fernando Montes visited newly-signed reliever Steve Crews property on Lake Nellie near Winter Haven. Tragically, all three pitchers were involved in a boat accident after the cookout. Olin and Crews sustained fatal injuries when the boat struck a neighbor's dock.

Charles Nagy was particularly affected by the loss of the two young pitchers, so it seemed appropriate to note this game, which was one of two where Nagy was credited with the victory and Olin with the save.

Game 51
June 10, 1959
Rocky Colavito 4 Home Run Game

Rocky Colavito came into Game fifty-one of the 1959 campaign in a 3 for 28 slump. The Indians were visiting Memorial Stadium in Baltimore for a Wednesday night matchup with the Orioles.

The Indians offense jumped on Baltimore starter Jerry Walker early. After retiring the first two batters, Walker gave up a single to Tito Francona and then walked Colavito. Indians left fielder Minnie Minoso drove a three-run home run into deep left field to give the Tribe an early lead.

Baltimore manufactured one run in the bottom of the first inning off a Gus Triandos sacrifice fly, but the Indians countered with a solo home run by Billy Martin in the top of the second. In the bottom of the second, the Orioles pulled within one run when Al Pilarcik recorded a two-RBI single with two outs.

In the top of the third inning, Colavito came up to bat for the second time. His two-run home run chased Walker from the game.

In the bottom of the fifth inning, he took reliever Arnie Portocarrero deep for a solo home run. Rocky's solo shot extended the Indians lead to 7-3.

Francona doubled in Woodie Held in the top of the sixth. With Francona on second, Colavito cranked another homer into left-center. It was his second off Portocarrero and third of the game.

Baltimore once again made the call to the bullpen. George Zuverink came on to pitch and got Minnie Minoso to pop out to end the inning.

The Orioles mounted a comeback in the bottom of the seventh inning. They bounced starter Gary Bell from the game with a four-run inning, including a bases-clearing double by Billy Klaus. The Indians lead was cut to 10-7.

With one out in the top of the ninth, Colavito crushed an inside fastball from Ernie Johnson and sent his fourth home run of the night over the right field wall. With that, he became only the eighth big leaguer to hit four home runs in a game. The Baltimore crowd honored him with a standing ovation.

Colavito later recounted an exchange he had with Herb Score before heading to the on-deck circle prior to that at-bat: "My roomie Herb Score is sitting on a ledge. I'm getting my bat, and he says 'C'mon, roomie, don't fool around and hit number four.' I said 'Roomie, I'm 3 for 28. If I get a single, I'll be tickled to death. He said 'Bullshit. Go up there and do it.' I said 'Yeah, right,' and went on deck."

It was forty-three years before another American League hitter repeated the feat. Mike Cameron did it for the Mariners in 2002. J.D. Martinez completed the four-homer feat most recently, for the Diamondbacks in 2017.

Game 52
May 31, 1996
Albert Belle Flattens Fernando Vina

Albert Belle was a prolific slugger with undoubtable anger issues. From cursing out reporters, to chasing kids with his truck on Halloween, and smashing the clubhouse thermostat, there are numerous anecdotes of his wrath. However, the highlight that is most often used to paint Belle as the bad guy is more nuanced than most people remember.

The Indians were in the middle of a weekend series in Milwaukee. Dennis Martinez was matched up with the Brewers' Ben McDonald. With one out in the top of the second inning, Manny Ramirez drove a laser shot home run down the left field left field line. He drove in Jim Thome to give the Indians an early 2-0 lead.

In the top of the third inning, Julio Franco dropped a single into left field. Franco took a lead off first, and McDonald attempted to pick him off but the throw was wide of the base. Julio took second on the error. Carlos Baerga smashed a single through the left side of the infield which put runners at the corners.

Albert Belle stepped in and added a run on an RBI single into left field. Eddie Murray came to the plate and hit a grounder between first and second. Fernando Vina fielded it, casually tagged Belle in the baseline, and completed the double play by throwing Murray out at first. The inning ended with the Tribe up 3-0, but first base coach Davey Nelson was incensed.

He had just told Belle to look out for the double play ball, and felt that Albert's play lacked situational awareness. In a later interview with Spike Lee on Real Sports with Bryant Gumbel Nelson recounted, "Now it's three outs. So Albert's standing out on the infield, and I go out there ... and I said, `Dammit Albert, what did I tell you? ' I said ... `You cost us a run, and you should have took the guy out. '"

Milwaukee pieced together four hits off Martinez and took advantage of a throwing error in the bottom of the third inning, the score was quickly tied at three runs apiece.

103

The Indians began to pull away in the middle innings. Kenny Lofton had an RBI single in the fourth and Eddie Murray drove in Belle with a line drive over second base in the bottom of the fifth.

Mike Potts came on in relief for the Brewers in the bottom of the seventh. After Carlos Baerga grounded out, he walked Albert Belle. Belle stole second, the throw from the plate skipped into center field and Belle advanced to third on the error. Potts walked Murray and was promptly sent to the showers in favor of Marshall Boze. Boze did not fare any better. The Tribe took advantage of two Brewer errors and scored four runs, extending the lead to 9-3.

After Dennis Martinez pitched a 1-2-3 seventh inning, Marshall Boze hit Belle with a pitch to lead off the top of the eighth. Jim Thome struck out. Belle was once again on first base with Eddie Murray at the plate. Murray bounced an almost identical grounder to Vina at second base. Vina turned to tag Belle and was met with a forearm shiver that sent him sprawling to the dirt. Murray was safe at first with a fielder's choice. He later scored the Indians tenth run on an RBI single by Tony Peña.

Back in the dugout, Belle said something to Indians reliever Julian Tavarez, reportedly telling him to throw at a Milwaukee batter. Tavarez's first pitch in the ninth went about five feet behind Brewers' catcher Mike Matheny. The benches emptied and the brawl was on.

Once the dust cleared, Indians reliever Jim Poole secured the final three outs and the 10-4 victory. Later, in the Spike Lee interview, Albert Belle reflected on the play, "I was going to make sure the next time it happens I wasn't going to be as lenient."

Game 53
June 1, 2007
Both Roberto Hernandezes Pitch in a 5-run Comeback

Fausto Carmona started this game against the Tiger's Mike Maroth. The Tigers jumped on the board early with a leadoff triple by Curtis Granderson to open the game and RBI singles by Placido Palanco and Sean Casey.

The Tigers led by four runs at three different points in the game. The first was after a two-run home run by left fielder Craig Monroe in the top of the sixth inning. Next, after they manufactured four runs on three hits off Indians relievers Tom Mastny and Aaron Fultz. Finally, after Fernando Cabrera walked in a run and Omar Infante had an RBI single off Roberto Hernandez in the top of the ninth inning.

Indians entered the bottom of the ninth down 11 runs to 7. The Tigers sent in closer Doug Jones. After a leadoff groundout by Grady Sizemore, Casey Blake singled and Jones walked Travis Hafner on five pitches. With runners on first and second, Victor Martinez launched one to deep left field for a three-run homer that brought the Indians within one run.

Jhonny Peralta knocked a line drive double down the right field line. Ryan Garko struck out. With two outs, Jones intentionally walked Trot Nixon to set up the force out. Josh Barfield drove a line drive to short right field, scoring Mike Rouse who had pinch run for Peralta. David Delluci, the ninth batter of the inning, stepped in and hit one sharply into short center field. His RBI single completed the comeback and gave the Tribe the 11-10 walk-off win. It was Jones' second straight blown save on his way to a league high eleven blown saves for the season.

Looking back, it is interesting to note that the pitchers who recorded the first and last outs for the Indians in this contest were both named Roberto Hernandez. Of course, we did not know that at the time.

The baseball world would later learn that starter Fausto Carmona had committed identity fraud and was actually named Roberto Hernandez. We also learned that he was three years older than he previously claimed. He missed much of the 2012 season, because

105

he did not have a valid visa to work in the United States. In July of 2012 he was granted a new visa under his true name He served a three-week MLB suspension for age and identity fraud and then returned to the Indians. He pitched only 14⅓ innings for the Tribe in 2012. He had some journeyman years with the Rays, Phillies, Dodgers, Astros, Jays, and Braves, but was never able to replicate the lights-out pitching of his early days with the Indians.

The Roberto Hernandez, who recorded out #27, was Roberto Hernandez the former All-Star who appeared in 28 games in relief for the Indians in the twilight of his seventeen-year MLB career. Luckily the Tribe offense was geared up to make up for the miscues of both Hernandezes on this evening.

Game 54
May 31, 1998
Jose Mesa's Last Save with Indians

Indians fans have always had a complex relationship with their closers. This is probably true for most teams, but the Jose Mesa era was the purest distillation of Cleveland's closer angst. Mesa's career 4.36 ERA is the highest of any pitcher with at least 150 saves. What can we derive from this statistic? Some of that average is from his early days as a starting pitcher. Most of it comes from giving Cleveland fans heartburn by giving up a run or two on his way to recording the save.

The Indians were north of the border, with Chuck Nagy facing Pat Hentgen in Toronto. Carlos Delgado led off the scoring with a two-run home run off Nagy in the bottom of the first.

Drink rails, dining areas, and concession stands facing the playing field have become commonplace throughout the MLB. In 1998, the Sight Lines restaurant inside the SkyDome was among the first spaces that were not enclosed in a concourse, but facing the action of the field. That made it even more surprising when Jim Thome cranked a home run deep into center field. It not only cleared the wall, but entered the open-air bar 60 feet above the playing field, cleared three rows of tables, and came to rest next to the dessert buffet.

Two batters later, Mark Whiten followed with a solo home run. David Bell and Omar Vizquel wrapped up the inning with RBI singles, bringing the score to 4-2 Indians.

With the bases loaded in the bottom of the fifth inning, Carlos Delgado touched up Nagy once again, with a ground ball that scored Alex Gonzalez.

Manny Ramirez made the score 5-3 in the top of the eighth inning with a single to short that scored David Justice from third base.

Jose Mesa entered the game in the bottom of the eighth inning. Earlier in the year he had been replaced in the closer role by Mike Jackson. Mesa retired the heart of the Blue Jays lineup, Jose

107

Canseco, Carlos Delgado, and Mike Stanley, in order on eleven pitches.

The Tribe added three more runs in the top of the ninth inning. With the added breathing room and his low pitch count, manager Mike Hargrove sent Mesa back out to close the game.

Tony Fernandez swung at Mesa's first pitch and lined out to the shortstop. Ed Sprague fell behind in the count and popped up the 0-2 pitch for an easy out in left field. Pinch hitter Felipe Crespo got aboard on a sharply hit ball over second base. Mesa got Alex Gonzalez to ground out to second and end the game. He booked his one-hundred-fourth and final save as an Indian. This figure places him fifth on the current list of franchise leaders.

Due to simmering resentments from his collapse in the 1997 World Series and faltering confidence in his stuff, Mesa needed a change of scenery. He was dealt to the Giants in July along with Shawon Dunston and Alvin Morman for Steve Reed and Jacob Cruz.

Game 55
June 16, 1965
Luis Tiant One-Hitter

On this Wednesday night in 1965, second-year pitcher Luis Tiant was matched up with Phil Ortega and a forgettable Washington Senators lineup. Tiant had been called up from AAA Portland halfway through the 1964 season after throwing a no-hitter and a one-hitter consecutively for the Beavers.

In the big leagues he had shown flashes of brilliance, but was mostly overshadowed by his friend from the Indians farm system, Sam McDowell.

Tiant had a brilliant night against the Senators (the version that became the Texas Rangers). He worked out of a bases-loaded jam in the second inning after hitting the leadoff hitter Frank Howard with a pitch. Joe Cunningham reached on a fielding error by Indians second baseman Pedro Gonzales. With Cunningham at second and Howard on third, Tiant intentionally walked Ed Brinkman to get to the pitcher Phil Ortega. He struck out Ortega and escaped with the scoreless tie intact.

In the bottom of the fourth inning, Leon Wagner came through with some run support when he rocked a three-run home over the Municipal Stadium wall.

Woodie Held got the only Senator hit, a single to lead off the top of the seventh inning.

Tiant helped out his own cause in the bottom of the seventh. Leon Wagner got aboard when Washington second baseman Don Basinglame booted a ground ball. Chuck Hinton moved Wagner over to second with a sacrifice bunt. The Senators intentionally walked Pedro Gonzales to pitch to Tiant. He drove Big Daddy Wags home with a single that made it 4-0 Indians.

Vic Davalillo reached on an error by the Washington shortstop to lead off the bottom of the eighth inning. Max Alvis slapped a single into center field that moved Vic over to second base. Rocky Colavito hit a grounder to third. Alvis was forced out at second, but Davalillo made it safely to third. With runners at the corners, Leon Wagner dropped an RBI single into right field which put the icing on the Tribe's 5-0 victory.

Tiant's final line was a complete game one-hitter. He walked three, struck out seven, and bailed the Indians out of their two errors.

Luis pitched the rest of the 1965 season with some persistent soreness in his arm and finished with an 11-11 record. He altered his delivery slightly to abate the soreness in his shoulder. He began to turn away from home plate during his windup. With this new motion, he broke through into the upper echelon of American League pitchers. In 1968, he led the American League with a 1.60 ERA and hits per nine innings with 5.3. He was selected as an All-Star in 1968 and had two more All-Star seasons with Boston later in his career.

Game 56
June 17, 1965
Sonny Siebert 15 Strikeouts

This is the first place in the Project where consecutive games appear. The day after Luis Tiant's one-hitter, Sonny Siebert was on the mound for the Tribe against the struggling Senators.

In the bottom of the first, Siebert gave up one of only three Senators hits on the day--a single to right field by Frank Howard. He struck out Willie Kirkland to end the inning.

Senators pitcher Bennie Daniels lost control of the game early. He gave up a leadoff walk to Larry Brown. Vic Davillo reached on an error by Senators shortstop Ed Brinkman. Max Alvis laid down a perfect bunt and beat the throw to first. With the bases loaded, Rocky Colavito, Leon Wagner, and Duke Sims hit a parade of RBI singles, giving the Tribe an early 4-0 lead.

Confident with this lead, Siebert mowed through the Sens for the rest of the game. He struck out the side in both the fifth and seventh innings. He scattered three hits and one walk, but no Senator advanced past first base after the first inning.

These were the fourth and fifth wins of what became a ten-game winning streak. The Tribe rode a 22-7 record in June to first place in the standings by July 2nd. The second half of the season was less successful; however, and came to a close with a fifth-place finish in the American League East.

Only eight Indians pitchers had recorded 15 strikeouts in a game up to this point. Sam McDowell did it just two weeks before against the Tigers. The mid-60's Indians were among the greatest strikeout-throwing rotations in team history. McDowell, Siebert, and Tiant set many team records that would not be matched until the 2014 Indians set a new MLB record for most strikeouts in a season by a pitching staff.

Game 57
June 14, 1958
Roger Maris' Last Home Run as an Indian

Every baseball fan knows the name Roger Maris as the first to break Babe Ruth's mark of 60 home runs in a season. Fewer know that he began his career with the Indians and developed that prolific power swing in the Tribe's farm system.

While playing for the Three-I League's Keokuk Kernels in 1954, manager Jo Jo White taught Maris to pull the ball to the opposite field. This transformed the talented prospect from a contact hitter into the power hitter that is remembered from his days in New York.

Maris helped the Indianapolis Indians win a minor-league championship in 1956 and then started the season in Cleveland in 1957. In his two years with the Indians, he slugged twenty-three home runs (14 in 1957 and 9 in 1958).

On June 14th, the Indians were in Washington to face the Senators (the ones that later became the Twins) in Griffith Stadium. Cal McLish was on the hill for the Indians.

Maris was hitting in the leadoff spot. He started the game by taking Senators starter Hal Griggs deep with a solo home run. The Indians manufactured two more runs in the inning and were out to an early 3-0 lead.

The Tribe extended that lead in the top of the third inning by way of a Preston Ward home run, and a wild pitch that scored Mickey Vernon from third. Washington made a call to the bullpen for Ralph Lumenti.

Lumenti struggled to find his footing. He walked McLish to load the bases. Next up, Maris drew a walk to force in a run and put the Tribe up 6-0. Billy Hunter grounded out to end the inning.

Washington got on the scoreboard with an RBI single in the bottom of the fifth inning, but could not sustain the rally.

Lumenti had not settled in. Rocky Colavito led off the Indians half of the sixth with a home run to deep left field. Lumenti walked Mickey Vernon. Russ Nixon dropped a double into left field which allowed Vernon to score. Nixon advanced on a wild pitch before Billy Moran smacked a single into left. Nixon came in to score, making it 9-1 Indians before Lumenti could record an out. Minnie Minoso drove in one more run before the inning came to close.

McLish was fading a bit when he gave up a solo home run in the bottom of the sixth to Neil Chrisley. Herb Score came in to pitch in the seventh inning and recorded a nine-out save.

The home run that led off the sixth inning was Maris' twenty-third and last as an Indian.

After the game, GM Frank "Trader" Lane squeezed in one more of his signature roster moves. Coming in just under the wire of the June 15th trade deadline, Lane dealt Preston Ward, pitcher Dick Tomanek, and Maris for Woodie Held and Vic Power. Lane had previously attempted to trade Maris for Yankees second-baseman Bobby Richardson. He was later quoted, "Before I let the Athletics have him, I made sure they wouldn't turn around and trade him to the Yankees. They assured me they would keep him themselves."

After the 1958 season, the A's did indeed send Maris to the Yankees and eventually into the record books.

Game 58
June 2, 2014
Masterson Throws 25 Consecutive Strikes

The Red Sox were visiting Progressive Field to start a midweek series. John Lackey was matched up against Justin Masterson in a potential pitcher's duel.

The Red Sox came out strong, loading the bases on Masterson before Jonny Gomes struck out swinging to end the inning.

Lackey gave up a five-pitch walk to leadoff man Michael Bourn. Bourn stole second before Asdrubal Cabrera struck out. Then, Lackey walked Michael Brantley. Jason Kipnis grounded out to first, advancing the runners to second and third. Lonnie Chisenhall slapped a single down the left field line which cleared the bases and gave the Tribe a 2-0 lead.

In the bottom of the third inning, Michael Bourn led off with a long fly to center. As the ball bounced around the outfield, Bourn motored around the bases for a triple. Asdrubal Cabrera made the score 3-0 when he slapped a single through the right side of the infield allowing Bourn to score.

In the top half of the fourth inning, Justin Masterson struck out Jonny Gomes with three pitches. Next up was Masterson's former teammate Grady Sizemore. Grady took the first strike, fouled the second pitch off his ankle, and struck out swinging. Stephen Drew took the first two strikes, and then was called out on a check swing on a ball in the dirt. nine pitches, nine strikes, three outs: an Immaculate Inning.

Not only did he strike out the side on nine pitches, but these nine were part of a run of 25 consecutive strikes from the top of the third inning to the top of the sixth. Overall, Masterson struck out ten Red Sox. 67 of his 105 pitches were strikes.

Despite a two-run Xander Bogarts homer off Bryan Shaw, the Indians bullpen was able to hold on and secure the 3-2 win.

Masterson was the first-ever Indian to complete the rare immaculate inning. There have been 95 immaculate innings thrown in MLB history to date. Three years later, Carlos Carrasco threw the Tribe's second immaculate inning in Game 85 of 2017.

In Game 20 of 2018, Yonder Alonso, Yan Gomes, and Bradley Zimmer fell victim to an Immaculate inning thrown by the Orioles Kevin Gausman. However, the Indians would still go on to win that game 2-1.

As for consecutive strikes thrown, Masterson's feat still stands as the franchise record. The MLB record is also held by a former Indian. Bartolo Colon, who threw 38 consecutive strikes for the Athletics against the Angels in April 2012.

Game 59
June 23, 1950
Luke Easter Hits Longest Home Run in Muni Stadium

In 1949, the Indians signed a contract with Luscious "Luke" Easter, one of the most prolific stars of the American Negro League. Playing in 1948 for the Homestead Greys against the New York Cubans, he hit a home run 475 feet from home plate and into the center field bleachers at the Polo Grounds.

At the beginning of 1949, only the Dodgers (Jackie Robinson), Indians (Larry Doby), and St. Louis Browns (Hank Thompson) were integrated. Easter was sent to AAA San Diego to get ready for the majors. He was only the second black player in the Pacific Coast League. When asked his opinion on integrating the PCL he told San Diego president Bill Starr, "Everybody likes me when I hit the ball." Easter certainly hit the ball, recording several record-setting home runs in PCL stadiums.

Easter joined the Indians August 11, 1949 and became the 11th black player in the MLB. He turned 35 in what was technically his rookie season in MLB. On June 23rd, 1950 Bob Lemon was pitching for the Indians against the Senators Bob Ross. Tribe shortstop Ray Boone opened up the scoring with an RBI single in the bottom of the second inning. Washington tied it up in the top of the inning as Eddie Yost scored Sam Dente on a fielder's choice.

In the bottom of the third with Dale Mitchell on second and Lemon on third, Easter hit a three-run home run off Senators starter Bob Ross making the score 4-1. Easter had another RBI in the bottom of the fourth when he scored Jim Hegan on a powerful line-out to left field.

In the bottom of the sixth inning, facing Joe Haynes, Luke Easter hit the most prodigious blast in the 61-year tenure of Cleveland Municipal Stadium. The ball traveled over the 475-foot mark in right center and cleared the auxiliary scoreboard. The estimated distance traveled was 505 feet. In 1960, Mickey Mantle hit the only other homer that travelled over the auxiliary scoreboard.

The Indians rode Easter's six-RBI day to a 13-4 victory. He would go on to finish the 1950 season with a .280 batting average, 28 home runs, and 107 RBIs.

After playing for the Rochester Red Wings and Buffalo Bisons in the International League well into his 50's, Luke Easter returned to Cleveland and was working as the chief union steward for the Aircraft Workers Alliance at the TRW plant in Euclid. One of his functions as steward was to cash paychecks for the union members and bring the cash back to the factory.

On March 29, 1979, he was held up by robbers after cashing the checks. During the robbery, Easter was shot. He was pronounced dead on arrival at Euclid Hospital. In 1980, the city park in Cleveland's Mount Pleasant neighborhood was named after him and a bust was erected in the park.

Game 60
June 23, 1931 (Second Game)
Indians Outscore Boston 23-0 in Doubleheader

The Indians were originally scheduled to face the Red Sox at League Park on this Tuesday afternoon. When the game originally scheduled for May 11th was postponed due to threatening weather, June 23rd became a traditional doubleheader consisting of Games 59 and 60.

Game 59 was something of a pitcher's duel for the first six innings. In the bottom of the sixth, the Indians broke the ice when Johnny Hodapp got caught in a pickle attempting to steal second. Ed Morgan was able to score from third before the Sox tagged Hodapp out.

Clint Brown threw a five-hit shutout for the Tribe while the Indians manufactured thirteen runs in the final three innings and coasted to a 13-0 victory.

In the second leg of the doubleheader, pitcher Willis Hudlin was even more brilliant. He threw a complete game one-hit shutout. No Boston base runner ever made it past first.

Earl Averill had seven hits in ten at-bats combined over the two games. His two-run double to right field in the bottom of the third inning basically put the game out of reach for the scuffling Red Sox.

The Indians hit 15 for 27 with runners in scoring position, which is always a recipe for success. Perhaps most interesting is the fact that the Tribe scored 23 runs in the two games combined with no home runs.

How often have the Indians put up consecutive double-digit scores in consecutive shutouts? Twice. 87 years later, the 2018 Indians beat the White Sox 12-0 in Game 73. The next day, they defeated the Tigers 10-0 in Game 74. With the decline of double-headers, the likelihood of seeing double-digit shutouts on the same day seems infinitesimally small.

Game 61
June 14, 1997 (First Game)
First Interleague Game

The Indians were in St. Louis for the first time since 1953 when the Browns moved to Baltimore and became the Orioles. Despite both teams being Charter members of their League (St. Louis since 1892 and Cleveland since 1901) they had never crossed paths in the World Series. The Indians faced Brooklyn in the 1920 Series, the Boston Braves in 1948, the New York Giants in 1954, and the Atlanta Braves in 1995.

Over 43,000 were in Busch Stadium for this new and novel matchup on a Saturday afternoon. Bartolo Colon faced off against Cardinals righty Andy Benes. In the bottom of the second, Benes helped out his own cause with an RBI single into right field. However, Marquis Grissom ended the inning on a spectacular throw. He caught Mike DiFelice trying to advance from first to third.

Bartolo Colon struck out looking on three pitches to lead off the third inning, confirming many fan's fears about American League pitchers attempting to hit in only a handful of interleague games.

In the bottom of the fourth, Colon gave up a leadoff home run to John Mabry and a double to Gary Gaetti. Gaetti was driven in by Mike DeFelice to make it a 3-0 ballgame.

The Indians bats finally came alive in the top of the seventh inning. After a leadoff ground out by Sandy Alomar, Marquis Grissom singled into right and then stole second. Brian Giles drove in Grissom with a line drive single to left field. After a fly out by Omar Vizquel, Julio Franco dropped a single into center field and advanced Giles to second. Jim Thome pushed both Giles and Franco across the plate with a deep line drive down the left field line which tied the game 3-3.

Albie Lopez came on in relief and pitched a 1-2-3 inning in the bottom of the seventh.

David Justice knocked a ground ball single into left to lead off the top of the eighth inning. Utility man Kevin Seitzer entered the game to hit in the pitcher's spot. Seitzer laid down a bunt which moved Justice over to second. Sandy Alomar was put out on a weak grounder to second.

With two outs, Marquis Grissom came through again. He smashed a single through the left side of the infield which brought in the go-ahead run. Grissom stole second base, and Brian Giles drew a walk. Omar Vizquel grounded one to second base. Cardinals second baseman Delino DeShields botched the throw to first and Vizquel was aboard on the error. The Indians took full advantage of the extra out. Julio Franco drubbed a line drive into right-center which scored two more runs. Jim Thome followed with his own single that sent Franco around to score.

With an 8-3 lead, Alvin Morman and Paul Shuey both chewed through the Cardinals lineup on eleven and fourteen pitches, respectively. This sealed the Indians first inter-league win. In the inter-league era, the Indians are 16-10 against the Cardinals and 137-146 overall through the 2019 season.

Game 62
June 11, 2009
Birds Distract Coco Crisp on Walk-off Hit

Both the Royals and Indians were struggling in 2009. Jeremy Sowers faced off against the Royals' Zack Grienke in a battle to stay out of the basement in the AL Central.

In the bottom of the third inning, Louis Valbuena led off with a double to left-center. Trevor Crowe advanced Valbuena to third on a well-executed sacrifice bunt. Victor Martinez drove him home with an RBI single.

The Royals took a 2-1 lead in the top of the fifth with RBI hits by David DeJesus and Billy Butler.

Throughout late spring in 2009, a flock of seagulls had been roving around the outfield and roosting in the rafters of Progressive Field. A week earlier with the Yankees in town, New York outfielder Nick Swisher remarked, "There's what, 8,000 seagulls out there? This ain't even the beach. It's Cleveland."

Indians spokesman Bob DiBiasio commented on the arrival of the birds and the difficulty in getting them to move on, "Gulls are riding the wind currents up the valley to the ballpark in search for food scraps to feed their young. The Indians are continuing to research ways to control this issue under the guidance of gulls being federally protected."

By the later innings, the birds were out in full force, filling the outfield gaps and taking flight to avoid batted balls. In the top of the eighth inning, KC extended their lead to 3-1 with a solo home run by Miguel Olivo.

In the bottom of the eighth, the Indians mounted a comeback. A single by Mark DeRosa and a five-pitch walk to Victor Martinez chased Grienke from the game. DeRosa scored on a grounder by Shin-Soo Choo that was mishandled twice by the Royals. Martinez was forced out at second, but two throwing errors left Choo on second when the dust cleared. Then, Jhonny Peralta doubled to score Choo and tie the game at 3-3.

121

Indians closer Kerry Wood came on and pitched a 1-2-3 ninth, but the Tribe were unable to break the tie.

The Royals were unable to get anything going against Matt Hedges in the top of the tenth inning. Mark DeRosa singled to center to lead off the Indians' half of the inning. Kyle Farnsworth issued a walk to Victor Martinez which moved DeRosa into scoring position. Shin-Soo Choo came to the plate and poked a single into the flock of birds in shallow center. Royals center fielder Coco Crisp charged in and appeared to have a play on the ball.

On one hop, the ball struck one of the gulls in the wing. The bird flopped around momentarily and then took flight. Crisp could only throw up his hands in disgust as the ball deflected away from him, allowing DeRosa to score the winning run.

After the game, Tribe coach Joel Skinner who has been with the organization both at Municipal Stadium and Progressive Field remarked about the birds, "It's never been this bad here or at the old ballpark. I just hope I don't get pooped on."

Game 63
June 22, 1980
Joe Charboneau Homers on the Way to Rookie of the Year

Joe Charboneau got his call-up after Andre Thornton went down with a knee injury at the end of spring training. After crushing a home run against the Angels on Opening Day, Cleveland was captivated with the rookie slugger. Soon after, sportswriter Terry Pluto gave Charboneau the moniker "Super Joe."

By mid-June, he was slugging homers and tall tales were growing among the fanbase. He broke rocks against his chest. He opened beer bottles with his eye socket. He was a bare-knuckle boxer before taking up baseball. He fixed a broken nose with plenty of whiskey and a pair of pliers. Super Joe never confirmed or denied the legends.

On June 22nd, the Indians were in Minneapolis to face the Twins. Bo Diaz and Miguel Dilone got the Tribe out to an early 2-0 lead. The Twins tied it up in the bottom of the second inning with a two-run single by Dave Edwards.

Super Joe singled to center to load the bases in the top of the third inning. After a flyball out by Toby Harrah, Jack Brohamer pushed Jorge Orta and Mike Hargrove across with a two-run double. Rick Manning drove in Charboneau to give the Tribe a 5-2 lead.

In the top of the fourth inning, Charboneau was back at the plate. He singled to left in an inning that saw the Tribe score one run on three hits but stranded two runners on base.

In the top of the sixth inning, Tom Veryzer led off with a double to left field. Miguel Dilone singled to move him over to third. Dilone then stole second to get himself into scoring position. Dell Alston knocked a triple into the left field corner, scoring Veryzer and Dilone. Mike Hargrove then drove in Alston with an RBI single. After a pitching change, Charboneau crushed Fernando Arroyo's pitch into the stands for a no-doubt two-run home run. The Tribe led 11 runs to 4.

The Twins would scatter a few more runs, but Super Joe's Home Run turned out to be the highlight of the day.

123

A week later on June 28th, Charboneau would become one of only three players to ever hit a home run into the third deck of Yankee Stadium. However, the Indians would go on to lose that game 11-10.

Super Joe finished the 1980 campaign with 23 home runs, and 87 RBIs. He became Cleveland's third AL rookie of the year. A local punk band's single *Go Joe Charboneau* reached No. 3 on the local charts.

The sophomore slump hits many major leaguers, but none fell off as dramatically as Super Joe. After hitting poorly in the early part of 1981, Charboneau injured his back sliding head-first into second base while playing for the AAA Charleston Charlies. He played only 70 more major-league games and has the fewest MLB appearances for any Rookie of the Year winner.

Game 64
June 9, 2014
Lonnie Chisenhall 15 Total Bases

Tris Speaker, Nap Lajoie, Rocky Colavito, Luke Easter, Victor Martinez, Joe Carter...Lonnie Chisenhall? Despite the pantheon of great all-around hitters that came before him, a solid case can be made that Lonnie Chisenhall had the best night of hitting in Tribe history on June 9, 2014.

The Indians were visiting the Rangers and facing Nick Martinez. With one out and runners on second and third in the bottom of the first inning, Chisenhall knocked a line drive single into center field. This pushed Cabrera across the plate and contributed to a three run, two hit innings.

The Rangers got one run back in the bottom of the first inning, but the Indians offense kept rolling. After a solo home run by George Kottaras and a two RBI single to right by Jason Kipnis, Lonnie launched a laser shot that just cleared the right field wall for a two-run home run. The Tribe ended the inning up 8-1.

George Kottaras picked up another RBI in the top of the third inning when he allowed David Murphy to score from third on a long sacrifice fly to center.

Texas closed the gap in the bottom of the fourth. Indians' starter T.J. House got into a jam after issuing a leadoff walk to Luis Sardinas. He struck out Daniel Robertson, but then gave up a double to Elvis Andrus which put runners at the corners. House's first pitch to Shin-Soo Choo bounced to the backstop and Sardinas came into score on the wild pitch. Choo grounded out to first, but Andrus came in to score.

In the top of the fourth inning, Michael Brantley rocked a solo home run to center. Jason Kipnis followed with a single, then stole second. Chisenhall sent a towering two-run home run out of the park to make the score 12-4.

The Rangers narrowed the lead to 12-6 in the bottom of the fourth when they scored two more runs off House. After Daniel

Robertson's RBI double, Terry Francona made the call to the bullpen for Scott Atchison.

In the Indians' half of the sixth, Michael Brantley got aboard with a line drive into the left field gap. Once again, Chisenhall drove a ball to center. This one stayed in the yard, but Michael Brantley was able to score from first.

Finally, in the top of the eighth with runners on first and third Lonnie uncorked a line drive down the right field line. It cleared the wall for his third home run and ninth RBI of the night.

The final scoreboard had the Indians on top 17 runs to 7 with eighteen hits.

Lonnie became the fourth player in MLB history with five or more hits, three home runs, and nine or more RBI in a game. The last to do it was Fred Lynn for the Red Sox in 1975. His fifteen total bases are one short of the club record. Rocky Colavito collected sixteen total bases in Game 51 of 1969 (see Page 101).

Game 65
July 10, 1947 (First Game)
Don Black Throws First No-hitter in Muni Stadium

Don Black was on his last chance. In 1945, he had been suspended by the A's for being so drunk that he passed out in a bowl of split pea soup. Disappointing results and continued personal struggles led Connie Mack to trade Black from the As' to the Indians following the 1945 season.

Black had flashes of brilliance in 1946, but had been optioned to minor league Milwaukee for the later part of the season.

In 1946, Bill Veeck purchased the Indians and began making many of his famous innovations. He immediately reached an agreement to broadcast all games on the radio. In 1947 he hired Larry Doby, breaking the color barrier in the American League. He moved the team to Municipal Stadium full-time, and he began mentoring Don Black.

Veeck himself was a recovering alcoholic and a proponent of Alcoholics Anonymous. Veeck agreed to pay off Don Black's outstanding debts if he would enter A.A. "Listen, give this thing a good try," he told Black. "You won't have to worry about your debts. I'm paying them all off. The only man you're going to owe is me, and I'm not going to be tough on you."

Less than five months after he joined A.A., Black was pitching behind Bob Feller as the Indians' number two starter.

On July 10th, Black was facing his old team in the first half of a double-header. The twin bill had attracted a rather large crowd for a weekday, despite the threat of rain in the forecast.

Black walked the first two Philadelphia batters on eight wide, nearly wild, pitches. After he struck out Elmer Valo, Ferris Fain grounded out, but advanced the runners. Eddie Joost was left on third when Sam Chapman grounded out to end the inning. That is the farthest any A's base runner would make it this afternoon.

Black pitched a 1-2-3 second inning, and then the heavens opened up. During the rain delay, Black remarked to some reporters, "Gee, I'm wild tonight. I don't seem to have it. I hope I can stick it out."

After a 45-minute delay, he did more than stick it out. After Jim Hegan broke the ice in the bottom of the second with an RBI single, Black helped out his own cause by scoring Joe Gordon with a sacrifice bunt. Tribe center fielder George Metkovich drove in Hegan with an RBI single of his own.

In the top of the third inning, A's left fielder Barney McKoskey was on base after a walk. Elmer Valo launched a ball to deep right field. Indians outfielder Joe Gordon sprinted toward the wall and made a dramatic over-the-shoulder catch on the hardest-hit ball of the game.

Black's slider was moving brilliantly and fooling A's hitters, but his tendency to be a little wild was almost his undoing. After walking Ferris Fain in the top of the sixth, Lou Boudreau made a mound visit. "I went over … when he walked Fain to tell him to slow down a little. We all knew he was going for the no-hitter."

Wiping sweat from his brow after every third pitch, Black faced the heart of the A's batting order in the top of the ninth. George Binks flied out to Dale Mitchell in left field. Ferris Fain grounded one back to Eddie Robinson at first. Eddie hustled back to the bag and made the out.

Sam Chapman hit a weak grounder back to the mound. Black fielded the ball, took a few steps toward first, and tossed the ball to Robinson to complete the no-hitter.

47,871 fans erupted in jubilation at the feat. It was the largest crowd to date to witness a no-hitter in the majors.

Later, Black reflected on the game "Never a drink made could give me the belt I got out of that game."

Game 66
July 3, 1939
Three Triples for Ben Chapman

The Indians were in Michigan with Bob Feller on the mound facing Detroit's Archie McKain.

In the bottom of the first, Chapman walked, but was ultimately left stranded at third.

With the score still tied 0-0, Chapman led off the top of the fourth inning with a triple. Hal Trosky grounded out to McKain, but the speedy Chapman was able to score.

Feller was cruising through the Tiger's lineup, and the score was still 1-0 when Chapman came up with two outs in the top of the sixth. He tripled again, but was stranded on third by a Hal Trosky groundout.

In the bottom of the sixth inning, the Tigers tied it up with a solo homer by Hall of Famer and former Indian Earl Averill, who played two years in Detroit in the twilight of his career.

Skeeter Webb led off the Indians half of the eighth with a fly out to center. Bob Feller got on base with a single. He advanced on a Rollie Helmsley hit. Bruce Campbell rocked a three-run home run to make it a 4-1 game. Chapman followed with his third triple of the day. Trosky grounded out to first, and Chapman was held at third. He was stranded again when Jeff Heath was called out on strikes.

Detroit brought in Roy Cullenbine pinch hit for Archie McKain in the bottom of the eighth. Cullenbine led off the Inning with a home run which cut the Indians' lead to 4-2. Feller completed the game with a final stat line of two runs on five hits, four walks, and two strikeouts.

Three triples in a game was *somewhat* more common before World War I when massive outfields were the norm. In some early cases, spectators were seated *in* the outfield when the grandstands were over-full. In some parks, ground rules dictated that balls hit into spectator areas were awarded three bases. Therefore three-triple games occurred once or twice a year in the early 20th century.

129

Since 1920, 29 players have hit three triples in a game. Five Indians have had a three-triple game, but only Campbell's occurred in what most would consider the modern era of hitting. The others were Elmer Flick in 1902, Bill Bradley in 1903, Nap Lajoie in 1904, and Shoeless Joe Jackson in 1912.

The latest player to hit three triples in a game was Denard Span for the Twins against the Tigers on June 29, 2010. For comparison, there had been eighty 3+ home run games between Al Bumbry's three-triple game in 1973 and Span's 2010 effort.

Although many of the massive outfields were still around in 1939, Campbell's three triples were not heavily assisted by odd dimensions. Briggs Field (later known as Tiger Stadium) would be recognizable to today's hitters.

If you have heard of Ben Chapman before, it is likely as part of Jackie Robinson's story. As manager of the Phillies in 1947, he heaped racist vitriol on Robinson from the dugout and encouraged his players to do the same. This was not a one-off performance. In 1934, nearly 15,000 New Yorkers signed a petition requesting Yankees fire Chapman because of his anti-Semitic remarks.

Despite that dark history, this game must be acknowledged as one of the preeminent feats of hitting and baserunning in Indians history.

Game 67
June 21, 1999
Jose Mesa Loses Game on a Wild Pitch in the 12th

Summer had arrived in Cleveland and the Indians were off to a strong start with 45 wins in their first 66 games. The Mariners were in town on this Monday night throwing Jamie Moyer against Bartolo Colon.

Colon and Moyer dueled through the early innings, and the score remained 0-0 until the bottom of the fifth. Alex Ramirez led off the Indians half of the inning with a ground-ball single to center. Jeff Manto executed a sacrifice bunt to move him over to second base, and Enrique Wilson drove Ramirez home with a line drive single to left.

Omar Vizquel led off the bottom of the sixth inning with a line drive single to center. He advanced to second on a wild pitch and stole third with Alex Ramirez at bat. With two outs on a 2-2 pitch, Ramirez shot a line drive through the hole on the left side of the infield scoring Vizquel and making the score 2-0 Indians.

Bartolo retired the Mariners in order in the seventh inning, but began to tire in the top of the eighth. After striking out Russ Davis on four pitches, he gave up consecutive singles to Dan Wilson and Brian Hunter. He got Alex Rodriguez to pop out after an eight-pitch at-bat and then the call was made for Paul Assenmacher to face Ken Griffey Junior.

Junior got the Mariners on the scoreboard with a line drive over second base. Paul Shuey was brought in to replace Assenmacher. With Edgar Martinez at the plate, Brian Hunter and Griffey executed a double steal. With both runners now in scoring position, Edgar looped a single into short right field and made the score 3-2 M's.

Jeff Fassero came in to pitch for the Mariners, and started off strong. He struck out David Justice and got Richie Sexson to ground out weakly back to the mound. He issued a walk to Jim Thome. Alex Ramirez worked through an epic at-bat and drew an 11-pitch walk. Robbie Alomar came in to pinch hit for Jeff Manto and loaded the bases with a single. Enrique Wilson drew a six-pitch walk to push Thome across and tie the game 3-3.

The Indians had the bases loaded in the bottom of the ninth inning, but Alex Ramirez struck out swinging to send the game into extra frames. The Mariners threatened several times, stranding baserunners in the tenth and eleventh innings.

In the bottom of the eleventh, the Mariners brought on former Indians closer Jose Mesa to pitch to the heart of the Indians order. He faced off against Omar Vizquel to lead off the eleventh. This is one of the few times in his post-Indians career that Mesa did not intentionally throw at Vizquel. The tension of extra innings was evidently enough to set aside their long standing feud.

Mesa retired the Indians side in order in the eleventh inning. He ran into immediate trouble in the twelfth when Jim Thome led off with a single. Alex Ramirez laid down a sacrifice bunt to move Thome into scoring position. Mesa intentionally walked Roberto Alomar to get to Enrique Wilson. Wilson singled to left to load the bases.

Mesa had recorded his first save against his former team earlier in the year, but had not faced this kind of pressure cooker situation against the Tribe. Chris Turner stepped to the plate. Mesa's pitch sailed inside and got past M's catcher Dan Wilson. Thome scampered home for the walk-off win.

This was the Indians ninth win in ten games. The 1999 team was known for late-inning drama. This was their eleventh win of the season in the final at-bat.

Game 68
July 1, 1951 (First Game)
Bob Feller's Third No-Hitter (But Not a Shutout)

On the first Sunday in July, the Tigers were visiting Municipal Stadium, and Bob Feller was set to face Detroit's Bob Cain.

With runners on second and third in the bottom of the first, Luke Easter grounded to short. Dale Mitchell scored from third and gave the Tribe the early lead.

In the Detroit half of the fourth inning, Tigers shortstop Johnny Lipon reached on an error by Tribe shortstop Ray Boone. With Jerry Priddy at the plate, Lipon stole second and advanced to third on a wild throw by Dick Kryhoski. George Kell lofted a long fly ball into left field. Lipon tagged up and scored the unearned run, tying the game at 1-1.

Feller issued two walks, but otherwise had the Tigers offense locked down. Feller later remarked to the Plain Dealer, "My fastball and curve were nothing to brag about so I was depending on the slider most of the time. The fast one got better as the game moved along and I used it quite a bit in the late innings."

In the bottom of the eighth inning, Sam Chapman had a one-out triple. Milt Neilson replaced him as a pinch runner. Luke Easter drove in the go-ahead run with a single to right field which scored Neilson easily.

Feller faced the heart of the Tigers batting order in the top of the ninth. He got Charlie Keller and George Kell to fly out to right and left field, respectively. Vic Wertz was up to bat with the Tigers down to their last out. A month earlier, Wertz had broken up Bob Lemon's bid for a perfect game.

Feller struck out Wertz to end the game and earn his third no-hitter. Three career no-hitters was the record at that time and brought Feller into rare air with Cy Young.

At this time, there have been 300 no-hitters officially recognized by Major League Baseball. 257 of them are in the time-scope of this Project (since 1901).

According to Baseball Reference, there have been ten recognized no-hit games that were not shutouts. Feller's was the second in baseball history. Dazzy Vance and the Brooklyn Robins No-Hit the Phillies in 1925, but Phillies first baseman Chicken Hawks got on base by way of an error in left field and scored on a sacrifice fly.

The Indians are the most recent victims of the no-hit non-shutout. Irvin Santana of the Angels no-hit the Tribe in Game 102 of the 2011 campaign. In that game, Eziquiel Carrera reached on an error by the Angel's shortstop, stole second, advanced to third on an Asdrubal Cabrera groundout, and scored on a wild pitch.

Game 69
June 15, 2019
Leonys Martin Steals Home

Outfielder Leonys Martin came to the Indians in a deadline-day deal at the end of July 2018. Just nine days later, he was placed on the injured list with an undisclosed illness. After some speculation, it was revealed that Martin was being treated for a life-threatening bacterial infection at the Cleveland Clinic.

After an intense offseason of treatment and rehabilitation, Martin was back on the Opening Day roster. While his return to baseball was nothing short of miraculous, it was clear by mid-June that Martin's production was going to be below past expectations.

The Tribe made the short trip north to face the Tigers for a weekend series, and Leonys started in center field against his former club. Shane Bieber was matched up with Gregory Soto.

In the top of the third inning, Oscar Mercado beat the throw to first on a high chopper and then stole second. After Carlos Santana struck out and Jordan Luplow walked, Jose Ramirez was up for the second time with runners on base and two outs. He lofted a ball to deep center which looked like a sure RBI-producer, but Tiger's centerfielder Harold Castro made an over-the-shoulder catch at a full sprint on the warning track to end the inning.

Bieber was perfect through the first four innings. He struck out six of the first twelve Tigers he faced.

Mercado got aboard once again in the top of the fifth inning with a bloop single. Carlos Santana followed with a single of his own. Jordan Luplow broke open the scoring when he sent a long fly ball onto the warning track in right. Nick Castellanos mis-played the carom off the wall, allowing Mercado to score. Jose Ramirez lined one into left field, and Santana made it 2-0 Indians with a sacrifice hit. Jason Kipnis' ground out advanced Luplow to third, where he was eventually driven in by catcher Kevin Plawecki.

Miguel Cabrera knocked a single through the left side of the infield to lead off the bottom of the fifth inning and break up Bieber's perfect streak. However, Shane found his footing and retired the next three Tigers in order. He only seemed to pick up momentum. He struck out the side in the bottom of the sixth.

Bieber started to scuffle in the bottom of the seventh, when he gave up a leadoff walk to Christin Stewart. The bases were loaded after singles by Castellanos and Cabrera. Brandon Dixson knocked a single into left to make it a 3-2 game. With runners on first and second, Bieber struck out Harold Castro and then got Ronny Rodriguez to ground into an inning-ending double play.

Leonys Martin poked a line drive into the right field corner and found himself on second base to lead off the top of the eighth inning. Francisco Lindor just missed on the pitch he was waiting for from Victor Alcantra. He slammed his bat to the ground in frustration. Martin returned to second, and then broke for third unexpectedly. He beat Stewart's throw into third base and felt emboldened against the disinterested Tigers.

As Alcantra began his motion on the 1-0 pitch to Carlos Santana, Martin broke for home. John Hicks caught the pitch and applied the tag, but Martin's slide poked the ball loose. His straight-steal of home put the Tribe up 4-2.

Oliver Perez relieved Bieber part way through the eighth inning. Brad Hand came on to pitch the bottom of the ninth and converted his 20th save of the season in as many attempts.

Game 70
June 20, 1996
Indians Defeat Roger Clemens in a Walk-off

It was always a joy to watch the juggernaut offense of the mid-90's go up against the era's best pitchers. Matching up with Randy Johnson, Pedro Martinez, David Cone, Kenny Rogers, or David Wells was usually a memorable battle, and often a playoff preview. You would be hard pressed to find a pitcher that typified the 1990's (steroids and all) like Roger Clemens.

The Rocket was matched up against Chad Ogea this Thursday night at the Jake. Ogea started off a bit rocky, issuing a leadoff walk to Jeff Frye and a single to John Valentin. However, he then got Mo Vaughn to ground into a double play and Jose Canseco to pop out to end the inning.

Jim Thome got the Indians on the board early, cracking an RBI double to deep left field that scored Julio Franco from first base.

The Sox took a 4-1 lead in the top of the third. A flurry of offense topped off by a two-run single by Reggie Jefferson put the Tribe in a bit of a hole.

The Indians began to climb back into things when Manny Ramirez led off the bottom of the fourth inning with a solo home run.

In the bottom of the fifth inning, Jim Thome was up with one out and runners on second and third. He grounded out to second, but Omar Vizquel was able to come around and score. This cut the Sox' lead to one run.

Thome came through for the Tribe again in the bottom of the eighth inning. He tied the game with a timely home run to deep right field. Clemens struck out Albert Belle, and then walked Manny Ramirez on five pitches. Eddie Murray drove the ball into short left field for a single, advancing Manny to second. Carlos Baerga had the opportunity to do some damage, but grounded into a 6-4-3 double play to end the inning.

Indians reliever Paul Shuey faced four Red Sox in the top of the ninth and held them scoreless. Mike Stanton replaced Roger Clemens on the mound for the Sox in the bottom of the ninth. Tony Peña led off the inning with a double. Jeromy Burnitz replaced Peña on the basepaths as a pinch runner. Omar Vizquel executed a perfect sacrifice bunt to move Burnitz over to third.

In his fifth plate appearance of the day, Kenny Lofton drove the game-winning single into center field. Burnitz scored easily from third and gave the Tribe their third (of an eventual nine) walk-off win in the 1996 campaign.

Game 71
July 16, 1995
Manny Ramirez "Wow!" Home Run

The red-hot Indians were trying to complete a four-game weekend sweep of the A's in mid-July of 1995. The Tribe were already running away with the Central Division, and every game seemed to have a new hero.

Oakland threw Todd Stottlemyre against "El Presidente" Dennis Martinez. Eckersley began his career in Cleveland as a hard-throwing starter. He threw a no-hitter for the Tribe in Game 41 of 1977 (see page 80). In 1987, he signed with his hometown Oakland A's and eventually became the most dominant closer of the era.

Rickey Henderson led off this Sunday afternoon game with a home run on the third pitch from Martinez. Four batters later, Geronimo Berroa took Martinez deep to left-center to put the A's ahead 3-0.

Manny Ramirez drew a walk to lead off the Indians' half of the second inning. Paul Sorrento flied out. Then, Herbert Perry blazed a line drive into right field that allowed Manny to advance to third. Tony Peña grounded one to the third baseman. Manny was able to race home, while the A's settled for throwing Peña out at first.

In the bottom of the sixth inning, the Indians loaded the bases on Stottlemyre, but Wayne Kirby ended the inning with a flyball out. Likewise, the A's loaded the bases in the top of the seventh. Dennis Martinez was able to work out of the jam when Stan Javier grounded out to short.

The A's went to their bullpen in the bottom of the seventh inning. Mark Acre came on to replace Stottlemyre. Carlos Baerga poked a single through the right side of the infield. Albert Belle smashed Acre's first pitch deep to left-center and gone, tying the game at 3-3.

The A's loaded the bases again in the eighth inning, but once again failed to score. Julian Tavarez and Todd Van Poppel pitched scoreless ninth innings, for their respective clubs.

The bullpens continued to battle, until the top of the twelfth when Stan Javier scored Ricky Henderson on a sacrifice fly off of Alan Embree.

The Indians came to bat in the bottom of the twelfth with the pressure mounting. The A's brought in Eckersley to try to slam the door. Carlos Baerga singled to left on Eck's second pitch. Things were looking grim after consecutive pop outs by Albert Belle and Jim Thome.

Mike Hargrove sent the speedy Kenny Lofton in to pinch run for Baerga. Lofton stole second with Manny Ramirez at the plate. Ramirez stepped back in and fouled off a handful of Eckersley fastballs. On the seventh pitch of the at-bat, Manny connected with one of those Eckersley fastballs in a big way. The two-run home run landed more than half way up the left field bleachers. As Manny rounded the bases, a TV camera caught the moment when Eckersley turned to see the ball leave the park and mouth "WOW!"

Interestingly, Eckersley is credited with coining the phrase I have used so often in this project "walk-off home run." He initially used the term to describe the home run he gave up to Kirk Gibson in Game 1 of the 1988 World Series.

Game 72
July 7, 1923
Largest Margin of Victory in Club History

In the first half of a Saturday double-header against the Red Sox, Stan Coveleski was matched up with Boston's Curt Fullerton at League Park.

The Indians unleashed an historic offensive onslaught. They scored at least one run in every inning, including a thirteen-run sixth that saw seven hits by seventeen batters.

In the bottom of the fourth, the Sox called on Lefty O'Doul pinch hit for Fullerton. O'Doul then stayed in to pitch. Lefty is known as one of the game's great hitters, having won two batting titles in 1929 and 1932. He holds the fourth highest career batting average at .349, and he helped to found Nippon Professional Baseball after World War II.

However, O'Doul also holds the distinction of giving up the most runs in a relief appearance with 16 in three innings, including the 13-run sixth.

Every Indian starter scored at least one run, and everyone but Frank Brower and Glenn Myatt had an RBI. Third baseman Rube Lutzke was four for five with six RBI and a walk in seven plate appearances. Shortstop Joe Sewell had three hits and two stolen bases—no lack of hustle in the blowout.

With a final score of 27-3, this game is fifth on the MLB all-time list for runs scored, and third all-time for margin of victory. Only the Rangers 30-3 drubbing of the Orioles on August 22, 2007 and the Red Sox 29-4 run romp over the St. Louis Browns on June 8, 1950 had larger margins of victory. The Tribe also holds the number four spot on the margin of victory list, with their 26-3 victory over the St. Louis Browns in Game 105 of 1948.

Game 73
July 18, 1995
Albert Belle Walk-off Grand Slam

The Indians were 14½ games ahead in the Central Division on July 18, 1995. It was the biggest pennant lead in franchise history to date. The California Angels, who were leading the West, were in town for a two-game series that would test both first-place clubs.

The Angels sent Mark Langston to the mound with a five-game winning streak. Spot starter Mark Clark, not far removed from Triple-A Buffalo, started for the Tribe.

California got out to a three-run lead, as Clark could not keep the ball inside the park. He gave up a solo home run to Tony Phillips in the top of the third inning, and a two-run shot to Jim Edmunds in the fifth.

In the Cleveland half of the fifth, the Indians manufactured three runs on five singles by Alvaro Espinoza, Ruben Amaro Jr., Carlos Baerga, Albert Belle, and Manny Ramirez. This parade of offense tied the ballgame at three runs apiece.

JT Snow got things started for the Angels in the top of the sixth inning with a single through the left side of the infield. Garrett Anderson got to Clark once again with a home run that just cleared the right field wall. The Angels pulled ahead again five runs to three.

Eric Plunk came into the game to relieve Clark. He pitched 1-2-3 seventh and eighth innings to hold the score at 5-3. However, the Indians were not able to get a runner past second base in either the seventh or eighth inning.

After Paul Assenmacher retired the side in the top of the ninth, the Indians were down to their last three outs. Angel's closer Lee Smith came on to pitch. At that time, Smith was the all-time saves leader with 456. He was one save behind Jose Mesa for the league high for the season.

Left-handed utility man Wayne Kirby was brought on to bat for Alvero Espinoza. He hit a sharp ground ball down the first base line. It kicked off the base, off the chest of the Angels first baseman and into foul territory. Kirby was safe at first. Jim Thome struck out, but not before Kirby stole second. A line drive single through the left side of the infield got Omar Vizquel aboard and advanced Kirby to third. With runners at the corners, Smith walked Baerga on four pitches to load the bases and set up a double play.

Smith quickly threw two strikes. A close pitch just missed the outside corner. Albert later admitted that he thought that may have been strike three. Then, Belle smashed a hanging slider 425 feet to dead center.

In a post-game interview Smith said, "I was trying to throw something in the dirt, out of the strike zone, but that's what happens when you hang sliders."

Belle's trip around the bases and subsequent curtain call were met with a deafening roar from the crowd of over 41,000. This was the fourteenth Indians victory in their final at-bat in 1995.

Game 74
June 20, 2008
Borowski Blows Save, Earns Win

The Indians were visiting the Dodgers in Chavez Ravine for an interleague game with a most compelling pitching matchup. Dodgers starter Clayton Kershaw would go on to win three Cy Youngs and an MVP award. The Indians were throwing Cliff Lee would go on to win the AL Cy Young in the 2008 season. However, neither accomplished pitcher would end up with the win.

The Indians took a 4-0 lead into the bottom of the eighth courtesy of a two-run homer by catcher Kelly Shoppach in the top of the third and RBI hits by Casey Blake and Jhonny Peralta.

After a groundout by Juan Pierre to lead off the first, Cliff Lee gave up a line drive single to Matt Kemp. Lee's pitch count was at 104, so manager Eric Wedge made the call to the bullpen.

Things unraveled quickly as Rafael Betancourt gave up an RBI double to Jeff Kent. Rafi was replaced on the mound by Rafael Perez, who gave up a single to James Loney, which scored Kent. Perez was able to get out of the eighth with the score 4-2.

Dodgers reliever Cory Wade quickly shut down the Indians in the ninth, using only eleven pitches to retire Shoppach, Delucci, and Sizemore.

Indians closer Joe Borowski came in to pitch the Dodgers half of the ninth. Angel Berroa sent Borowski's second pitch into right field for a single and Russel Martin followed with a double. Borowski struck out pinch hitter Blake DeWitt, but then gave up an RBI single to Juan Pierre.

Pierre stole second, and Borowski intentionally walked Matt Kemp to load the bases and set up the double play. Jeff Kent grounded one to the shortstop and was put out, but not before Martin crossed the plate for the tying run. Because he entered the game with a two-run lead and gave up the tying run, Borowski was charged statistically with a blown save.

With two outs in the top of the tenth, Jhonny Peralta knocked a double into right field, scoring Ryan Garko and Franklin Guttierez.

Masahide Kobayashi came to the mound to try and hold on to the Indians lead. Kobayashi was one of three players to record 200+ saves in Japanese professional baseball. In 2008, the Indians brought Kobayashi to Cleveland to convert him to an MLB closer.

Kobayashi retired the Dodgers side, giving up only one hit to Russell Martin. He was awarded the save. This was his fourth of six saves in his MLB career. Selfishly, I wish that he had worked out, because I loved hearing Tom Hamilton say "Kobayashi."

After blowing the initial save opportunity, Borowski was awarded the win because the Indians scored the winning run while he was the pitcher of record. This is an interesting statistical twist. Wins are traditionally the most-cited statistic for pitchers, along with Earned Run Average. However, an entry in the win column for a closer is a *negative*, because it indicates that he blew the save opportunity. The save statistic was developed to better measure the particular job of a closer. Later, the "hold" was developed for middle-inning relievers.

Borowski led the American League in saves in 2007 and contributed greatly to the Indians playoff run, but clearly did not have his best stuff in 2008. He was designated for assignment a few weeks later on July 4th.

Game 75
June 28, 1992
Indians Win After Jacobs Field Groundbreaking

The corner of Carnegie and Ontario did not always look like it does today. In the 1920's, Central Market sat in the middle of Ontario Street just north of Eagle Avenue. At the time, the corner of Carnegie & Ontario was the confluence of Woodland Ave, Broadway, and Ontario Street. A tangle of streetcar lines converged at the market before heading north to Public Square. Businesses located in what is now the footprint of the ballpark included the National Biscuit Company, Cottage Creamery, and A.L.Ehrbar Cigar Company.

A 1951 aerial photograph shows the dense neighborhood of offices and warehouses that stood where the ballpark is now. The old Central Market burned down in 1949. Its operations moved into the Eagle Street Market located where the Gateway Parking Garage is today.

In May 1990, Cuyahoga County voters narrowly approved the "Sin Tax" which added a charge of 1.9 cents on a can of beer and 4.5 cents on a pack of cigarettes for 15 years. This revenue stream opened the door for the creation of the Gateway Economic Development Corporation and the construction of both Jacobs Field and Gund Arena.

On June 28, 1992, the Indians invited Mel Harder who had thrown the first pitch in Municipal Stadium to throw a ceremonial first pitch at the Gateway construction site. Charles Nagy and Sandy Alomar Jr. were the battery representing the current Indians that would move into the new stadium at the start of 1994.

After the speeches and photo opportunities at the construction site, Dennis Cook started against Jack Morris and the Blue Jays back down on the Lakefront at Municipal Stadium.

It was a high-scoring affair. Joe Carter and John Olerud both homered off Cook in the first inning, giving the Jays a 3-0 advantage out of the gate.

The Tribe answered by sending all nine batters to the plate in the bottom of the first. Kenny Lofton dropped a leadoff bunt down the third base line and raced to first. Felix Fermin blooped one over the shortstop's head to get aboard and put Lofton on third base. Carlos Baerga hit a grounder past the Jay's first baseman and Lofton came around to score. Albert Belle grounded into a double play, but Fermin was able to score.

With two outs, Carlos Martinez dropped a single into left field. Morris issued consecutive walks to Mark Whiten and Glenallen Hill. With the bases juiced, Jim Thome scorched a single through the left side of the infield, scoring two. Finally, Sandy Alomar skied a popup that was caught by Jay's catcher Pat Borders to end the inning. The Tribe had taken a 4-3 lead.

Carlos Baerga extended that lead to 5-3 in the bottom of the second with an RBI single.

Former Indian Joe Carter tied things up in the top of the seventh with a two-run single into short left field. Jeff Kent put the Jays on top in the top of the eighth with a solo home run off reliever Steve Olin.

The speedy Alex Cole drew a walk to lead off the bottom of the eighth. Mark Whiten laid down a sacrifice bunt to move Cole into scoring position. Paul Sorrento socked a go-ahead home run over the center field wall.

Eric Plunk pitched a 1-2-3 ninth to earn a save and close out a celebratory day in Indians history with a 7-6 victory.

Game 76
June 28, 2016
Lindor Steals Home on Throw to Second

The 2016 Indians were 16 games over .500 and visiting the last place Braves for an interleague matchup. Corey Kluber was matched up with Matt Wisler.

Wisler struck out Carlos Santana to start the game, but then gave up consecutive singles to Jason Kipnis and Francisco Lindor. Jose Ramirez scored Kipnis with a single into right field, and Lindor advanced to third.

With Lonny Chisenhall at the plate, Jose Ramirez broke to steal second. Atlanta catcher AJ Pierzynski's throw was off the mark. When it was bobbled by shortstop Eric Aybar, Lindor broke for home. Both runners were safe and the Indians ended the frame up 2-0.

Corey Kluber retired the first 15 Atlanta batters in order and was untouched until he gave up a single to Eric Aybar in the bottom of the sixth inning. Emilio Bonifacio followed with another single. Aybar and Bonifacio eventually came around to score on an RBI single by Ender Inciarte. Inciarte was thrown out trying to stretch the hit into a double and the inning ended with the score tied 2-2.

Kluber mowed through the Braves lineup once again. He eventually pitched eight innings, gave up three hits, one walk, and recorded seven strikeouts. Michael Martinez pinch hit for Kluber in the top of the ninth. The Braves had a wild inning. They gave up three runs on two hits, an error and a wild pitch. Carlos Santana had the game-winning hit.

Indians closer Cody Allen came in to hold the 5-2 lead. Despite a solo home run by Jace Peterson, Allen was able to record the save and preserve the Tribe's winning streak (this was win number 11 out of an eventual 14 from June 17 to July 1)

Game 77
June 26, 1998
Bartolo Colon Battles Ricky Gutierez in a 20-Pitch At-Bat

On a hot Friday night, the Astros were visiting Jacobs Field for an interleague matchup. Both were talented clubs coming into mid-season form. The Indians were nine games ahead in the Central Division, while Houston led the NL central by five games.

The Indians were throwing ace Bartolo Colon against the Astros Pete Schourek. Colon faced his first challenge in the top of the third inning. He walked Ricky Gutierrez to lead things off. Brad Ausmus singled to center. A Craig Biggio single plated Gutierrez. Bill Spiers was up next. Spiers grounded into a 4-6-3 double play, but Ausmus managed to score from third, putting the Astros up 2-0.

The Tribe was all fundamentals in the bottom of the third inning. Omar Vizquel had a leadoff single, and stole second. Shawn Dunston laid down a bunt to move him over to third. Manny Ramirez came through with a single that sent Omar around to score.

Colon continued to pitch both efficiently and effectively. Through seven innings he had given up only five hits and a single walk on 84 total pitches.

In the bottom of the seventh inning, Manny Ramirez was on first after a fielder's choice. With two outs, the Indians got a rally going. Manny stole second and then Houston reliever Mike Magnante walked Jim Thome. Sandy Alomar drove in Ramirez with a line drive double into center field. David Justice drew a walk to load the bases.

Still with two outs and the bases loaded, Mark Whiten drove Magnante's fourth pitch through the left side of the infield to score Thome and Alomar. Travis Fryman struck out to end the inning, but the Indians had taken a 4-2 lead.

Astros shortstop Ricky Gutierrez stepped in against Colon to lead off the top of the eighth inning. Gutierrez swung and missed at the first pitch. On the second pitch, Gutierrez took another big cut. The

149

bat slipped out of his hands and spiraled into the stands for the second strike. He fouled off the third pitch, and things began to get interesting. The fourth pitch was a ball outside. Gutierrez fouled off another, and then pitch number six was another ball outside. Now on a 2-2 count Gutierrez fouled off six straight pitches. Pitch thirteen was a ball in the dirt and the crowd was beginning to buzz. Gutierrez then fouled off *another* six straight pitches.

At this point, Bartolo had thrown more pitches to the Houston shortstop than he had thrown in any other *inning* of this game (17 in the third was the largest pitch count). On the 20th pitch of the at-bat, Gutierrez struck out swinging. The crowd gave the pair a standing ovation. A quick check with Elias Sports Bureau revealed that this was the longest at-bat for which there were reliable records.

In 2012, High Heat Stats analyzed the average pitches per plate appearance. In 1998, the average pitches per plate appearance was 3.7. This record-breaking at-bat was 5.4 times longer than a standard at-bat of the time.

Closer Michael Jackson recorded the last three outs of the game and was awarded the save.

In 2018, Brandon Belt of the Giants and Angels pitcher Jaime Barrias surpassed this record with a 21-pitch at-bat. Belt eventually flied out.

Game 78
July 2, 2015
Urshela's Odd Hitting Streak

Closing out the 2014 season, Giovanny Urshela was regarded as the Indians top prospect. He was called up to the Majors on June 8, 2015, and made his debut in Game 59.

By Game 77, Gio has already accomplished something (however odd) that no Indian had ever done. Jason Lukehart of SB Nation noted that Urshela had one hit--and no more--in twelve consecutive games. A search of the baseball reference database revealed that Rocky Colavito had one hit--and not more than one--in eleven consecutive games in 1958, making Urshela the franchise leader for this very odd distinction.

Keeping a hitting streak going is widely regarded as one of the most difficult accomplishments in baseball, where a 30% success rate at the plate can make you an All-Star. However, hitters on a hot streak usually succeed well past the minimum. Urshela's streak to this point included eleven singles and a home run. He batted .293 during these twelve games—good, but nothing groundbreaking.

Gio's single hit came in the top of the fourth inning. He hit a line drive to center off the Rays' Alex Colome. He advanced to second on a single by Michael Bourn, tagged up on a Roberto Perez fly out, and was driven home on a line drive by Jason Kipnis. Urshela scored the Indians' fifth run of the night. They went on to win 8-1 behind a brilliant start by Carlos Carrasco. Cookie struck out thirteen and only gave up one hit in 8 ⅔ innings of work.

Urshela extended his one-hit streak to 15 games. He was unable to get a hit in Game 81, which was a 5-3 loss in Pittsburgh.

Game 79
July 19, 1909 (First Game)
Neal Ball Turns First Unassisted Triple Play

Cy Young was pitching for the Indians at League Park against Charlie Chech and the Red Sox in the first game of a Monday double-header.

The play-by-play of the game has been lost to history, but plenty of newspaper accounts preserve the box score and much has been written about the events that make this game notable, even 110 years later.

With the Naps up 1-0 in the top of the second, Boston's Heinie hit a lead-off single. Jake Stahl moved Wagner over to second base with a bunt single. The hit-and-run was initiated with Amby McConnell at the plate. McConnel lined the 3-2 pitch up the middle and Wagner was on his way to third on contact.

Neal Ball leaped to spear the line drive as it passed directly over second base. The ball stuck in his glove, and he landed on the second base bag, forcing out Wagner who was most of the way to third. Stahl attempted to reverse course, but Ball ran him down between first and second to record the third out.

The play happened so quickly, that initially there was some confusion. Cy Young asked Ball why he was headed to the dugout. "That's three outs," he deadpanned. Once fans at League Park realized what they had seen, they showered the field with their hats in celebration.

Ball himself later recounted the play, "I didn't think there was a chance of getting it but I was on the move toward second and I gave it a try anyhow. It was dead over the bag by then so I jumped and the darned thing hit my glove and stuck. The rest was easy. Wagner was way around third base somewhere and when I came down on the bag he was out. I just stood there with my hands out and Stahl ran into them. He was halfway down when the ball was hit and couldn't stop. That's all there was to it. I can still remember how surprised I was when the ball hit in my glove."

It often seems that a player that makes a spectacular defensive play follows it up with offensive heroics. Whether this is due to adrenaline, or a run of good luck, it was certainly true for Neal Ball. With the crowd still cheering the triple play, he hit Chech's first pitch of the third inning deep into League Park's expansive outfield. He rounded the bases for an inside-the-park home run.

The Naps would go on to win the game 6-1.

There have been only 15 unassisted triple plays in Major League History. The Indians are the only team to have recorded three. In addition to Ball's triple play, Bill Wambganss recorded the only unassisted triple play in the World Series. It came in Game 5 of the 1920 Series against Brooklyn. Asdrubal Cabrera put out three at once in a loss to the Blue Jays in Game 38 of the 2008 season.

Ball remains the only player in MLB history to record an unassisted triple play and a home run in the same inning, a feat that is unlikely to ever be matched.

Game 80
July 6, 1997
Sandy Alomar Jr. (Maybe) Sets Franchise Record

Although he is best known for his defense, leadership, and ability to call a game from behind the plate, Sandy Alomar, Jr. put together one of the best summers of hitting in a generation during May, June, and early July of 1997.

On this night, the Indians were trying to close out the first half of the season with a sweep of the Royals. Orel Hershiser was on the mound against Tim Belcher.

Alomar extended his hitting streak in the bottom of the second with a ground ball single to third base. He beat the throw down the line on the weak grounder. Unfortunately, he was stranded as Matt Williams and Brian Giles both flied out.

Tony Fernandez grounded out to start the Cleveland half of the third inning. Omar Vizquel got the offense started with a line drive single into center. Marquis Grissom lofted a fly ball into center. Tom Goodwin caught it for the putout, but Omar was able to tag and advance to second. Kevin Seitzer drew a five-pitch walk. Jim Thome drew a second walk to load the bases. Manny Ramirez put the Tribe ahead in a big way, with a towering grand slam into the left field bleachers.

However, the Royals surged in the top of the fourth, hanging seven runs, including a three-run double by Scott Cooper, on Hershiser and chasing him from the game.

Matt Williams leadoff home run in the bottom of the fourth and a two-run double by Kevin Seitzer tied the game at 7-7.

Jose Mesa held the Royals at bay for 3 and ⅔ innings, one of his longest outings of the year.

In the bottom of the eighth inning, Omar Vizquel came through with a two-out single into center field. Gregg Olson came on for the Royals in relief. Omar broke for second on Olson's first pitch. He slid into second safely. Marquis Grissom punched a single past the shortstop and drove in Vizquel for what turned out to be the winning run. Michael Jackson pitched the ninth and was awarded the win.

This was the last game before the All-Star break. While most of the team enjoyed several days off, Jim Thome and Sandy Alomar returned to Cleveland for the first All-Star Game at Jacobs Field. Sandy hit the game-winning home run off Shawn Estes and was named the MVP of the All-Star Game in front of the hometown crowd.

Sandy could not keep the streak alive after the All-Star break, but the 30-Game streak is regarded as the longest in team history. Some record-keepers note a possible 31-game streak by Nap Lajoie in 1906, but the records are unreliable this early in baseball history, and there are differing accounts.

During the streak, Alomar slashed .422/.455/.595. He had 11 home runs at the break, including a streak of five straight games with a home run in April. "I'm in a zone. Everything looks like a beach ball," he said in one post-game interview.

The one benchmark that Sandy's streak did not achieve was the longest streak by a catcher. This is notable because that mark is held by Sandy's old rival, Benito Santiago. Santiago put together a 34-game streak for the Padres in 1987. This performance, along with his ability to throw out baserunners from his knees, kept Sandy out of the San Diego lineup in the late 1980's and eventually led to his trade to the Indians.

Game 81
July 3, 2009
Choo Four Hits, Seven RBI

At the beginning of 2009, Shin-Soo Choo signed a one-year deal with the Indians. Choo was 27 and still on the hook for two years of military service in his native South Korea before age 30.

Choo was coming off a strong 2008 season in which he was the Player of the Month for September. In the MLB off-season, the Korean national team had taken Japan to extra innings in the final of the World Baseball Classic.

The 2009 Indians were dead last in the American League at 32 and 49 for the season and were looking to get some good vibes going against the worst team in the AL West, the Oakland A's.

The A's jumped out to an early 2-0 lead, but the Indians offense was the key to this game. Travis Hafner got things started with a solo home run in the bottom of the second inning.

Ben Francisco hit a weak grounder to third base to lead off the Indians' half of the third inning. Bobby Crosby rushed his throw to first and it skipped away from Nomar Garciaparra. Asdrubal Cabrera grounded out, but Francisco was able to advance to second. A's starter Trever Cahill issued a walk to Grady Sizemore. Victor Martinez had a long fly out down the left field line.

Choo stepped in with two outs and drove in Ben Francisco with a single to center. Travis Hafner drew a five-pitch walk. Jhonny Peralta hit another grounder to third base. Crosby threw this one away as well. Two runs scored as the ball skipped away toward the dugout. The Indians took a 4-2 lead thanks to the A's miscues.

Choo chased starter Trevor Cahill from the game with a two-run double down the left field line in the bottom of the fourth. Santiago Casilla came on to pitch for the A's. Choo broke for third as Casilla made his first pitch of the night to Travis Hafner. Choo safely swiped second base. Jhonny Peralta drove him in with a single through the left side of the infield. By the end of the inning, the Tribe was up 8-3.

The Indians scored five more runs in the bottom of the fifth inning, as A's reliever Santiago Casilla could not right the ship. Asdrubal Cabrera had a two-run double. Choo blasted a three-run homer to deep right-center.

In his fifth plate appearance, Choo led off the bottom of the seventh inning with a home run that squeaked by the right field foul pole. The Indians went on to win 15-3.

Choo's final stat line went 4 for 5 with seven RBI and a stolen base.

After the MLB Season, Choo again joined up with the Korean national team. They earned a gold medal in the Asia Cup, and Choo earned the military exemption that he had long sought. At 1,542 games and counting, Choo is the longest tenured and most accomplished Korean position player in the MLB.

Game 82
July 3, 1968
Luis Tiant 19K in Ten Inning Complete Game

The Indians were hosting the Twins for a four-game series leading up to the Fourth of July holiday. After splitting the first two games, Luis Tiant was on the mound against the Twins Jim Merritt.

Tiant pitched brilliantly, but was challenged early. With Twins on first and second in the top of the second inning, he struck out Minnesota shortstop Jackie Hernandez, looking to end the inning. Although Tiant scattered six hits, no Twins base runner made it past first base until the top of the tenth inning.

Merritt had an outstanding night for the Twins as well. He struck out seven Indians, gave up only four hits and a walk as the scoreless game stretched into extra frames.

In the top of the tenth, Rich Reese doubled to left field for the Twins. Frank Quilici followed with a well-executed bunt that moved Reese over to third. With runners at the corners and no outs, Tiant struck out John Roseboro, Rich Rollins, and Merritt in quick succession to end the threat. Take a moment to reflect on how different the game is today. In the top of the tenth inning, with a runner in scoring position and two outs, the Twins sent the *pitcher* to bat.

Indians left fielder Lou Johnson led off the bottom of the tenth with a single, and advanced to second on an error. With Johnson in scoring position as a result of the miscue by Jackie Hernandez, Tribe catcher Joe Azcue stepped to the plate. Azcue knocked a single into right field, easily scoring Johnson and sending the Indians into the holiday on a winning note.

Tiant finished 1968 with a league-leading 1.60 ERA, and a 21-9 record. Seven of his twenty-one wins were shutouts. His nineteen strikeouts stand as the franchise record for any single game.

Game 83
July 16, 1946
Indians Employ the "Ted Williams Shift"

After the conclusion of World War II, most of Baseball's stars returned to the game in 1946. On this Tuesday afternoon, Bob Feller was on the hill for the Indians against Tex Hughson at Fenway Park. Feller had recently returned from the Navy. Another all-time great who stepped away from baseball to serve in the war effort would step in against him: Ted Williams.

Two day before, the Indians had a doubleheader with the Red Sox. In the opening game, player-manager Lou Boudreau went 5-for-5 with four doubles and a homer. Ted Williams hit three home runs and went 4-for-5. All of his hits were to right field. This was not the first time Boudreau's hitting was overshadowed by Williams.

Boudreau won the AL batting crown in 1944 with a .327 average; however, this honor always came with the asterisk that Williams was busy serving as a second lieutenant in the Marine Corps in between winning his six batting titles.

Between games, Boudreau proposed a radical solution. When Ted Williams came to the plate in the second game, the Indians defense changed their alignment *drastically*. When Williams saw the shift for the first time, he turned to the umpire and said, "What the hell is going on out there? They can't do that."

They could, though. Boudreau had checked the rules. The current edition of the MLB Rulebook is 184 pages long. The clause that implicitly allows a defensive shift is rather succinct: 5.02(c) "Except the pitcher and the catcher, any fielder may station himself anywhere in fair territory."

The Tribe's shifted defense held him to only one hit in the second game of the twin bill, but Cleveland lost 6 to 4.

Seeing the success of his new strategy, Boudreau continued to apply the shift when facing Williams. Two days later in Game 83, the Indians got on the board early when a long fly out by Pat Seerey allowed George Case to tag and score. Ken Keltner made the lead 2-0 with a home run to lead off the top of the second inning.

Heinz Becker led off the Indians' half of the fifth with a double. He was driven in by catcher Jim Hegan. Pat Seerey led off the top of the sixth with another home run to make the score 4-0.

In the bottom of the sixth, Ted Williams beat the shift with a line drive to center field that went for a triple and scored Johnny Pesky from second.

Jim Hegan answered with an RBI-triple of his own in the top of the seventh inning. This extended the Indians' lead to 5-1.

Williams singled to left in the bottom of the eighth, but it came to naught as Feller retired the next three Red Sox in order. All told, Feller gave up three runs on nine hits but it was good enough to get the complete game win. He squashed a late comeback attempt that included a two-run double by Dom DiMaggio in the bottom of the ninth. Williams went two for five with the triple noted above as the only highlight.

Boudreau would continue to use the shift against Williams throughout the mid-1940's. Cardinals manager Eddie Dyer used the same tactic against Williams to win the 1946 World Series. Eventually he trained himself to be less of a pull hitter, but that required major adjustments to his approach.

The shift has become commonplace over the last decade, thanks to statistical analysis. Still, it is hard to overstate how shocking this was to the baseball establishment at the time. Lou Boudreau is remembered not only as a talented hitter in his own right, but also as an innovative manager who knew the rules and how to bend them.

Game 84
July 3, 2018
Second Game Winning Grand Slam in a Row

On July 2nd, Francisco Lindor hit a grand slam in the top of the fourth inning to break a 2-2 tie against the Royals. These would go on to be the game-winning runs.

On this night in Kansas City, the Indians got out to an early lead, scoring two runs off Danny Duffy in the top of the first. The Royals answered in the bottom of the first when Lucas Duda sent a home run over the bullpen in right field to tie the game at 2-2.

In the bottom of the second with Adalberto Mondesi on second base, Whit Merrifield blooped a hit just out of reach for Rajai Davis who was charging in from center. Mondesi scored after the ball dropped and rolled past Davis. Merrifield scored from first on Rosell Herrera's line drive over third base. This put KC up 4-2.

Edwin Encarnacion walked to lead off the top of the sixth inning. Brandon Guyer was hit by Danny Duffy's fourth pitch. Yonder Alonso loaded the bases with a single. Catcher Yan Gomes stepped in and smashed Duffy's 1-0 pitch into the Indians bullpen in left field. Gomes' grand slam put the Tribe ahead 6-4, but the lead was far from safe.

The Royals had the tying run at second base in both the eighth and ninth innings. In the eighth, Royals catcher Salvador Perez was on second with Hunter Dozier at the plate. Dozier sent a ground ball through the left side of the infield, which was run down by Rajai Davis. Perez hesitated rounding third base as Davis threw to the cutoff man Francisco Lindor. Lindor spun and threw a strike to Gomes at the plate. Perez was initially called safe, but the play was reviewed and the out was confirmed.

In the bottom of the ninth, Mondesi and Merrifield were aboard for the Royals with only one out. Cody Allen struck out Rosell Herrera and got Salvador Perez to fly out to deep left to end the game and record the four-out save.

Game 85
July 7, 2006
Travis Hafner Hits Fifth Grand Slam Before All-Star Break

The Orioles were visiting Jacobs Field on a beautiful summer Friday night. Both teams were slightly below .500 and looking for an identity. CC Sabathia was matched up with Baltimore's Kris Benson.

Grady Sizemore led off for the Tribe with a single into center field. Left fielder Jason Michaels followed with his own line drive single into center. Ronnie Belliard got the Indians on the scoreboard with a sacrifice fly that allowed Grady to tag and score.

Jeff Conine got aboard for the O's in the bottom of the second with a line drive single. Ramon Hernandez popped out. Kevin Millar worked into a full count. On Sabathia's payoff pitch, Conine was running. Millar swung and missed, Victor Martinez fired to second and the inning ended on a strike out-throw out double play.

In the bottom of the second, Jhonny Peralta lofted a double into the left field gap. Ramon Vazquez singled into right field. Peralta came around to score the Tribe's second run on a liner by Franklin Gutierrez. Grady Sizemore hit a ball that looked like it had a chance to leave the park, but was tracked down in deep center field. Jason Michaels hit one sharply to third base. Vazquez was put out at home on the fielder's choice. Ronnie Belliard notched a two-out single.

Travis Hafner stepped in with two outs and the bases loaded. Pronk sent Benson's first pitch over the wall with great gusto. The line-drive grand slam was Hafner's fifth of the year. He is the only player to hit five grand slams before the All-Star break.

CC Sabathia faced the minimum number of Orioles through three innings. Even with a 7-0 cushion he did not lose focus. Overall, he struck out seven and gave up only three hits in this complete game shutout. The Indians would go on to win 9-0 on seventeen hits.

Hafner tied Don Mattingly for the all-time mark of six grand slams in a season in Game 117 (see page 224).

Game 86
July 15, 1994
The Corked Bat Heist

In the middle of July 1994, the Indians and White Sox were in the midst of a race for the central division title and Albert Belle was becoming one of baseball's preeminent sluggers.

The Indians were up 1-0 in the bottom of the first after an RBI single by Carlos Baerga when Albert Belle stepped to the plate. White Sox manager Gene Lamont approached home plate umpire Dave Philips and asked Philips to inspect Belle's bat.

Philips could not find anything obviously amiss with the bat, but asked that it be taken to the umpires' locker room for further analysis after the game.

The game continued, but the Indians dugout was tense. Manager Mike Hargrove and the rest of the Indians knew that the bat was likely corked and that Belle would be suspended during the pennant chase. Relief pitcher Jason Grimsley offered to retrieve the bat. He noted that the various sections of the clubhouse under Comiskey Park were divided by cinder block walls with a drop ceiling.

Grimley changed from his cleats to a pair of tennis shoes, donned batting gloves, and took off his jersey. He pushed a tile out of the drop ceiling in the Indians locker room and prepared to head up.

Grimsley later said that Belle had not brought a single bat to Chicago—batting practice or game bat—that was not corked. So, he packed one of Paul Sorrento's bats in plastic and took it with him into the Comiskey Park ceiling.

Grimsley crawled through the drop ceiling, and encountered a member of the grounds crew when he removed a tile in the wrong room. However, he eventually found the umpire's locker room and switched the Sorrento bat for the one that had been confiscated.

The confiscated bat, along with all of Belle's other corked bats were spirited out of the park by Indians staff as the game was going on.

In the top of the third, Carlos Baerga drove in Kenny Lofton with another RBI single, making the score 2-0.

Sox catcher Ron Karkovice led off the bottom of the third with a triple and then scored on an Ozzie Guillen groundout to cut the Indians' lead to 2-1.

Eddie Murray gave the Tribe an insurance run in the top of the fifth inning when he drove in Baerga with a two-out RBI double.

The Indians went on to win 3-2, but the drama would continue. Returning to their locker room, the umpires found the White Sox general manager who informed them that there had been a break-in. The White Sox had the locker room treated as a crime scene and brought in a former FBI agent to investigate.

Eventually, Indians GM John Hart presented the White Sox with the original bat for further analysis on the condition that the player responsible for the break-in would not be punished or prosecuted. Jason Grimsley's Mission Impossible-style caper was known only to the Indians until 1999 when Grimsley did an interview with Buster Olney in *The New York Times.*

When the original bat was analyzed it was, of course, found to be corked. Belle was given a ten-game suspension, but the pennant race never materialized as the 1994 season ended on August 12th with the beginning of the player's strike.

Game 87
July 13, 1963
Early Wynn's 300th Win

Hall of Fame pitcher Early Wynn came to the Indians in 1948 after eight seasons with the Senators and two years serving in World War II. Early in his career he was known as an aggressive power pitcher who was quick to brush batters back off the plate. He once said, "A pitcher will never be a big winner until he hates hitters." He was also known to knock runners down at first base with bean balls disguised as pickoff attempts.

Ten years into his baseball career, Wynn could no longer rely entirely on velocity and swagger. He credited Mel Harder with re-making his career. Harder taught Wynn how to throw a curveball, and he became part of one of the most talented pitching rotations in history along with Bob Feller, Bob Lemon, and Mike Garcia.

He pitched for nine years with the Indians, leading the World-Series bound 1954 squad with 23 wins. Wynn was traded to the White Sox after the 1957 season where he pitched until the end of 1962. The White Sox released Wynn at the end of the season with 299 total wins.

The Indians reached out to Wynn on June 1, 1963. He was at home in Florida and unhappily retired. The 43-year old felt that he had more innings left in his arm. Wynn pitched a complete game in his first game back in the rotation, but was the hard-luck loser in four consecutive outings.

On July 13, the Indians were visiting the Kansas City Athletics in Missouri's Municipal Stadium and Wynn was on the mound again seeking his elusive 300th win. Second baseman Larry Brown put the Tribe ahead early with an RBI single that drove in Joe Romano.

The A's tied it up in the bottom of the fourth when George Alusik sent Wynn's pitch over the Muni Stadium wall for a lead-off home run.

Wynn led off the top of the fifth inning with a single, and advanced to second on a Dick Howser hit. KC's Moe Drabowsky walked Max

165

Alvis to load the bases. Then Joe Adcock knocked a single scoring Wynn and Howser. After another walk, Drabowsky's day was done. Al Luplow knocked in another two runs before Romano was gunned out at home trying to score from first base.

The Royals loaded the bases to lead off the bottom of the fifth inning, then Jerry Lumpe tried to stretch a double into a triple. Three runs scored, including a young Tony LaRussa who was on base as a pinch runner.

Woodie Held pinch hit for Wynn in the top of the sixth. With five innings in the books and a 5-4 lead, Wynn could not lose the game but his teammates would have to hold on for the win.

Reliever Jerry Walker gave up only three hits and two walks in his four innings of work. His talented pitching along with two further insurance runs sealed Wynn's place in the history books as the 14th MLB pitcher to achieve 300 wins.

Wynn made one start after this game, and spent the rest of the year in the bullpen. He retired at the end of the 1963 season with exactly 300 wins, and a lifetime ERA of 3.54. He struck out 2,334 batters in 4,564 innings across parts of four decades.

The 300 win club currently stands at 24 pitchers, and is not anticipated to grow anytime soon. Randy Johnson is the most recent addition, having earned his 300th win in 2009. Lefty Grove is the only other pitcher to have retired with *exactly* 300 wins.

Game 88
July 19, 1982
Toby Harrah Gets Tribe Back to .500

After three seasons with the Tribe, Toby Harrah was not pleased with the direction the Indians were taking. He did not mince words. "I am tired of playing .500 ball or being the spoiler. It has been the same every year and I'm sick of it. We need a more balanced bullpen... We need a team that doesn't have 12 designated hitters and 6 first basemen. All of this is management's fault."

In mid-July of 1982, the Indians were once again in 6th place in the AL East, ahead of only the Blue Jays. The day before, the Indians celebrated a rare walk-off win on a pinch-hit RBI triple by Bill Nahrodny.

On this Monday evening in July, a sparse crowd of under 12,000 was scattered around Municipal Stadium to see the Indians take on the Oakland A's. Steve McCatty started for the A's while the Tribe sent Lary Sorenson to the mound.

Indians' second baseman Larry Milbourne bookended the previous night's performance with a leadoff triple in the bottom of the first. He was driven home by a Toby Harrah groundout to get the Tribe on the board 1-0.

The A's tied things up in the top of the third when Ricky Henderson walked with two outs, stole second, and was driven home by a Dwayne Murphy single to center field. A two-run homer by Jeff Newman put Oakland ahead 3-1.

Von Hayes doubled to right to lead off the bottom of the fourth. After fly-outs by Rick Manning and Ron Hassey, Carmello Castillo drove Hayes in with a single past the shortstop. The Indians had cut the A's lead to one run.

The teams continued to battle through the middle innings, with Oakland notching another run on a Jeff Burroughs homer in the top of the sixth inning.

Von Hayes had another leadoff hit in the Indians half of the sixth, Ron Hassey drove Hayes in with a single to right.

In the bottom of the ninth, the Indians were down a run with one out and the bases loaded. Larry Milbourne lofted a sacrifice fly to right. Rick Manning tagged up to score the tying run.

Down to their final out, Toby Harrah stepped to the plate and smacked a sharp one to third base. It should have been an easy out to send the game to extra innings. However, A's third baseman Wayne Gross botched the throw to first. As the ball skipped toward the first base dugout, Jack Perconte hustled home to give the Tribe their second walk-off win in as many nights. It put the team back at .500 with a 44 and 44 record for the season.

Harrah played all 162 games of the 1982 season for the Indians. He had the best hitting season of his career. He finished the year batting .304 with .183 hits, 25 home runs, and 100 runs scored. However, the Indians would finish 78-84 and once again 6th in the AL East.

Game 89
July 16, 2004
50 Total Bases and Back-to-Back-to-Back Home Runs

The Indians entered this game against the Mariners with a 43-46 record. They were 4.5 games back of the division-leading White Sox. Cliff Lee was on the mound in the Emerald City against Travis Blackley.

Blackley got off to a rough start. He loaded the bases in the top of the first and forced in a run on a five-pitch walk to Travis Hafner. He eventually retired first baseman Lou Merloni, but the Tribe had the early 1-0 lead.

In the bottom of the third inning, Omar Vizquel led off with a line drive single into center field. Matt Lawton took Blackley's 1-1 pitch deep to right field to make the score 2-0. Victor Martinez followed him with a home run of his own. Not to be outdone, Casey Blake stepped in and sent the 2-1 pitch up and out of the park for back-to-back-to-back home runs!

Clearly struggling with control, Blackley hit Travis Hafner, sending Pronk to first. Lou Merloni knocked a ground-ball single into left center. Jody Gerut doubled to right field, scoring Hafner. Mariner's skipper Bob Melvin had finally seen enough of Blackley. He brought on J.J. Putz to face Coco Crisp with no outs and Merloni on third. Crisp popped out, but Ronnie Belliard was able to push across the sixth run of the inning before Putz retired the side.

Cliff Lee pitched effectively, until the bottom of the fourth, when he gave up a three-run home run to Mariners third baseman Justin Leone.

Ron Villone replaced Putz on the mound for the Mariners in the top of the sixth inning, and immediately got himself into a bind. He walked Vizquel to lead off the inning, and then hit Matt Lawton. With those two on base, Victor Martinez crushed the 0-1 pitch for a three-run home run which extended the Tribe lead to 10-3.

George Sherill came on to pitch for the M's in the top of the seventh inning. He quickly got Crisp and Belliard out on consecutive fly balls.

169

Then Omar Vizquel punched a grounder into center field. Matt Lawton hit a liner down the right field foul line which allowed Vizquel to advance to third. Victor Martinez came through again when he smashed a single over the second base bag and into center. Both Vizquel and Lawton were able to come around to score. Casey Blake struck out swinging, but not before the Tribe had extended the lead to 12-3.

Travis Hafner bounced one into the seats to lead off the Indians half of the eighth inning. Coco Crisp sent him home with an RBI single into center field.

The hits kept coming for the Indians in the top of the ninth. Ben Broussard, Victor Martinez, and Travis Hafner each hit a solo homer off Julio Mateo. Mateo hit Lou Merloni with a pitch, and was pulled from the game in favor of Mike Meyers. Jody Gerut stepped in against Meyers, worked into a full count, and took the payoff pitch to deep right field. The fourth homer of the inning put the Tribe up 18-3.

Looking for a reversal of August 5, 2001 (see page 209), the Mariners mounted a comeback in the bottom of the ninth against Tribe reliever David Riske. Riske gave up three runs on two hits. Eric Wedge called on Rick Wright to get the final out of the game. The Tribe prevailed 18 runs to 6.

In all, the Indians scored 18 runs on 21 hits, including eight home runs. The Indians would not hit back-to-back-to-back homers again until Game 72 of the 2019 Season when Jake Bauers, Roberto Pérez and Tyler Naquin hit theirs against off of Drew Smyly and the Rangers.

Game 90
July 14, 2002
Bill Selby's Walk-Off Grand Slam Stuns Mariano Rivera

A sellout crowd packed Jacobs Field for the Sunday finale of this weekend series with the Yankees. Chuck Finley took the hill for the Tribe against the Yankees' Mike Mussina. The Indians trailed almost immediately, as the Yankees manufactured four runs off five singles in the top of the first inning.

Mussina retired the first nine Indians he faced, while the Bombers tacked on an additional run in the top of the third via a Jason Giambi double. New York scored two more runs in the fourth inning to make it a 7-0 ballgame.

The Indians began to climb back into things in the bottom of the sixth. Omar Vizquel hit a one-out line drive single to left. Ellis Burks followed with another liner into left. Jim Thome cranked Mussina's second pitch deep and over the center field wall.

Tribe reliever Mark Wohlers retired the Yankees in order in the top of the seventh. Ramiro Mendoza replaced Mussina on the hill in the bottom of the seventh inning. Omar Vizquel drove in third baseman John McDonald with an RBI double.

Both bullpens pitched scoreless eighth innings. Ricardo Rincon made quick work of the Yankees in the top of the ninth. The bottom of the ninth arrived with the score Yankees 7, Indians 4.

New York brought their legendary reliever Mariano Rivera in to close the game. Rivera had already recorded 215 of his eventual career 652 saves coming into the 2002 season. In the previous season, he had given up only five home runs in 71 relief appearances. Joe Torre and the Yankees felt that the game was in more than capable hands.

The Indians comeback kindled quickly. John McDonald led off the bottom of the ninth with a line drive single to right. Backup catcher Eddie Perez knocked a single into right, advancing McDonald to third. Einar Diaz came into pinch run for Perez while Chris MacGruder stepped to the plate. MacGruder grounded to short, and Diaz was forced out at second. McDonald scored on the play, bringing the score to 7-5.

Omar Vizquel singled to right, advancing MacGruder to third. With runners at the corners, Ellis Burks hit a line drive to deep left field. It dropped in for a double that plated MacGruder and put Omar on third. With the winning run now at second base, Mariano intentionally walked Jim Thome to load the bases and set up an inning-ending double play. Travis Fryman struck out swinging on three straight pitches, leaving the Indians down to their last out.

Career utility man Bell Selby stepped in. He pulled Rivera's fifth pitch deep down the right field line. It was called a foul ball, but many insist that a puff of chalk was visible. A double into the corner would have easily won the game, but Selby trotted back to the batter's box to face a 2-2 pitch from the game's most legendary closer. He later told a Plain Dealer interviewer, "When they talk about somebody dying or coming close to death, they talk about how your whole life flashes before your eyes. I can remember by the time I got halfway to first and realized it went foul, on the walk back, so many things went through my mind... I remember walking back, going, 'That was my pitch. No, no, no. Clear your thoughts. Just relax. You've proven to yourself now you can get to the ball. Stay relaxed and breathe a little bit.'"

On some advice from hitting coach Eddie Murray, Selby choked up on the bat and dug in again. He sent Rivera's pitch hooking near the right field foul pole. It cleared the right field wall and dropped into the bullpen, unleashing pure joy from the sellout crowd.

In a later interview Mariano stated, "It was where I wanted it. It was there. He hit my best pitch. I can't get upset at that." This was the first grand slam that Rivera had allowed in his seven-year career. He would not give up another until 2010.

This iconic Indians moment was one of 11 career home runs for Selby, who played in 122 games across parts of five MLB seasons.

Game 91
July 19, 1974
Bosman Misses a Perfect Game Due to His Own Error

The Oakland A's were two-time World Series champions coming into the 1974 season. The largest Municipal Stadium crowd of the season so far, over 48,000, filed in to watch the opening matchup of the series. It was a pitching duel between perennial Cy Young candidates Catfish Hunter and Gaylord Perry. The Tribe dropped that game 3-2.

On the next evening, Dick Bosman started for the Indians against Oakland's Dave Hamilton. These two carried over the pitching duel from the previous evening. Hamilton retired the first six batters he faced, while Bosman was perfect through three innings.

In the bottom of the third inning, Indians first baseman Tommy McCraw led things off with a single to right field. Joe Lis homered to give the Indians a 2-0 lead.

In the top of the fourth inning, Bosman struck out Bill North. Bert Campenaris grounded out to third. Third baseman Sal Bando hit a slow roller between the mound and third base on a checked swing. Bosman hustled over to field the ball, turned and threw quickly to first. The ball skipped off the end of McCraw's glove. Bosman was charged with an error and Bando ended up at second.

He later said, "I had enough time, but because I had to go a long way to get the ball, I thought I had to hurry. My throw just sailed away from McGraw." Reggie Jackson struck out to end the inning.

The A's made the call to the bullpen in the bottom of the fourth after Buddy Bell drove in John Ellis on a double to left field. McCraw grounded to short off Blue Moon Odom, allowing Bell to score from third. After four innings, the Tribe was up 4-0.

Shortstop Frank Duffy kept the no-hitter alive in the top of the fifth inning with an incredible throw from deep in the hole to put the speedy Joe Rudi out at first. Bosman continued to mow through the Athletics order.

To date, Bosman had pitched four one-hitters in his career, including a no-hit bid against the Yankees that lasted into the eighth inning. "After the fifth, after the sixth, my feeling was that I wasn't going to screw this one up," Bosman said. "I was confident in myself that day that I wasn't going to make a physical mistake."

Bosman was in new territory when he came out to pitch the top of the ninth. Dick Green grounded out to third. Jesus Alou (uncle to Moises) grounded out to second. Bosman struck out Bill North swinging for the 27th out. He used only 72 pitches.

There have been 303 recognized no-hitters in MLB history, 260 of them in the "modern era" since 1901. Bosman's remains the only one that would have been a perfect game, if not for his own error. The A's went on to win their third consecutive World Series that fall, making Bosman's no-no an interesting blip in the history of one of baseball's great dynasties.

Game 92
July 11, 2013
Danny Salazar Defeats Cy Young Winner in His MLB Debut

Danny Salazar started the 2013 season in Akron, moved up to Columbus, and was called up to make spot start in this Thursday afternoon businessman's special. The Indians were limping into the All-Star break with a 47-44 record.

The Blue Jays were wrapping up a midweek series in Cleveland. Toronto would throw reigning Cy Young winner R.A. Dickey against Salazar in his first big-league appearance. Manager Terry Francona has said that he prefers to have new players make their debut in day games, so that they don't have all afternoon to become anxious. The noon start time certainly seemed to benefit Salazar.

Salazar came out firing and struck out Blue Jays leadoff man Jose Reyes on five pitches to start the game. After a 1-2-3 inning, Asdrubal Cabrera staked Salazar to a lead with a solo home run in the bottom of the first inning.

Salazar had the home crowd behind him as he struck out the side against the heart of the Jays order in the top of the second inning. He got Adam Lind, Colby Rasmus, and Maicer Izturis all swinging. His fastball routinely reached 97 to 99 MPH on the radar gun.

The veteran knuckleballer and the rookie battled back and forth until the sixth inning. Jays catcher Josh Thole dropped a single into left to lead off the sixth inning. Salazar got an ovation from the crowd for holding the Jays hitless to that point. Salazar got the next two Jays out, but did not fare as well against Jose Bautista. Bautista tied the game with an RBI double down the left field line.

Dickey's knuckleball lost some of its movement around the sixth inning. He hit Michael Brantley and walked Ryan Raburn. After Brantley stole second, he walked Mark Reynolds to load the bases. Lonnie Chisenhall poked a single into left, which scored Brantley easily. The throw in from future Indian Rajai Davis missed the mark, allowing Raburn to score as well.

Rich Hill replaced Salazar in the top of the seventh inning and retired the side in order. Following that success, Cody Allen retired the Jays with no damage in the eighth.

Ryan Raburn drew a walk to lead off the bottom of the eighth inning. Then Carlos Santana knocked a fly ball to deep right. It got past a diving Jose Bautista for an RBI triple that put the Tribe up 4-2.

Closer Chris Perez came on to pitch the ninth inning. Perez was an effective closer, but his saves rarely came without drama. After recording the first two outs, Adam Lind doubled to right. Colby Rasmus singled through the right side of the infield. Lind scored and cut the Indians lead to one run. After a passed ball and a walk, Perez got Rajai Davis to fly out to left. Despite the heartburn, he recorded the save and gave Salazar the win in his major league debut.

Salazar struck out seven Blue Jays on 89 pitches. This was the most strikeouts for an Indians pitcher in his MLB debut since Luis Tiant struck out 11 Yankees in 1964.

With his quality spot start, Salazar took some pressure off the overworked Indians bullpen, but also got himself an entry in the history books as only the fourth pitcher to defeat the reigning Cy Young winner in his MLB debut.

Game 93
July 21, 1978
Mike Paxton Strikes Out Four in the Fifth Inning

A matchup between the last-place Mariners and second-to-last place Indians in mid-summer 1978 would be entirely forgettable if not for an event that happened only for the 16th time in MLB history. Mike Paxton had gone 10-5 in his first major league season. He was with Boston the year before, and had developed into a competent member of the Indians rotation in 1978.

The Tribe got the offense going in the bottom of the second inning. Andre Thornton and Bernie Carbo drew back to back walks. Then catcher Gary Alexander singled to load the bases. Jim Norris flied out and everyone had to stay put. Second baseman Duane Kuiper grounded to short, scoring Thornton, while Carbo was forced out at first. Then Tom Veryzer singled, driving in Carbo. Rick Manning followed with a two-run double to center. The Indians were up 4-0 after three innings.

Paxton struck out Dan Meyer to lead off the top of the fifth inning, but the third strike was mishandled by Greg Alexander. Meyer took first on the passed ball. Paxton then retired Bruce Bochte (not to be confused with Bruce Bochy, Giants manager), Tom Paciorek, and Bill Stein all on strikeouts. Paxton became only the sixteenth pitcher to retire the side with four strikeouts.

The Tribe would score another seven insurance runs and go on to an 11-0 rout of the lowly Mariners. Mike Paxton would finish 1978 with a 12-11 record, but the Indians finished 74-85 and in sixth place.

Five Cleveland pitchers have had four-strikeout innings. Guy Morton in Game 51 of 1916, and Lee Stange in Game 136 of 1964 preceded him. Paul Shuey K-ed four in Game 33 of 1994 (see page 66) and Chuck Finley in Game 12 of 2000. Finley is the only MLB-er to have two four-strikeout innings. His other record book entry was with the Angels in 1999.

Game 94
July 13, 2014
Mike Aviles Throws Out Runner at First from Foul Ground

Great defense often does not get highlighted in this kind of retrospective, because it does not show up as readily in box scores and stat sheets. However, a great outfield double-play can be as memorable as any other baseball feat.

Trevor Bauer was facing John Danks and the White Sox in a Sunday afternoon affair at Progressive Field. The Sox' Connor Gillespie knocked a single into right field to lead off the inning. Gordon Beckham hooked Bauer's 2-2 pitch down the left field line. Mike Aviles raced across the outfield and made the catch right on the chalk. He turned and threw a 280-foot strike to Carlos Santana at first. The throw beat Gillespie by half a step to record the 7-3 double-play.

In the bottom of the second, Yan Gomes pushed Ryan Raburn across the plate with an RBI single up the middle giving the Indians an early 1-0 lead.

Bauer and Danks scattered quite a few hits throughout the middle innings, but the score remained 1-0 as the teams headed into the top of the eighth. The White Sox took advantage of a rough inning by Bryan Shaw. Gillespie scored on a Gordan Beckham single after taking second on a wild pitch. Leury Garcia put the Sox ahead with a single into center field that scored Beckham. Shaw was credited with a blown save.

The White Sox had bullpen problems of their own in the bottom of the eighth inning. Javy Guerra gave up a leadoff single to Nick Swisher. Then Yan Gomes sent a home run out just inside the right field foul pole to put the Tribe back on top 3-2.

Cody Allen retired the Sox in order in the top of the ninth to record his 12th save of the season and put the Indians back at .500 with a 47-47 record.

Game 95
July 14, 2013
Fan Catches Four Foul Balls in One Game

Only 15,400 fans spun the turnstiles for this Sunday afternoon matchup with the Royals. Enthusiasm was low, despite the Indians being just one game back from the Central Division lead. That left plenty of room for Greg Van Niel to snag foul balls.

Van Niel caught four foul balls over the course of the game. He caught number one, two and four on the fly, directly to his seat. He retrieved number three off the ground a few seats away.

"Three of them were catches and one was a ball I picked up off the ground," said Van Niel. "The third one, I think was the hardest one ... I ended up sprawled across a few rows, and I got some cheese on myself. But the other ones were just a matter of being in the right place at the right time."

He kept three of the balls for the young family members who were at the game with him, and tossed the fourth to a child in his section.

Van Neil said that he had never caught a Major League foul ball before, despite being a season ticket holder just one section over from the lucky spot.

In on-the-field action, Jason Kipnis put the Indians up early with a sacrifice fly in the bottom of the first that scored Michael Bourn.

The Royals scored two runs in the top of the second and another two in the top of the fourth. Ubaldo got the first out of the fifth inning, and then was replaced by reliever C.C. Lee.

The bottom of the sixth inning started with the Tribe down 4-3. Lonnie Chisenhall drew a walk. Drew Stubbs cracked a line drive single down the left field line. Michael Bourn laid down a perfect sacrifice bunt which moved the runners over. Asdrubal Cabrera delivered a two-run double into the right field gap. Jason Kipnis smashed a liner into center. Cabrera came around to add an insurance run. The Indians were up six runs to four.

The bullpen combination of Bryan Shaw, Joe Smith, and Chris Perez held off the Royals through the final third of the game to seal the 6-4 victory.

Honorable Mention:
July 25, 1928 - First Indians Radio Broadcast Airs

Owner Alva Bradley had agonized over the decision whether to allow radio broadcast of Indians games for years. Some owners thought that broadcasts boosted interest in their club, others maintained that free access to real-time baseball would depress attendance. By mid-summer of 1928, Bradley elected to let WTAM broadcast all games live from League Park, except for on Sundays.

Billy Evans and Tom Manning called the first game, a 10-2 win over the Red Sox featuring left fielder Charlie Jamieson going 3 for 5 with two RBI.

Game 96
August 3, 1960
Manager-For-Manager Trade

The Indians were visiting the Senators in the Nation's Capital at Griffith Stadium. Mudcat Grant was pitching for the Tribe against Washington's Jack Kralick.

Johnny Temple led off the game with a single into centerfield. Ken Aspromonte put the Tribe ahead with a two-run home run to deep left.

In the bottom of the first, Lenny Green knocked a triple into center field. After striking out Harmon Killebrew, Mudcat threw a wild pitch that allowed Green to score from third.

Hitting in the nine-hole, Grant led off the top of the third with a single. Ken Aspromonte drove him in with a double into left field to extend the Indians lead to 3-1.

Washington cut the Tribe's lead to one run in the bottom of the third. Billy Consolo poked a single into right field. Lenny Green drove him in with a clutch two-out double.

The Senators took a brief lead with a two-run home run by Faye Thornberry in the bottom of the sixth inning, but the Indians offense got going in the bottom half of the inning. Tito Francona led things off with a single into left field. With two outs, Senators shortstop Billy Consolo mishandled a Johnny Temple grounder and Temple reached on the E6. Tito Francona was able to score from second.

Consolo committed a second straight error on Aspromonte's ground ball, further extending the inning. Harvey Kuenn and Vic Power hit consecutive RBI singles to give the Tribe the 6-4 lead.

Mudcat grant had another RBI single in the top of the eighth that sealed the 7-4 victory. Grant recorded a complete game, six strikeout performance.

After Game 96 is when things got interesting.

The Indians GM was the infamous "Frantic" Frank Lane, or "Trader" Lane who dealt ballplayers left and right. Lane was already infamous for shipping Rocky Colavito out of town prior to the 1960 season.

After the win in Washington, Lane traded manager Joe Gordon to the Tigers straight up for their manager Jimmy Dykes. Joe Gordon was a Hall-of-Fame second baseman in his own right who spent the prime of his career winning championships with the Yankees. Jimmy Dykes was also a talented infielder, playing primarily for the Athletics in the WWI era. He is still the franchise leader in doubles for the A's.

This is the only time in MLB history that a manager has been traded for another manager. The fact that the trade came mid-season and in the middle of a road trip only made it more puzzling.

JoJo White served one game as the Indians manager, presumably to allow the skippers to travel to their new cities. White's only managerial experience was a win against the Orioles in Game 97.

Ultimately it was just another Trader Lane publicity stunt. Both teams were sub-.500 before the manager swap, and both teams finished below .500 and out of the playoff race in 1960.

Game 97
July 24, 2012
Suicide Squeeze by Aaron Cunningham

The division-leading Tigers came into Progressive Field riding a five-game winning streak and sent Doug Fister to the hill against Ubaldo Jiminez.

Carlos Santana led off the bottom of the second inning with a line drive double into the gap. Johnny Damon put the Tribe on the scoreboard. He turned on Fister's first pitch for a line drive single into center field which scored Santana easily.

Jason Kipnis doubled down the left field line to start off the Indians' half of the fourth inning. Michael Brantley got aboard when he beat out a ground ball to third. Kipnis held at second. Carlos Santana punched a single between first and second to score Kipnis. Brantley ended up caught in a rundown, which saw Detroit first baseman Cecil Fielder sprinting across the infield on the wild play to tag out Dr. Smooth. When the dust settled, the Indians were up 2-0.

Joe Smith replaced Ubaldo to pitch the top of the seventh inning. After retiring the first two batters, he issued a walk to Quintin Berry. Unfortunately, Miguel Cabrera was up next. Smith fell behind 2-0 to Miguel, who crushed the next pitch over the center field wall to tie up the game.

After a Carlos Santana fly-out in the bottom of the seventh inning, Travis Hafner launched a low line drive which ricocheted off the wall in left center. Hafner was safe at third with a head-first slide.

Lou Marson was brought on to pinch run for the clearly-winded Hafner. Marson took off toward the plate on the 1-1 pitch to Cunningham who laid down a perfect bunt back to the pitcher. Fister fielded the bunt cleanly, but his throw home was rushed and got away from catcher Alex Avila. Marson scored on the suicide squeeze and Cunningham took second on the error.

Vinnie Pestano and Chris Perez held up the 3-2 lead to secure the win and end the Tiger's winning streak. In reference to the blown save Smith said, "It was like my big truck was sitting on top of me

183

and somebody lifted it off...The guys bounced right back after I messed up."

Less than 24 hours later, Cunningham was designated for assignment to make room on the roster for first baseman Brent Lillibridge who had been acquired just before Game 97. Manager Manny Acta had high praise for Cunningham, but his .197 average in 97 appearances was not enough to keep him on the big-league team.

Game 98
July 25, 2017
Two Grand Slams, Encarnacion Walk-off in Extras

Mike Clevinger was pitching against his old team as the Angels came into Cleveland for a midweek series. The Angels sent Jesse Chavez to the mound.

Both Clevinger and Chavez threw 1-2-3 innings to start the game, but the Indians offense woke up in the bottom of the second inning. Edwin Encarnacion laced a double to center field to lead things off. Jose Ramirez followed with a line drive double of his own. Encarnacion came around to score. After striking out Carlos Santana on three pitches, Chavez suffered a sudden loss of control. He walked Austin Jackson and Yan Gomes to load the bases. Then he issued a third consecutive walk to Gio Urshela to hand the Indians their second run.

Facing a 3-1 count with the bases loaded, Bradley Zimmer was not content to take pitches and wait for another walk. He sent one over the wall in right center and into the bullpen for his first career grand slam.

After a pop-out by Francisco Lindor, Michael Brantley followed with a home run of his own. The Tribe sent eleven batters to the plate and scored seven runs on four hits in the inning.

The Angels narrowed the lead to three runs in the top of the third inning, when Kole Calhoun took Clevinger deep with a three-run homer. Luis Valbuena took advantage of an Indians' error to drive in Andrelton Simmons for an RBI single.

The Indians chased Chaves from the game in the bottom of the third, while Clevinger held on until the top of the fifth. After giving up another home run to Luis Valbuena, Terry Francona made the call for Nick Goody and both bullpens were at work. Valbuena's home run put the score at Cleveland seven, Anaheim six.

In the top of the sixth inning, Goody gave up a leadoff single to Kaleb Cowart. Yuniel Escobar sent a line drive down the right field line.

185

Cowart scored comfortably, but Escobar got caught in a rundown trying to stretch the hit into a triple and was tagged out at third.

With the game now tied, the bullpens battled on into extra innings. In the eleventh Anaheim called on reliever Bud Norris. After being held scoreless for eight innings, the Tribe offense surged back. Bradley Zimmer drew a seven-pitch walk to lead off the inning and then stole second base. Norris could not find his command against Francisco Lindor. On a 3-2 count, Norris' pitch got away from backup catcher Juan Graterol, allowing Zimmer to take third.

With no outs and runners at the corners, the Angels elected to intentionally walk Michael Brantley to set up a potential double-play. The Angels shifted into a five-man infield. Edwin Encarnacion stepped in and sent Norris first pitch deep into the Cleveland night for a walk-off grand slam.

Bradley Zimmer later said, "You could put the whole team on the infield and it's not going to work. The guy was made for situations like that."

Game 99
August 8, 1948 (Second Game)
Comeback Win Over Yankees

The Indians, Yankees, and Athletics were in a race for the American League pennant throughout the 1948 season. A chance to see the hated Yankees always brought crowds to Municipal Stadium, but August 1948 was on another level. The four-game weekend series (including a Sunday double-header) set a three-day attendance record of 188,081 through the gates.

The Indians had prevailed in the first game of the doubleheader with an 8-6 win led by a two-home run game by first baseman Eddie Robinson. Robinson's second homer of the game, a two-run shot off of Joe Page, sealed the victory for the Tribe.

In the second game, the Indians threw spot starter Steve Gromek against the Yankees rookie Bob Porterfield who was making his major league debut in front of 73,000+ at Municipal Stadium.

In the top of the fourth inning, Larry Doby robbed Yankees first baseman George McQuinn of a home run when he raced toward the wall, perfectly timed his jump, and brought the ball back into play.

With two outs in the bottom of the fifth, Eddie Robinson rocked his third home run of the day (the first two came in game one of the double-header) over the right field wall. It was only his 13th homer of the season, but he was certainly in a groove on this August afternoon. The solo shot put the Indians up 1-0.

The Yankees answered with some of their own two-out magic in the top of the sixth inning. Billy Johnson singled to left. When Phil Rizzuto stroked a single down the right field line, Johnson hurried hard for third. Larry Doby fired the ball from right field to third base, but struck Johnson in the back. The ball ricocheted off Johnson and into the stands near third base. Doby was charged with a throwing error, despite the cross-diamond display of strength, and Johnson was given home plate to tie the game 1-1.

Gromek allowed only four hits over his seven innings, and the only run on the board was the unearned one.

Indians second baseman Joe Gordon led off the bottom of the seventh inning with a single. Johnny Bernardino moved Gordon over to second with a sacrifice bunt. Porterfield elected to intentionally walk the red-hot Eddie Robinson and pitch to Jim Hegan. Hegan knocked a single into center field that scored Gordon and put the Tribe up 2-1.

Ed Klieman pitched two strong innings of relief. He faced only seven Yankee batters on the way to securing the Indians third victory of the weekend in front of the record-setting crowd.

The 1948 Indians ended the regular season with a 97-58 record. They tied the Red Sox for the pennant, and beat Boston in a one-game playoff at Fenway Park. The Tribe advanced to the 1948 World Series where they returned to Massachusetts to face the National League's Boston Braves. The Indians won the series in six games. The Indians currently have the second-longest major league championship drought. The only franchise that has gone longer since their last championship is the Arizona Cardinals of the NFL, who last won a football championship in Chicago in 1947.

Game 100
July 22, 2014
Indians Take Advantage of Egregious TOOTBLAN

One of the best developments to come from sports blogging and sports Twitter has been the invention of increasingly specific and weird statistics. In 2008, Tony Jewell coined the term TOOTBLAN in his now defunct Cubs blog Wrigleyville23. Short for Thrown Out On the Basepaths Like a Nincompoop. More precisely, Jewell defined it "In short, it is any out a runner makes on the basepaths while attempting to take an extra base - whether advancing from second to third on a ground out (with no runner on first); attempting to stretch a single into a double, a double into a triple, and so on; or getting thrown out while advancing on a flyball. It also applies to base runners who are picked off or who are doubled out on a line drive."

Jewell was using this measure to feed further statistical analysis that adjusted on-base percentage to account for errors on the basepaths. However, in the intervening years, it has become popularized as a hashtag for the sort of videos that would make Sportscenter's "Not Top 10."

Danny Salazar started for the Tribe in this Tuesday night contest against Yohan Pino of the Twins at Target Field in Minneapolis.

Pino retired the first three Indians he faced, but began to get in trouble in the top of the second inning. Carlos Santana led off the inning with a line drive down the right field line. Then Pino hit Lonnie Chisenhall with his 0-2 pitch. Nick Swisher poked a hit into center to load the bases. After a Yan Gomes strikeout, David Murphy drove a line drive into right scoring Santana and Chisenhall. A sacrifice fly by Mike Aviles put the Tribe up 3-0.

The Twins challenged Salazar in the bottom of the fourth. With runners at the corners, Sam Fuld drove in Oswaldo Arcia with a grounder to first, but Salazar struck out Brian Dozier to quell the threat. The Tribe held the score at 3-1 Indians

Carlos Santana smashed a solo home run to deep right field in the top of the fifth, but it was the Indians' only hit of the inning.

189

In the bottom of the seventh, Brandon Dozier scored the Twins only other run with a line drive home run that cleared the wall near the left foul pole. After a Trevor Plouffe strikeout, Kendrys Morales stepped in against Indians reliever Scott Atchison.

Morales blooped a single near the left field line. He made a wide turn at first and dug for second as Indians cup-of-coffee outfielder Chris Dickerson fielded the ball on one hop, wheeled and threw to second. The throw was a bit low, sending Jason Kipnis sprawling into the dirt. However, Morales' slide brought him about four feet short of the base. He popped up and attempted to hopscotch over and around Kipnis' tag, but Kip managed to tag his cleat. Morales confidently called himself safe, but umpire Brian O'Nora did not agree. The TOOTBLAN ended the Inning.

The Indians put together a four hit ninth inning, including RBI doubles by Yan Gomes and Carlos Santana. A two-run single by Chris Dickerson, put the Tribe up eight runs to two.

Carlos Carrasco made a non-save appearance in the bottom of the ninth. Despite issuing an early walk to Danny Santana, Carrasco was able to close out the game and seal the victory.

Game 101
July 29, 1928
Indians Defeat Yankees with 24 Singles

The Indians and Yankees were at the corner of 66th and Lexington for this Sunday afternoon contest. Joe Shaute was pitching for the Tribe against George Pipgras at League Park.

Bob Meusel got aboard with an infield single. Babe Ruth knocked a single into right field. Meusel took advantage of an error by Indians right fielder Homer Summa to score from first base. Shaute regained his composure and got both Lou Gehrig and Mark Koenig to pop out to end the inning.

The Indians batted around and then some in the bottom of the first. They sent thirteen batters to the plate. Langford singled, Lind walked, Sewell singled, and Johnny Hodapp doubled to score two. Morgan had a two-RBI single, and Summa singled. Yankees manager Miller Huggins called for Wilcy Moore out of the bullpen.

Wilcy did not fare much better than Pipgras. George Gerken singled. Wilcy struck out Luke Sewell. Then Ed Morgan scored on a fielder's choice hit by Joe Shaute. Sam Langford grounded out with the bases loaded, but forced Langford out. Carl Lind had a two-run single before Joe Sewell finally grounded into the third out. The score was 8-1 Indians after the first inning.

After the Yankees were retired with only one hit in the top of the second, Wilcy Moore returned to the mound. Hodapp singled. Ed Morgan hit into a fielder's choice, but ended up safe due to the Yankee second baseman's error. Gerken singled again, and Sewell cleared the bases with a triple into League Park's ample outfield. Myles Thomas was brought in to relieve Moore on the mound.

Thomas lasted only four batters. Shaute reached base on Tony Lazzeri's second error of the inning at second base. Then Langford, Lind, and Joe Sewell singled in succession. The Yankees called on Hank Johnson to stop the bleeding. Johnson gave up consecutive RBI singles to Hodapp and Morgan out of the gate. Homer Summa recorded the second out of the inning on a sacrifice fly that scored

Hodapp. George Gerken struck out to end the second inning. The score was Cleveland 17 New York 1.

The teams traded runs in the third, and New York tacked on another in the top of the fourth by way of an Earle Combs double. Hank Johnson survived until the bottom of the sixth inning, when the Indians struck again with two outs. With Johnny Hodapp on second, Luke Sewell, Shaute, Langford and Lind hit consecutive singles. Archie Campbell came on for New York to relieve Johnson.

Joe Sewell and Johnny Hodapp hit the fifth and sixth consecutive two-out singles for the Tribe before Ed Morgan grounded out to end the inning. The score was 24-3

Babe Ruth and Leo Durocher had RBI hits in the ninth to close the deficit to 24-6. The Indians final batting line was 24 runs on 27 hits and 4 walks. They were 19 for 31 with runners in scoring position. The game stood for a time as the most singles in a nine-inning game, but was surpassed by the Milwaukee Brewers when they hit 26 singles against the Blue Jays in 1992.

Game 102
August 4, 1932 (First Game)
First Win in Cleveland Municipal Stadium

The Cleveland franchise played its first 31 seasons at League Park in the Hough neighborhood on Cleveland's east side. City Manager William R. Hopkins proposed a downtown stadium in the early 1920's. Several Cleveland real estate magnates began pushing for the construction of a massive multi-use facility on the Lake Erie shore. Most notable among these were the Van Sweringen brothers who built the Terminal Tower complex and Alva Bradley, who also owned the Indians at the time.

In 1928, the citizens of Cleveland voted on a "$2.5 million levy for a fireproof stadium on the Lakefront." The vote needed 55% approval to pass. 59% of Cleveland voters approved the stadium levy.

Walker & Weeks Architects and Osborne Engineering teamed up to design and construct the massive multi-use facility.

Municipal Stadium hosted the Indians for the first time on Sunday July 31st, but the Tribe lost that game and the contest on Monday to the Athletics. The team had some time to reflect on those losses, with a Tuesday off day and a rain-out on Wednesday.

The weather cleared on Thursday and the teams set out to play two. In the first game, Oral Hildebrand started against the Sox Bob Kline.

Joe Vosmik led off the bottom of the second inning with a triple into the spacious new outfield. Ed Morgan drove him in with another triple. Luke Sewell grounded out to short, and then Bill Cissell scored Morgan on a sacrifice fly. The Tribe were up 2-0 quickly.

In the bottom of the third, Dick Porter hustled for the club's third triple of the afternoon on a hit into the left field gap. Johnny Burnett plated Porter with a single into right field.

Hildebrand issued a walk to Roy Johnson to lead off the top of the fourth. He gave up a single to Smead Jolley that advanced Johnson to third. Dale Alexander hit into a 4-6-3 double play, but Johnson hustled home to get Boston on the scoreboard.

Kline and Hildebrand had a pitcher's duel going through the middle innings. Kline retired the Indians side in order in the fifth, sixth, and seventh innings. Hildebrand scattered just three hits from the fifth through the eighth inning.

Gordon Rhodes came in from the Sox bullpen in the bottom of the eighth, and the offense came alive. Hildebrand knocked a single into left field, but he was forced out on a Dick Porter grounder. Johnny Burnett smacked one into the left field gap that went for a triple. Porter came around to score. Earl Averill sent one down the right field line that went for the team's fifth triple of the day. Burnett came in to score. Joe Vosmik sent another down the right field line that went for a double, scoring Averill. Ed Morgan laid a bunt down the third base line and Vosmik held at second. Bill Cissell sent him home with a single into left. After this flurry of offense, the Indians were up 8-1.

Hildebrand gave up one run on two hits in the top of the ninth, but got Rabbit Warstler to ground into a game-ending double play. The Indians finally got to celebrate a victory in the new Municipal Stadium clubhouse.

At the time, Municipal Stadium was the largest baseball park in the world with a seating capacity of 72,000. It was only surpassed by parks used in a temporary capacity—Los Angeles Colosseum by the Dodgers, and Mile High Stadium by the expansion Rockies. It hosted the All-Star Game in 1935, 1954, 1963, and 1981.

The "Mistake by the Lake" saw it all from the highs of the 1948 and 1954 World Series to the low of 10-cent beer night.

The Indians moved to the south end of downtown in 1994, kicking off a renaissance for the team and the life of the city. After the Browns moved to Baltimore, Municipal stadium was quickly demolished. 5,000 cubic yards of stadium concrete was dumped in two locations in Lake Erie. The two "stadium reefs" are located off Perkins Beach and directly north of Euclid Hospital. They continue to provide recreation for generations of Clevelanders, and occasionally a familiar blond-colored brick will wash up on a Lake Erie beach.

Game 103
July 31, 2009
Tribe Comes Together After Shocking Trades

The Indians had just traded Cy Young winner Cliff Lee to the Phillies and fan favorite Ryan Garko to the Giants. In the afternoon prior to Game 103, the Indians traded beloved catcher and clubhouse leader Victor Martinez to the Red Sox for Justin Masterson, Nick Hagadone, and Bryan Price. The Indians were classic sellers at the trade deadline, as they were 43 and 60 going into July 31st and 11 games behind the division-leading Tigers at the trade deadline.

Those same Tigers were in town for a Friday night contest at Progressive Field. Fausto Carmona was throwing against Detroit's Edwin Jackson. Both pitchers took a minute to find their footing. Fausto gave up two runs on three hits in the top of the first.

Grady Sizemore led off the Indians' half of the first with a single through the left side of the infield. Asdrubal Cabrera battled Jackson into a full count. On the ninth pitch of the at-bat, he sent one over the right field wall for a game tying two-run homer.

Shin-Soo Choo gave the Tribe a 3-2 lead in the bottom of the fourth inning when he doubled in Trevor Crowe, who had reached on an error to lead off the inning.

Taiwainese reliever Fu-Te Ni came in to pitch for the Tigers in the bottom of the sixth inning. He gave up a leadoff single to Trevor Crowe and then a line-drive RBI double to Asdrubal Cabrera. After hitting Choo in the next at-bat, Ni was pulled with the score 4-2. Ryan Perry took the mound for Detroit and got the final two outs of the inning.

Maglio Ordonez drove a double into left field off Tribe reliever Tony Sipp to lead off the eighth inning. Marcus Thames grounded one to first. Brandon Inge closed the gap for Detroit when poked a ground ball single into center that scored Maglio Ordonez to make it a 4-3 ballgame.

Trevor Crowe led off the bottom of the eighth with a triple--his third hit of the night. Grady Sizemore drove him in with a single through the right side of the infield to extend the lead to 5-3.

The Indians had acquired Kerry Wood as a free agent to be their closer after the steep decline of Joe Borowski in 2008. Wood had secured fourteen saves with the Tribe to date. He gave up a line drive single to left to Placido Palanco to lead off the bottom of the ninth inning. Carlos Guillen stepped in and cranked Kerry's 3-1 pitch deep into right center. Although he retired the next three Tigers on eight pitches, he was credited with his fifth blown save of the season and the game went to extra innings.

Jhonny Peralta led off the bottom of the thirteenth inning when he knocked a line drive down the right field line for a double. Utility man Jamey Carroll, who had pinch run for Travis Hafner in the bottom of the ninth, stepped in. Carroll sliced a single just inside the first base bag to drive in Peralta and give the Tribe an emotional walk-off win.

The next day, a Victor Martinez bobblehead promotion was planned for Game 104. Despite V-Mart's departure, the bobbleheads were distributed as planned. Six days later, the promotional team awkwardly went ahead with a Victor Martinez chest protector backpack giveaway—a case study in why not to schedule player-specific promotions a week after the trade deadline.

Game 104
August 1, 1990
Five Steals for Alex Cole

As the month of August opened, the Indians were eight games back of the frontrunning Blue Jays in the American League East. The visiting Royals were dead last in the AL West. They were sixteen games behind Oakland, making this game...pretty much irrelevant except for the arrival of Alex Cole.

Cole made his first appearance with the Indians on July 27, 1990. Cultivated as an outfielder with blinding speed on the basepaths, Cole was eager to prove himself at the big-league level.

The Royals jumped out to an early lead against Greg Swindell. Bill Pecota got things started with a double. He was driven in by Gerald Perry's line drive single to center.

Alex Cole led off the bottom of the first by drawing a walk. With left fielder Mitch Webster at the plate, Cole stole second. Webster flied out, and Jerry Browne came to bat. Cole stole third. Browne knocked a double into left field, and Cole's run tied the game at one run apiece.

In the bottom of the third inning, Alex Cole was hit by Mark Davis' pitch. Mitch Webster popped out. Again, with Jerry Browne at the plate, Cole stole second. By the third inning, he had three stolen bases without yet recording a hit.

In the bottom of the fifth inning, the Tribe offense got going. Tom Brookens doubled into center field to get things started. Alex Cole poked a single through the right side of the infield to score Brookens. Cole stole second and then was driven home by Mitch Webster's double into center field. Not to be outdone, Webster stole third with Jerry Browne at the plate. Browne's sacrifice fly plated Webster to make the score 4-1 Indians.

Cole singled to left in the bottom of the seventh, stayed put on a Webster fly-out, and then stole second with Browne at the plate for his fifth steal of the day.

197

Greg Swindell pitched into the eighth inning, but his day was done after giving up consecutive singles to Gerald Perry and Danny Tartabull. Closer Doug Jones entered the game and retired the next three Tigers on six pitches.

Jones returned to pitch the top of the ninth, and got the next three Tigers on fly ball outs as well. He got the six-out save and closed out a historic day for Cole.

Twenty-seven players have stolen five or more bases in a single game under the modern rules. Eddie Collins stole six bases for the Athletics twice in the 1916 season, a feat which was unmatched until Carl Crawford stole six for the Rays in 2009.

Alex Cole shares the franchise records for stolen bases in a game with Kenny Lofton. Lofton Stole five in Game 133 of 2000.
Alex Cole stole five bases again in Game 26 of 1992.

Game 105
July 29, 2013
Giambi Becomes Oldest MLBer with a Walk-off Home Run

Zach McAllister was facing John Danks as the Indians were making a late-July surge into the playoff race against the scuffling White Sox. The Tribe entered this game 2½ games back of division-leading Detroit.

Jason Giambi was hitting under .200 in his spot appearances so far in 2013. Although he was a clubhouse leader and mentor to many of the younger players, there was plenty of speculation that trade-deadline maneuvering would bump him off the roster.

In the bottom of the second inning, Asdrubal Cabrera grounded one to Alexei Ramirez at shortstop. As Cabrera hustled down the line, Ramirez botched the throw to first. Asdrubal was safe on the E5. Ryan Raburn knocked a double through the left side of the infield, advancing Cabrera to third. Asdrubal scored on a sacrifice fly by Carlos Santana to put the Tribe up 1-0 early.

McAllister held the Sox scoreless through five innings, scattering only two hits on his first two trips through the lineup. In the top of the sixth inning, McAllister got two quick outs against De Aza and Alexei Ramirez. Alex Rios started the White Sox two-out rally with a double down the right field line. Adam Dunn drove Rios home with an almost identical double. On McAllister's very next pitch Paul Konerko singled to center, driving in Dunn for the go-ahead run.

Danks walked Michael Bourn and Nick Swisher to lead off the bottom half of the sixth. Jason Kipnis laid down a bunt down the third base line. He beat the throw to first to load the bases. Asdrubal Cabrera grounded to short and was put out at first, but Bourn scored the tying run.

McAllister recovered, pitching a 1-2-3 seventh. Then a combination of Cody Allen, Rich Hill, and Chris Perez held down the 2-2 tie, bringing the Tribe up in the bottom of the ninth.

Jason Giambi came on to pinch hit for Mark Reynolds. He crushed a 1-1 pitch from right-handed Sox reliever Ramon Troncoso over the center-field wall and into the batter's eye greenery.

After an ice-water bath from his teammates, Giambi quipped "I might catch pneumonia. I'm too old to get a bucket of cold water dumped on me."

With that blast, Giambi became the oldest player in MLB history to hit a game-ending home run. He was 42 years, 202 days old. Hank Aaron was 45 days younger when he set the previous mark in 1976. Giambi also safeguarded his role as the clubhouse leader and veteran guru for the Tribe's run to the wildcard game.

Game 106
August 13, 1948
Satchel Paige Pitches a Complete Game Shutout at Age 42

Satchel Paige is sometimes referred to as, "the greatest player ever excluded from Major League Baseball." Paige dominated the Negro Leagues beginning in the late 1920's, through the 30's, and into the 1940's. Paige even played for a time for the Cleveland Cubs in 1931. It was the first time that he had played in a city with a white major league team. He later said, "I'd look over at the Cleveland Indians' stadium [League Park]. All season long it burned me, playing there in the shadow of that stadium. It didn't hurt my pitching, but it sure didn't do me any good."

In 1948, Bill Veeck gave Paige a tryout for the Indians. While Veeck is considered a P.T. Barnum-like figure for his odd moves and promotions, his contributions to the integration of baseball are often forgotten. The innovative owner had signed Larry Doby as the first black player in the American League in 1947, and he saw that Satchel still had something in the tank.

While there was some outcry that signing Paige was merely another publicity stunt, Bob Feller leaned into the controversy. "Maybe Mr. Veeck did want some publicity, but he wanted a pitcher, too," he wrote. "There was only one guy around who could fill both orders. That was Ol' Satch."

Paige earned his first MLB win—as a 42-year-old rookie—on July 15th against the A's. He won his first MLB start against the Browns on August 3rd. He had often drawn large crowds for Negro League games or barnstorming tours, but few expected the turnout in Chicago when the Indians went to visit the White Sox.

When Paige was announced as the starter for the Friday night contest, all of the reserved seats were snapped up. It had been over a decade since Comiskey had sold out so early in advance of a White Sox game. Eventually, 51,013 would pack the South Side ballpark, including Heavyweight Boxing Champion Joe Louis.

201

The Tribe scored first in the top of the fifth inning. Larry Doby tripled to start things off. Jim Hegan hit a fly ball deep to left. Pat Seerey tracked it down, but Doby was able to tag up and score

The Tribe extended the lead to 2-0 in the eighth. Ken Keltner dropped a single into left field. Dale Mitchell drove him in with another single into left.

In the top of the ninth inning, Lou Boudreau led off with a single into right. Eddie Robinson hit a ball sharply to second that was mishandled by Don Kalloway. Boudreau advanced to third and Robinson was safe on the E4. Larry Doby lofted a single into left field which allowed Robinson to score. Doby picked up his second stolen base of the day, with Ken Keltner at the plate. Keltner flied out. The Sox opted to intentionally walk Jim Hegan to pitch to Paige. Doby and Hegan executed a double steal, and the Sox catcher committed an error allowing Doby to score. Paige grounded out, but not before the score was 5-0 in Cleveland's favor.

Satch pitched brilliantly, never facing more than four White Sox in an inning until the ninth. He was tested a bit in the final frame, when Luke Appling and Pat Seerey hit consecutive one-out singles. Paige recovered and retired the next two Sox to finish off the complete game shutout.

Paige went 6-1 over the partial season, and was a critical part of the Tribe's run to the 1948 World Series. He garnered twelve votes for Rookie of the Year. When he was asked about his fourth-place finish in the voting, Satchel said that he would have declined the honor if elected, since "I wasn't sure what year the gentlemen had in mind."

Game 107
July 30, 2014
Kluber Throws a Maddux

First off, "What's a Maddux?" Sportswriter Jason Lukehart invented the term. In short, the starting pitcher must toss a shutout, and he must throw fewer than 100 pitches. It is named, of course, for Greg Maddux whose ruthlessly efficient pitching style typifies this type of performance.

There was no more marquee pitching matchup of the 2014 season than Felix Hernandez facing Corey Kluber. The two met on a Wednesday night at Progressive Field.

The first 4½ innings were played in under an hour as Kluber and Hernandez each mowed through the opposing lineup. King Felix had a perfect game going through four innings, until he walked Carlos Santana to lead off the fifth.

Lonnie Chisenhall followed with a double into right field, which put Santana comfortably at third. Nick Swisher grounded a slow roller to second, Santana and Chishenall held at their bases, and Swisher beat the throw to first. David Murphy hit a grounder to first. The M's forced Carlos out at home. With the bases still loaded, Yan Gomes came through with a two-run double.

With the 2-0 lead, Kluber pitched even more confidently and efficiently. He needed only seven pitches to retire the Mariners side in the top of the seventh inning.

The Indians did not threaten in the bottom of the seventh, and the Klubot returned to pitch the eighth. Kyle Seager grounded out on the second pitch. Logan Morrison struck out looking on three perfectly located strikes. Kluber got Mike Zunino to squib a weak grounder on the first pitch he saw. After a six pitch eighth inning, Kluber had thrown eight shutout innings using only 77 pitches.

The Tribe went quietly in the bottom of the eighth, and Kluber quickly returned to the mound looking for the final three outs. On a steady diet of nasty sinkers, Brad Miller, James Jones, and Dustin Ackley all grounded out to end the game. Kluber's 85 pitches established a new Indians record for fewest pitches in a shutout. 69 of his 85 pitches were strikes.

Terry Francona later said, "He threw 16 balls. My math is horrendous, but that's like two an inning?"

Although Kluber's league-leading 18 wins were not quite enough to put the Indians in the postseason in 2014, they were enough to win him the AL Cy Young award when he garnered seventeen first place votes over Felix's thirteen.

Game 108
July 31, 1963 (Second Game)
Four Consecutive Home Runs

The Angels and Indians were both in the basement of the American League in 1963. So, it is no wonder that only 7,822 came through the turnstiles on the Lakefront to see the second half of a Wednesday double-header. However, those few faithful fans witnessed something that has not occurred in Indians history before or since.

The Angels jumped out to an early 1-0 lead when first baseman Lee Thomas took Pedro Ramos deep for a two-out solo home run in the top of the first inning.

In the bottom of the third, Ramos helped out his own cause with a solo home run of his own which evened the score.

Back at the top of the order, Tito Francona singled, followed by another single from Larry Brown. With runners at the corners, Willie Kirkland drew a walk to load the bases. The Angels had seen enough from starter Eli Grba and brought Don Lee in from the bullpen. Lee struck out Max Alvis and appeared to be out to a strong start, until Fred Whitfield rocked a home run into the upper deck in right field to put the Tribe ahead 5-1.

Ramos tallied ten strikeouts through the first six innings, keeping the Angels to just the one early run.

Reliever Paul Foytack had pitched the bottom of the fifth inning for the Angels, and returned for the sixth. He struck out catcher Joe Azcue and Al Luplow flied to right. The two-out magic returned for the Tribe as Woodie Held homered to deep left. Pedro Ramos stepped in and smashed his second home run of the game. Tito Francona followed with a third straight homer to right. Rookie second baseman Larry Brown got his first homer in the majors for back-to-back-to-back-to-back long balls.

The Angels called on reliever Jack Spring to bail out shell-shocked Paul Foytack. Spring gave up consecutive singles to Willie Kirkland

205

and Jerry Kindall, but he finally ended the inning when Fred Whitfield grounded out to first.

Ramos gave up four runs on four hits in the top of the seventh inning, including a two-run homer by future Indian Leon Wagner.

Ramos pitched into the ninth inning, but was beginning to tire. After he struck out the leadoff man Joe Koppe, he gave up a single to Albie Peterson. Jim Fregosi reached on an error by third baseman Max Alvis. With runners on first and second, Tribe skipper Birdie Tebbets called for Gary Bell to come on in relief. Bell got Lee Thomas to hit into a game-ending 4-6-3 double play.

Only one team had ever hit back-to-back-to-back-to-back homers before. In 1961 Eddie Mathews, Hank Aaron, Joe Adcock, and Frank Thomas did it for the Boston Braves. The Indians were the first to complete the streak off a single pitcher.

The last team to hit back-to-back-to-back-to-back homers was the Washington Nationals. In 2019, Howie Kendrick, Trea Turner, Adam Eaton, and Anthony Rendon hit theirs off Craig Stammen and the Padres.

Game 109
August 24, 1919
Ray Caldwell Struck by Lightning On the Mound

Tris Speaker took a chance on Ray Caldwell mid-season. Caldwell had recently been cut by the Boston Red Sox due to his declining performance and issues with alcoholism. His former manager Miller Huggins later wrote of Caldwell, "[He] was one of the best pitchers that ever lived, but he was one of those characters that keep a manager in a constant worry. If he had possessed a sense of responsibility and balance, Ray Caldwell would have gone down in history as one of the greatest of all pitchers."

Caldwell showed his ability to pitch brilliantly on this August afternoon against Connie Mack's Athletics. He also showed incredible fortitude after a crazy turn of events.

In the bottom of the fourth inning, Rollie Naylor walked Indians shortstop Ray Chapman. Player-manager Tris Speaker drew a second walk. Joe Harris hit a sacrifice fly that moved both runners over. Third baseman Larry Gardner grounded out, but plated Caldwell. With two outs, Bill Wambsganss hit a sharp grounder to the shortstop. The A's Joe Dugan fielded it, but blew the throw to first. As the ball skipped away, Speaker was able to score from third on the error.

In the top of the fifth, George Burns of the A's reached on a hit by pitch. He was driven home by a Cy Perkins grounder. This cut the Indians' lead to 2-1, but Caldwell was pitching confidently.

A slight but steady rain had been falling for most of the game, as dark clouds scudded off Lake Erie in the way that they often do in late summer, but the game continued. Caldwell had the A's down to their final out. With Joe Dugan at the plate, there was a sudden crack of thunder and a blinding flash. Players and fans alike dove for cover. After a moment, others had recovered but Caldwell lay sprawled on the mound.

The shock knocked off Indians catcher Cy Perkin's helmet and mask. Several players later said that they felt the shock in their legs, conducted upward by their metal cleats. "We all could feel the tingle of the electric shock running through our systems, particularly in our legs," umpire Billy Evans later reported.

Caldwell slowly got up from the mound and assessed the damage. He had slight burns on his chest and tingling all over. Witnesses speculated that the lightning had struck the metal button on top of his cap, ran through his body, and exited out his metal spikes. Caldwell described the experience to the Cleveland Press, "Felt just like somebody came up with a board and hit me on top of the head and knocked me down."

After a few minutes to shake off the mighty jolt, the players re-took their positions, including Caldwell, to get the final out. Dugan hit a grounder to Larry Gardner at third base, who completed the throw to first and sealed the complete game win for Caldwell.

Caldwell's overall pitching line: nine innings, three strikeouts, two walks, and one near-death experience.

Game 110
August 5, 2001
The Impossible Comeback

The 2011 Seattle Mariners were one of the best ballclubs ever assembled. They had a .360 On Base Percentage for the season. They ended the regular season with an MLB record 116 wins. Seattle came into this game with a record of 80-30. Dave Burba was matched up with Aaron Sele in a late-summer contest that saw a good Indians team facing the juggernaut from the west.

That summer, I was in high-school. My girlfriend was hosting an exchange student from Talinn, Estonia. The game was nationally televised, and the wraparound weekend series had been hyped all week. We decided that on Sunday night, we would try to teach the exchange student about baseball.

Burba pitched a 1-2-3 inning to start the game, but quickly began to unravel in the second. Al Martin and Mike Cameron hit consecutive doubles to score Seattle's first run of the night. After a fly out by Carlos Guillien, Burba issued a walk to David Bell. With runners on first and second, Tom Lampkin doubled down the right field line to score Cameron. Ichiro drove in Bell and Lampkin with a line drive single to left. The Mariners were up 4-0 very quickly.

Burba gave up three consecutive singles to load the bases in the top of the third, and manager Charlie Manuel had seen enough. Reliever Mike Bacsik was called from the bullpen to make his first major league appearance. Bacsik would later become a historical footnote for giving up Barry Bond's 756th home run while pitching for the Nationals. The M's sent ten batters to the plate against Bacsik and scored eight runs in the frame. The Indians found themselves in a 12-0 hole against the best pitching staff in baseball.

Down 12 runs, Charlie Manuel decided to give some starters a rest. Juan Gonzalez, Robbie Alomar, Ellis Burks, and Travis Fryman all came out of the game after their second at-bat. Kenny Lofton later remarked that he, "wanted to stay in the game for some reason. [Maybe] I had a girlfriend there."

209

Jim Thome hit a two-run homer in the bottom of the fourth inning to end the shutout, but Seattle quickly regained their 12-run margin scoring twice in the bottom of the fifth.

Russel Branyan gave the Tribe offense a jolt to lead off the cranked a home run to left center off Aaron Sele to lead off the bottom of the seventh inning. After retiring Marty Cordova and Will Cordero, Sele began to fade. Backup catcher Einar Diaz singled to center, and then Sele walked both Kenny Lofton and Omar Vizquel.

John Halama was brought in from the Seattle Bullpen. He faced Jolbert Cabrera who lined a two-RBI single into left field that cut the lead to 14-5, Seattle.

In the bottom of the eighth, Jim Thome led off with a home run off Halama. Russel Branyan took first when Halama hit him with his first pitch. Marty Cordova followed with a homer that made the deficit 14-8. Omar drove in one additional run in the eighth with a double to right field. The Indians had cut the Mariner's lead to five runs.

Rich Rodriguez pitched a 1-2-3 top of the ninth for the Tribe. He used only seven pitches and got the offense, which was now beginning to feel a little spark, back to the plate.

Facing a five-run deficit in the bottom of the ninth, Ed Taubensee led things off with a single into center field. Jim Thome flied out to right. Russel Branyan struck out on three straight pitches, and things were looking grim.

Marty Cordova hit a line drive into deep left field. It dropped for a double, leaving Taubensee on third base. The Mariners called to the bullpen for Jeff Nelson. Nelson walked Wil Cordero, and the bases were loaded.

Einar Diaz singled to left, pushing Eddie Taubensee and Marty Cordova across the plate. Seattle was up 14-11, but Lou Pinella made the decision to go to his star reliever. Kazuhiro Sasaki had expected to have the night off when the M's were up twelve runs. Now, he entered the game looking for the final out. Kenny Lofton took Sasaki's second pitch through the left side of the infield for a single, and the bases were juiced again.

Vizquel worked Sasaki into a full count. On the eighth pitch of the at-bat, Omar hit one sharply over the first base bag. It skipped under backup first baseman Ed Sprague's glove and out toward the foul pole. Kenny Lofton, showing his characteristic speed, but on aging legs at this point in his career, dug hard to score from first. The bases-clearing triple tied the game at 14 runs apiece. The Tribe had closed the 12-run deficit over the course of just three innings.

I turned to the exchange student. "That is not usually how this works," I told her for about the fifth time in the last hour.

Both teams would fail to score in the tenth inning. The Indians' controversial recent acquisition, John Rocker, came on to pitch the top of the eleventh. Rocker struck out the side against the bottom third of the M's order.

Einar Diaz flied out to lead off the Indians' half of the eleventh. Kenny Lofton got aboard with a line drive single to center. Omar singled again to move Lofton into scoring position. This brought Jolbert Cabrera to the plate. Cabrera swung at Jose Paniagula's first pitch and shattered his bat, sending fragments out to third base and the ball into short left. Lofton raced from second and rounded third. Mark McLemore threw a strike from left field to the plate, but Lofton slid in under the tag to deliver the walk-off victory.

After the game, Lofton was beyond enthusiastic, "I can't explain it. It was unbelievable. I've never been in a game like that in my life. My voice is gone from hollering so much. It was fun. Wow."

Game 111
August 4, 1996
Kenny Lofton Climbs the Wall to Rob BJ Surhoff

The 1990's Indians were primarily known for their offense. However, of all the great Indians moments of the late 1990's, the most famous image is a defensive play. The clip is so iconic and instantly recognizable that it was included in the SportsCentury montage that ESPN ran in the final moments of New Year's Eve 1999.

On a Sunday afternoon in August, the Indians entered this game against the Orioles with the best record in the American League. The Orioles threw Rocky Coppinger against Brian Anderson.

In the bottom of the third, Kenny Lofton led off the inning by drawing a six-pitch walk. With Omar Vizquel at the plate, Lofton stole second and then third. After Vizquel drew his own walk, Jim Thome plated Lofton with a sacrifice fly.

Cal Ripken, Jr. led off the top of the fourth inning with a scorching line drive double into left field. Rafael Palmero followed with a fly ball to deep right. Ripken tagged up and headed to third. Manny Ramirez tracked down the fly ball and fired across the field to Thome at third base. The throw beat Ripken for the rare 9-5 double play. Bobby Bonilla took Anderson's second pitch deep to left and onto the home run porch, tying the game at one run apiece.

The Tribe broke the 1-1 tie in the bottom of the fifth inning when Lofton homered to right field. Omar Vizquel got aboard with a single into right field. Jim Thome punched a single through the right side of the infield which scored Vizquel from second base. Thome's RBI gave the Tribe a 3-1 lead.

After replacing Anderson, Paul Shuey gave up a solo home run to Jeffery Hammonds to make it a 3-2 ballgame in the top of the seventh inning.

In the top of the eighth, with Raphael Palmero on first, BJ Surhoff came to bat. Shuey fell behind to Palmero and into a 3-0 count. Surhoff took the 3-0 pitch to deep right-center. Omar Vizquel later

212

shared, "I thought that ball was going to be a homer. Period. I dropped my head and I said, 'Damn, man.'"

Kenny Lofton had not given up on the play. He raced toward the path of the ball. Lofton was originally recruited to the University of Arizona on a basketball scholarship. He is the only person to have played in both an NCAA Final Four and a World Series. Arizona Wildcats head coach Lute Olson once said of Lofton, "He's quick and a great leaper."

This was never more evident than at this moment when Lofton barreled toward the bullpen wall, leapt off the warning track, found a foothold on some padding that protected the bullpen door and vaulted three feet above the right field wall to bring back what would have been a go-ahead homer for Surhoff.

After Eric Plunk struck out Eddie Murray for the final out of the inning, the energized Indians came to bat. They sent fifteen men to the plate and scored eleven runs on eight hits, including a three-run double by Jose Vizcaino, a three-run home run by Jim Thome, and another three-run homer by Brian Giles.

Jose Mesa pitched a 1-2-3 ninth, but was clearly not eligible for a save in the 14-2 victory.

Honorable Mention:
August 16th, 1920 - Ray Chapman is Killed by a Pitch

While not a positive story, Chapman's is a unique one. He was struck in the temple by a pitch that he likely never saw. The Yankees' Carl Mays was a submarine-style pitcher known to scuff and soil the ball (as was legal at the time). It was nearing twilight when Chapman, a talented hitter who is still sixth on the all-time list of sacrifice hits, failed to track the pitch and was struck squarely in the head. He collapsed to his knees and was helped off the field. He died hours later in a New York hospital. Chapman remains the only MLBer ever to pass away as a direct result of an on-field injury.

Game 112
August 8, 1961
Four-Run Comeback Ends with a Walk-off Passed Ball

The 1961 Indians were a largely forgettable team, although they were playing above-.500 baseball at this point in the season. The lowly Washington Senators were in town. Just over 5,000 fans came to the lakefront to see Bennie Daniels take on Barry Latman.

Washington scored first in the top of the fourth inning. Latman walked left fielder Gene Woodling. Two batters later, Bob Johnson put the Sens on the board with a two-run home run to dead center.

An inning later, Washington right-fielder Chuck Hinton tacked on another run with a solo homer to center.

Bennie Daniels had given up only two hits through four, but issued two walks to lead off the bottom of the fifth inning. With Willie Kirkland and Bubba Phillips on base, Tribe catcher John Romano blooped a single into left field to score Kirkland and make it a 3-1 game.

In the top of the eighth inning, Washington touched up Indians reliever Bobby Locke for two more runs. Danny O'Connell sent one back up the middle. It was fielded by second baseman Johnny Temple. Temple sailed the throw to first, and O'Connell found himself on second base. Bud Zipfel grounded out to first base, but O'Connell advanced to third. Gene Woodling sent one into the right field gap that went for a double and scored O'Connell. Marty Keough came in to pinch run for Woodling, and was driven in by a Bob Johnson single. Washington had extended their lead.

Facing a 5-1 deficit, Woodie Held led off the bottom of the eighth with a strikeout. Chuck Essegian pinch hit for the pitcher Bobby Locke and rocked a home run to deep left field off Daniels. Johnny Temple recorded a quick flyball out. Two consecutive singles by Don Dillard and Tito Francona chased Daniels from the game.

Senators reliever Mike Garcia came on to pitch with runners on first and second. He gave up consecutive two-out singles to Kirkland,

214

Phillips, and Romano which tied the game. He was pulled in favor of Dave Sisler who recorded the final out of the eighth.

The teams played through a scoreless ninth inning. In the top of the tenth, the Senators threatened. They had runners on first and third with one out, but Marty Keough popped a fly to second base. Johnny Temple made the catch for the first out, and threw home to get Hinton who was running on contact. The inning-ending double play was yet another break for the Tribe in a game where luck was on their side.

In the bottom of the tenth, Sisler and backup catcher Gene Green could not get on the same page. Don Dillard led off with a double to center. Tito Francona walked, and then both runners advanced on a passed ball with Willie Kirkland at the plate. Kirkland eventually drew a walk. With the bases loaded and Bubba Phillips at the plate another ball skipped away from Green. Dillard hustled home to snatch a victory on the second passed ball of the inning.

Game 113
August 12, 2016
Indians Steal Eight Bases on Way to 13-3 Win

The 2007 Indians were my favorite team to watch pitch. The 1995 team was my favorite to watch hit. The magic of the 2016 squad came on the basepaths. Rajai Davis, Jose Ramirez, Francisco Lindor and plenty others were always pushing to take an extra base.

Carlos Carrasco was pitching against the Angels' Tyler Skaggs on this hot August Friday night. Carrasco got off to a rocky start. He gave up a solo home run to Kole Calhoun, a double to Mike Trout, and a single by Albert Pujols that scored Trout. The score was 2-0 before the Indians came to bat.

Rajai Davis drew an 11-pitch walk, then stole second on Skaggs second pitch to Jason Kipnis. On the very next delivery, Rajai broke for third and arrived safely. Kipnis poked a line drive single into left which sent Davis around to score. With two outs, Kipnis stole second but Jose Ramirez struck out to end the inning.

Carrasco got into a groove and threw a 1-2-3 second inning. Brandon Guyer led off the bottom half of the second with a solo home run that tied the game at 2-2.

Kole Calhoun got aboard to lead off the bottom of the third inning with a double into center field. Calhoun advanced to third on a wild pitch with Albert Pujols at the plate. Pujols put the halos ahead 3-2 with a grounder to third that allowed Calhoun to score.

Jose Ramirez singled to right to lead off the bottom of the fourth inning. Ramirez swiped second with Brandon Guyer at the plate. After Guyer fouled out, Ramirez stole third with Abe Almonte at bat. Almonte knocked a line drive into center field to score Jose and tie things up at 3-3.

The Tribe pulled away in the bottom of the fifth with four runs on five hits. Rajai singled into left field, and then got his third steal of the night. Jason Kipnis sent an RBI-double into the left field gap. Francisco Lindor blooped a single into short right field which scored

216

Kipnis from second. Mike Napoli lined one sharply into left field for a single. Jose Ramirez grounded one weakly to third base. Napoli was forced out at second, but Ramirez beat the throw to first to avoid the double-play. Jose Ramirez swiped his third base of the evening to get back into scoring position. Brandon Guyer sent a liner into short right field. Guyer's hit allowed two runs to score, but Brandon himself was put out at second trying to stretch it into a double. Abe Almonte struck out to end the inning with the Tribe up 7-3.

The Indians added two more runs in the bottom of the sixth inning thanks to an RBI single by Lindor. Frankie got the club's eighth steal of the night. Then Mike Napoli drove in Jason Kipnis to make it a 9-3 ballgame.

Jose Ramirez added a solo homer in the bottom of the seventh inning off Angels' reliever Jose Valdez. Ramirez added another insurance run in the bottom of the eighth when he smashed a line drive into the right field gap. This allowed Jason Kipnis to score for the third time. Brandon Guyer drove in Lindor and Ramirez with another liner down the right field line.

Brian Shaw and Zach McAllister both pitched 1-2-3 innings in relief as the Indians would continue to pile on toward a 13-3 victory.

When asked what made Skaggs so easy to run on, manager Terry Francona said simply, "You've got a lanky left-hander on the mound who's young."

The Indians had not had eight stolen bases in a game since Game 128 of 1917. Right fielder Braggo Roth stole four bags in that contest against the Washington Senators. Joe Harris added two steals along with one each from Tris Speaker and Bill Wambsganss.

Game 114
August 13, 1999
Robbie Alomar's Diving Catch Ends the Game

The Indians were 17 games ahead in the Central Division and cruising toward a fifth straight division title. Chuck Nagy was scheduled to start against the Orioles' Scott Erikson.

Nagy did not allow a runner past second base until the top of the fifth inning. After Delino DeShields singled to center, he advanced to second on a Brady Anderson walk. DeShields and Anderson executed a two-out double-steal to get into scoring position. Mike Bordick took Nagy's second pitch deep into left field. Richie Sexson leaped for the ball and made a backhanded catch. Sexson crashed into the outfield wall, but hung-on for the inning-ending putout.

With two outs in the bottom of the fifth inning, Richie Sexson was on third base after a single and two ground outs. Dave Roberts smashed a ground ball single into right field. Sexson came in to score, but Roberts was thrown out trying to stretch the hit into a double.

Former Indian Albert Belle tied things up in the top of the sixth inning when he drove home BJ Surhoff with a ground ball single to right.

Omar Vizquel led off the bottom of the sixth inning with a seeing-eye single through the right side of the infield. Robbie Alomar attempted to bunt him over, but the bunt was fielded by first baseman Will Clark and flipped to shortstop Mike Bordick at second to force out Vizquel. Despite the failed bunt attempt, Manny Ramirez put the Tribe ahead. He crushed a home run to deep right center that put the Indians in the lead 3-1.

Paul Shuey replaced Nagy to start the top of the eighth inning. He gave up a leadoff single to Brady Anderson. After a Mike Bordick fly-out, BJ Surhoff singled to center. With runners at the corners, Albert Belle drove in two more runs with a line drive double. Shuey was credited with a blown save, and Ricardo Rincon came on in relief.

After putting Jeff Conine on base with a hit-by-pitch, Rincon got Will Clark to ground into a 1-6-3 double play. That ended the inning with the score tied 3-3.

Scott Erikson returned to pitch the bottom of the eighth, but did not last long. Dave Roberts reached on an error and was moved over to second on a sacrifice bunt by Omar Vizquel. Robbie Alomar drove him home with a sharp line drive into right field. Manny Ramirez stepped in and launched his second two-run homer of the day.

With the O's down 6-3, Jesse Orosco came to the mound in relief. This was Orosco's 1,071st appearance in the majors. This tied him with Dennis Eckersley for the all-time lead. Orosco broke into the majors in 1979 and went on pitching until 2003. He eventually amassed 1,252 appearances. He is one of only twenty-nine big leaguers to have played in four decades.

Mostly a matchup pitcher later in his career, Orosco struck out Jim Thome and gave up a single to David Justice. He was replaced by Scott Kamienecki who got Richie Sexson to ground out to end the inning.

Michael Jackon came on to close the game for the Tribe. He struck out Charles Johnson, and got Delino DeShields to ground out. With the grounds crew kneeling next to the tarp as rain threatened, Jackson walked Rich Amaral. Amaral advanced to second as Jackson focused on Brady Anderson.

Anderson hit a ground ball sharply between first and second base. Ranging *far* to his left, Robbie Alomar snagged the grounder. He spun on his knees and threw a no-look strike to Jim Thome at first base.

Anderson later remarked, "I wasn't surprised. Anybody else, yes. But Robbie is one of the greatest second basemen ever."

Game 115
August 14, 1987
Tom Candiotti Knuckleballs His Way to Victory Over the Yankees

Tom Candiotti was the Indians' Opening Day starter for 1987. Candiotti was a bright spot on a dismal Indians team that normally dragged him down with poor run support. Coming into this mid-August game, he had a 6-11 record and the Tribe were dead last in the American League, 24½ games behind front-running Toronto.

Candiotti had seen some success against the Yankees, including a one-hitter in Game 105 at Municipal Stadium earlier in the season.

Throughout the 1986 season, Phil Niekro mentored Candiotti who was making the conversion to a full-time knuckleball pitcher.

In this matchup, Candiotti faced former Indian Tommy John (of ligament surgery fame) in a Friday night tilt at Yankee Stadium.

The Yankees kicked off the scoring in the bottom of the first inning. Willie Randolph got aboard with a ground ball single. Don Mattingly stepped in and crushed a Candiotti knuckler for a two-run home run.

Pat Tabler and Corey Snider singled for the Tribe in the top of the second inning. Tommy John walked Brook Jacoby to load the bases. This brought up Indians catcher Andy Allanson. Allanson poked a single into left field. Tabler and Snider crossed the plate to tie the game at 2-2.

Gary Ward led off the Yankee half of the second inning with a double. Catcher (and future Indians coach) Joel Skinner scored Ward with a sacrifice fly to right.

The Tribe re-took the lead in the top of the fourth inning. Brook Jacoby dropped a single into center field. Andy Allanson's double into left field put Jacoby on third. Brett Butler placed another single into center that allowed both runners to score. With the Indians back on top, the Yankees called to the bullpen for reliever Brad Arnsburg.

Arnsburg got the final two outs of the fourth inning and sat the Tribe down in order in the fifth inning.

220

Dan Pasqua led off the top of the fifth with another homer off Candiotti. Later in the inning with runners at first and third Don Mattingly put the Yankees ahead once again with an RBI single.

Brook Jacoby scored the tying run with a solo home run off Arnsburg in the top of the sixth inning. Arnsburg retired the rest of the Tribe lineup in order through the sixth, seventh, and eighth innings.

Jacoby stepped in against Arnsburg again in the top of the eighth. For the second time in as many at-bats, Jacoby sent one over the Yankee Stadium wall for the go-ahead run.

Jacoby finished the night with three runs scored on three hits, one walk, and two RBI. Doug Jones pitched a 1-2-3 ninth inning to record his fourth save of the season.

Candiotti pitched 7⅔ innings. He gave up five runs on nine hits but it was good enough to beat the Yankees in their second straight matchup. Candiotti continued throwing the knuckler into the 1999 season. By then, he had passed the torch to Tim Wakefield as the only knuckle-first pitcher in the league.

Game 116
August 17, 1933
Earl Averill Hits for the Cycle

On this Thursday afternoon, Monte Pearson was throwing for the Tribe against George Earnshaw and the rest of Connie Mack's Athletics. The Indians were splitting time between League Park and the newly-opened Municipal Stadium. This game took place on the Lakefront where the outfield was immense.

Earl Averill got the Indians' first hit of the game, a two-out double into left field in the bottom of the first inning. Joe Vosmik sent him home with a single into center field. Averill came around to score before Vosmik was put out at second trying to stretch the single into a two-bagger.

In the bottom of the third inning, Monte Pearson got aboard for the Tribe with a single to right field. Bill Cissel smashed a two-run homer over the left field wall. Again, with two outs, Averill knocked one into the right field corner. By the time the A's Lou Finney ran it down, Averill was safe at third. Once again, Vosmik pushed Averill across the plate with a single. The third inning ended with the score 4-0 Indians.

The A's sent nine men to the plate in the top of the fifth inning, scoring three runs on four hits to cut the Tribe lead to one run.

The Indians countered by working through thirteen batters in the bottom of the fifth. Milt Galatzer led off with a walk. Bill Cissel laid down a sacrifice bunt which moved Galatzer to second base. Earl Averill stepped in and had his third hit of the day, a single into right field. Galatzer came around to score. A's right fielder Lou Finney botched the throw to the plate and Averill was able to advance to second. Joe Vosmik doubled into right field and Averill was able to come around to score. Jim Peterson's day was done, and the A's brought in Rube Walberg in relief.

The hit parade continued against Walberg. Odell Hale flied a double into left field. Willie Kamm knocked another double into left which scored Hale and Vosmik. Roy Spencer blooped a single into center field. Monte Pearson smashed a single into left field which scored

Boss and Spencer. Milt Galatzer got the Tribe's eighth straight hit with another single into left field.

As the eleventh man up, Averill walked in his fourth appearance. Joe Vosmik grounded out to end the inning. The Tribe scored seven runs on eight hits, bringing the score to 11-3.

Cleveland added two more runs in the bottom of the sixth off rookie pitcher Bobby Coombs. The Philadelphia Inquirer later wrote that Coombs was "the fourth lamb offered up for sacrifice." Harley Boss and Roy Spencer both collected RBIs to put the Tribe up by ten runs.

In the bottom of the seventh with Cissel on second, Averill clubbed a home run over the Muni Stadium wall, completing the Indians first cycle since Bill Bradley in Game 136 of 1903.

Dib Williams had an RBI single for the A's in the top of the eighth, but the A's would not threaten as Monte Pearson secured the complete game win with a final score of 15-4.

Averill's cycle was the 62nd in major league baseball since 1901. It was the second of nine cycles in Indians history.

Game 117
August 13, 2006
Hafner Ties Mattingly for Season Grand Slam Record

The Tribe was wrapping up a weekend series with Kansas City with a Sunday afternoon tilt between Jeremy Sowers and the Royals' Luke Hudson.

Sowers gave up two quick hits, but then retired the Royals on a pop-out by Mike Sweeney and a line-drive to third base. Andy Marte caught the liner and tagged out David DeJesus as he was diving back to the bag.

The Indians put the game way out of reach early on. Hudson loaded the bases immediately. He issued a walk to Grady Sizemore. Jason Michaels singled. Then he walked Travis Hafner. Victor Martinez followed with a two-run single into right. Shin Soo Choo plated another pair with a ground ball single into left field. Ryan Garko punched another single into left field. Jhonny Peralta reached on an error, and Joe Inglett singled to load the bases once more. Hudson worked Andy Marte into a full count, but issued a walk to force in a run. Grady Sizemore pushed Peralta across the plate with another ground ball single. Hudson finally recorded an out against the tenth batter he faced when he got Jason Michaels to strike out swinging in his second at-bat.

Travis Hafner stepped in and launched a no-doubt line drive grand slam home run into the bullpen in right field. Pronk's grand slam put the Indians up 11-0 before the second out was recorded.

Victor Martinez got his second hit of the inning with a double to left. KC skipper Buddy Bell had seen enough. He called for Todd Wellmeyer to replace Hudson on the mound. Wellmeyer promptly retired Choo and Garko to end the eight-hit eleven-run inning.

Ryan Garko added a solo home run in the fourth inning. It was one of only two hits that Wellmeyer gave up in 6⅔ innings of work. It would have been a very respectable outing for Wellmeyer, if he had not come in with an eleven-run deficit.

Franklin Gutierrez replaced Grady Sizemore in center field in the fifth inning. In the eighth, Gutierrez, perhaps feeling left out of the earlier offensive explosion, smacked a solo homer of his own. Jeremy Sowers and the bullpen cruised to the 13-0 victory.

Hafner's grand slam was his sixth of the season. The only other player to hit six grand slams in a season is Don Mattingly. Mattingly spread his throughout the 1987 season. Hafner is by far the fastest to achieve the feat, since Mattingly hit his fifth and sixth late in September. Interestingly, Mattingly never hit another grand slam *after* 1987.

Unfortunately, Hafner did not get to write his own line in the history book, he was hit by a pitch in Game 133 and missed the entire month of September with a broken hand.

Hafner ended the season with a .659 slugging percentage and 1.097 OPS. He hit a total of 42 homers and drove in 117 in his best hitting campaign. While belting six grand slams is a personal achievement and a testament to Pronk's clutch hitting, it also indicates that the top of the order got on base *a lot*.

Honorable Mention
August 24, 1945 - Bob Feller Returns from Navy, Strikes out 12

As with many of the baseball greats of the 1940's, a significant chunk of Feller's career was given up to service in World War II. After three years in the Navy, mostly aboard the USS Alabama, Feller returned to the Indians mid-season in 1945.

His first game back was against the Tigers on a Friday night in Municipal Stadium. Over 46,000 fans came out to welcome Feller home and see him throw a complete-game four hitter. He struck out twelve Tigers in the 4-2 win.

Game 118
August 13, 1984
Joe Carter Walks Off the Yankees in the 11th Inning

Joe Carter has one of the most famous walk-off hits in baseball history. This is not that one. However, it does display the clutch hitting he was known for throughout his 18-year career.

Carter arrived in Cleveland as part of a trade with the Cubs in June 1984. Cleveland fans accused the front office of dumping salary when they dealt pitchers Rick Sutcliffe and George Frazier and catcher Ron Hassey to Chicago for Carter, Mel Hall, and Don Schulze. GM Phil Segui insisted that he was building a nucleus of young talent and wanted to see what these newcomers could do.

While the 1984 squad continued to struggle, Joe Carter was a bright spot. The night before, he accounted for all six of the Tribe's runs against Ron Guidry and the Yankees. Carter got the start in left field for the series finale on this Monday evening.

Brett Butler led off the Indians' half of the first with a triple, but was put out on a fielder's choice when Joe Carter sent one back to the pitcher. Julio Franco followed with a single that advanced Carter to third. Andre Thornton walked to load the bases. The Tribe jumped out to an early lead when Pat Tabler drove home Carter with a sacrifice fly, and Carmello Castillo singled in Franco. Chris Bando walked to juice the bases once again. Brook Jacoby knocked a two-run single, but Bando was thrown out trying to go from first to third. The inning ended with the score 4-0.

The Yankees made up some ground in the top of the third. Omar Moreno led off with a single. Tribe starter Roy Smith issued a walk to Bob Meacham. Tim Foli and Don Mattingly came through with consecutive RBI singles to cut the Tribe's lead in half.

In the bottom of the fourth, starter Jim Deshaies got in trouble once again. Bando and Jacoby got on base with consecutive singles. He walked Mike Fischlin. The Yankees brought Mike Armstrong from the bullpen to attempt to clean things up. Brett Butler hit a sacrifice fly to center which scored Bando from third. However, Fischlin was put out at second trying to stretch it into a double.

The Yankees slowly but surely closed the gap. Butch Wynegar had an RBI single in the top of the sixth inning. Don Mattingly singled Bob Meacham across with a single in the seventh. Omar Moreno tied the game with an RBI double in the eighth. The blown save was hung on Ernie Camacho.

Tribe reliever Steve Farr held onto the 5-5 tie through the eleventh inning. Brook Jacoby knocked a single to get things started in the bottom half. Bernazard hit a double that advanced Jacoby to third. The Yankees intentionally walked Brett Butler to load the bases and set up a potential double play. Joe Carter stepped in and poked the game-winning hit into left field to send the Indians home a winner.

Game 119
August 18, 2016
Naquin Pinch Hits the Game Winner

The White Sox were wrapping up a midweek series at Progressive Field. The Indians had just activated Danny Salazar from the 15-day disabled list to start against the Sox' Carlos Rodon.

Salazar walked three of the first four batters he faced. Justin Morneau drove a bases-clearing double into left-center. Morneau was left on base, but the Sox were out to an early 3-0 lead. Salazar did not return to the mound for the second inning.

Kyle Crockett pitched a 1-2-3 inning of relief for the Indians. Then, Mike Clevinger took over for the Tribe in the top of the third. He held the Sox scoreless through the top of the seventh.

The Tribe got on the scoreboard in the bottom of the fifth inning. Carlos Santana led off with a double down the left field line. Jose Ramirez drove him in with a ground ball smashed through the left side of the infield.

In the bottom of the sixth inning, Roberto Perez slapped a leadoff single into right field. Jason Kipnis bounced one into the stands for a ground rule double that put Perez on third. Francisco Lindor slapped a single into short right field to make the score 3-2 Sox.

After Dan Otero replaced Clevinger in the top of the seventh inning, JB Shuck bunted Tim Anderson from second to third. Omar Narvaez poked a grounder through the left side of the infield to give the Sox an insurance run.

Abe Almonte drove a liner into the left field gap with one out in the bottom of the seventh. Almonte came around to score on a Rajai Davis ground ball double. The Sox called on Nate Jones who struck out Jason Kipnis to end the inning.

Jones stayed on to pitch the bottom of the eighth. Francisco Lindor grounded out. Mike Napoli worked Jones into a full count, then drew a walk on the seventh pitch. A wild pitch sent Mike Napoli to second and into scoring position. Carlos Santana struck out looking, but

Jose Ramirez quickly picked him up with a single into right that allowed Napoli to score the tying run.

Andrew Miller pitched a scoreless ninth inning to hold on to the 4-4 tie.

In the bottom of the ninth, Abe Almonte led things off with a double into center field. Terry Francona signaled Roberto Perez to bunt Almonte over to third. However, Jacob Turner's first pitch skipped away from Narvaez behind the plate for a passed ball that put Almonte on third.

Now in a swing-away situation, Terry Francona decided that he could do better than Roberto Perez, who was hitting .108 at the time. He called on Tyler Naquin as a rare mid-at-bat pinch hitter.

On Turner's first pitch to Naquin, he lofted a fly ball to deep center. Almonte was able to tag and score the winning run for a walk-off sacrifice fly.

Francona later said, "Tyler Naquin was sitting over there by the bat rack for a couple of days, ready to hit. ...We didn't have to go find him. He was ready, and it showed."

Game 120
August 19, 2016
Naquin Walk-off Inside the Park Home Run

This is the second place in the Project where consecutive games appear. The first (see page 109) was a pair of brilliant pitching performances. In this case, we have two examples of dramatic clutch hitting.

After a walk-off win for the Tribe the night before, the Blue Jays came to town for a weekend series. The Indians matched up Trevor Bauer with Francisco Liriano. The Jays were hanging to a fractional game lead in the east with a formidable hitting lineup, while the Indians were out ahead of the Tigers by seven games going into the weekend.

Bauer got in trouble early. He walked Michael Saunders in the top of the first. With two outs, Russel Martin sent a line-drive home run over the left field wall. The Indians found themselves in an early 2-0 hole.

Liriano allowed only two hits through five innings. In the bottom of the sixth, Jason Kipnis got aboard with a line drive single to right field. With Lindor at the plate, Kipnis advanced to third on a passed ball that skipped away from Russel Martin. Mike Napoli drove Kipnis home with a single to left field.

In the seventh inning, Joaquin Benoit came on to pitch for Liriano. For the second straight night, Naquin entered the game as a pinch hitter. He replaced Brandon Guyer as a better matchup against Benoit. Naquin struck out swinging. Benoit retired Almonte and Perez for the 1-2-3 inning.

Jays reliever Jason Grilli faced only four batters in the eighth inning to hold on to the 2-1 lead.

After eight innings of five-hit baseball, Trevor Bauer's day was done. Jeff Manship was called from the bullpen to pitch the top of the ninth against the meat of the Toronto order. Manship got Russell Martin to fly out to short. He struck out Melvin Upton, Jr. on three pitches.

Ezequiel Carrera worked him into a full count, but Manship struck him out looking.

Roberto Osuna came on to pitch for the Jays in the bottom of the ninth. Carlos Santana popped one up behind the plate for the first out. Jose Ramirez stepped in. He took Osuna's 0-2 pitch deep down the right field line and over the wall to tie the game at 2-2.

Naquin battled through a series of fastballs and nearly struck out on Osuna's fourth pitch, which he barely tipped. On the fifth pitch of the at-bat, Osuna lost one out over the plate, which Naquin squared and drove to deep center. For a moment it was unclear if the ball would be a home run, off the wall, or caught by a leaping Michael Saunders.

As Saunders was leaping at the wall, Melvin Upton Jr. had slipped hustling over from second. Upton eventually ended up with the ball, but not before doing the splits and facing *away* from home plate.

As Upton attempted to hit the cutoff man from the seat of his pants in right field, Naquin was rounding third. Mike Sarbaugh gave him the green light, and Tyler dug for home. It was clear that there would be a play at the plate, and nearly as clear that Naquin would be successful. The Indians bench had cleared well before Naquin touched home and struck his now-iconic pose.

This victory put the Indians 20 games over .500 for the season and set the tone for one of the great post-season runs in team history. It also put Naquin firmly into the Rookie of the Year discussion. He went on to finish third in the voting behind Michael Fulmer of the Tigers and Gary Sanchez of the Yankees.

As a footnote, this was the first time in MLB history that a game-tying home run was followed by a walk-off inside-the-park home run.

Game 121
August 20,1992
Indians Spoil Tapani's 3-Hitter

The Indians started Rod Nichols against Twins workhorse Kevin Tapani on this Thursday night. The Twins were 6 games back in the AL West, but had a talented core. The Tribe were out of contention in the AL East, but young players like Albert Belle, Sandy Alomar, Paul Sorrento, and Jim Thome were beginning to make some noise.

Tapani pitched masterfully, holding the Indians hitless through the first six innings. The only Cleveland baserunner was Paul Sorrento who drew a walk in the bottom of the second.

Nichols scattered a hit or two in nearly every inning, but managed to escape without too much damage. The Twins only run against Nichols came in the top of the fifth inning when Chuck Knoblauch drove a double into right field. After Randy Bush advanced Knoblauch to third on a groundout, Kirby Puckett sent him home with a double down the right field line.

In the bottom of the seventh inning, Mark Whiten took Tapani's first pitch deep over the Muni Stadium wall to tie the game at one run apiece. Tapani retired the next nine Indians in a row to send the game to extra innings.

Carlos Baerga flied out for the first out of the tenth inning. Tapani issued a six-pitch walk to Albert Belle. That gave the Indians their first base runner since the top of the fifth. Paul Sorrento stepped in and slapped a line drive down the left field line. Belle motored around from first to score the winning run.

Tapani was the ultimate hard-luck loser. He went ten innings, gave up only three hits and two walks. The Twins supported him with eleven hits, but could not push them across the plate. The Twins left eight men on base and were a miserable 2 for 11 with runners in scoring position.

Game 122
August 14, 2003
Travis Hafner Hits for Cycle While Cleveland is Blacked Out

The Indians were wrapping up a midweek series in Minneapolis with a Thursday-afternoon getaway game. Before push notifications for every score and endless Twitter updates, most working people were not engaged with this game in real time. Despite the history-making moments in this game, not many Clevelanders remember it. Many of them even did not even see the highlights from the Metrodome.

Brian Anderson was matched up with Brad Radke of the Twins. Radke retired the side in order in the top of the first. Anderson returned the favor in the bottom half of the inning.

Ben Broussard lined one right back at Radke to lead off the second inning. Ryan Ludwick popped a foul behind the plate which was easily tracked down by Minnesota catcher Matt LeCroy. Travis Hafner opened up the scoring with a solo home run on Radke's first pitch of the at-bat. It was a towering drive to right field that landed somewhere in the "hefty bag" covering the collapsible seating sections used for Vikings' games.

In the top of the third inning, Casey Blake bounced one into the seats and scored Jhonny Peralta with the ground-rule double.

With two outs in the top of the fourth, Hafner slapped a bouncer over Brad Radke on a check swing. The ball found its way between the second baseman and shortstop. As it dribbled into the outfield, Pronk raced around first, and slid into second for a double.

Anderson scattered just five hits through the first six innings and the Twins never really threatened.

The Tribe broke things open in the top of the seventh when Hafner chopped one in front of the plate and beat Matt LeCroy's throw to first. The catcher's throw sailed past the first baseman and Hafner took second on the throwing error.

Josh Bard bunted Hafner over to third. He scored on a ground-rule double by Jhonny Peralta. The Tribe would add three additional runs in the seventh to bring the lead to 6-0.

After another 1-2-3 inning by Anderson, Ben Broussard led off the Indians' half of the eighth with a single. Ryan Ludwick struck out swinging and brought Hafner up with a shot at the record books. Clearly a triple would be a tall order for Hafner, who was not known for his speed on the basepaths. He sent a line drive into the right-center gap, perfectly placed between the outfielders. It skipped to the wall on the Metrodome turf. Torii Hunter fielded the ball up against the wall and double-clutched before hitting his cutoff man. By the time the relay came to third, Hafner was in safely with a head-first slide.

Anderson eventually gave up a home run to Matt LeCroy and was chased from the game. Reliever David Cortes gave up two additional runs while closing out the bottom of the ninth, but was more than serviceable in getting the Tribe to the 8-3 victory.

Hafner's final line was 4 hits, 2 RBI in 5 plate appearances. His mother, Bev had driven 400 miles from Sykeston, North Dakota to see her son at the nearest ballpark. Hafner became the seventh Indian to hit for the cycle. Rajai Davis and Jake Bauers have done it since.

The game in Minnesota ended when it was 3:36 p.m. in Cleveland. Around 3:10 p.m., various transmission lines and substations in the First Energy power system began tripping off. At 4:09 all Cleveland Public Power customers were completely in the dark. Eventually, over fifty million people in eight states and parts of Canada would be without electricity. With Clevelanders scrambling to empty fridges, procure generators, or drink beers with their neighbors under the stars, few were paying attention to the sports day's highlight reel. Hafner's cycle slipped from notoriety into trivia almost as soon as it happened.

Game 123
September 8, 1995
Indians Clinch Division for First Time in a Generation

The Indians came into this Friday night contest just a hair shy of a .700 winning percentage. They were a whopping 23½ games ahead in the Central Division. The Orioles threw Kevin Brown against veteran Orel Hershiser.

In the bottom of the third inning, Sandy Alomar took first base on a hit-by-pitch. Kenny Lofton advanced him to third when he scorched a single into right field. Alomar scored on a sacrifice fly by Omar Vizquel for the first run of the game. Carlos Baerga lined one into short right field, and then Albert Belle drew a walk. Eddie Murray drove in both baserunners with a two-out single over second base that put the Tribe up 3-0.

Hershiser gave up his first hits of the night in the top of the fourth inning. They were consecutive singles by Curtis Goodwin and Rafael Palmero. With runners at the corners, Bobby Bonilla hit a grounder to first. Paul Sorrento scooped it up and fired it to Vizquel for the force at second. Vizquel sent it back to Sorrento for the double-play while Goodwin scampered home to cut the lead to 3-1.

Brown and Hershiser battled through the middle innings. Harold Baines smacked a line drive double into left field for the Orioles in the top of the seventh. Jeff Huson drove him in with another double to make the score 3-2, Cleveland. Mike Hargrove made the call to the bullpen for Paul Assenmacher.

Assenmacher got the last out of the seventh inning and the first two of the eighth. Julian Tavarez came in to match up with Bobby Bonilla and recorded the final out of the eighth.

Jose Mesa came to the mound for the top of the ninth inning with the one-run lead intact. He retired Cal Ripken on a groundout to short and Harold Baines on a fly ball to right. He put the tying run aboard by issuing a walk to Chris Hoiles. Jeff Huson popped his 0-1 pitch into foul territory beyond third base. Jim Thome caught the fly, and the Indians were headed to the postseason for the first time since 1954.

Prior to the game, knowing that the clinch was possible, Manager Mike Hargrove made a request of the scoreboard crew. He asked that Garth Brooks "The Dance" be played during the post-game celebration. The Dance was a favorite of former Indians closer Steve Olin who died in a boating accident during Spring Training of 1993.

Hargrove later said, "I thought it would mean a lot to anyone who was there [at the time of the accident]. For those who weren't there it had no significance, but it was still a good song. It was a tribute to those guys, to their families. It was part of our promise to never forget them. We didn't tell anyone that we were going to do it. For those who knew, there wasn't a dry eye to be seen. I saw Charlie Nagy; tears were rolling down his face."

Of course, the 1995 Indians would later run into the woodchipper that was John Smoltz, Greg Maddux, and Tom Glavine. Jose Mesa would go from second in the Cy Young voting to an all-time Cleveland villain, and the window of contention would eventually close without a World Series ring. But for this day, Cleveland was on top of the baseball world.

Game 124
August 23, 1986
Andre Thornton Walk-off Pinch Hit

The 1986 Indians were playing just above .500 ball, but they were one game out of last place in the American League East. A crowd of over 40,000 came down to the Lakefront to see the first place Red Sox. Knuckleballer Tom Candiotti was starting against Tom Seaver in the marquee pitching matchup of the weekend.

In the top of the third, Wade Boggs struck first for the Red Sox when he rocked a solo home run off Candiotti.

The Tribe bounced back in the bottom of the third inning when Brook Jacoby led off the inning with a single. Seaver walked Tribe catcher Chris Bando. Jacoby advanced to third on a fielder's choice and was driven home by Julio Franco's single. Joe Carter had another base hit, which put runners on second and third with one out. Mel Hall grounded out, but Tony Bernazard hustled home to give the Indians a 2-1 lead.

The Indians extended their lead in both the fourth and fifth innings. An RBI single by Chris Bando and a solo home run by Joe Carter, gave the Indians a 4-1 lead.

The Tribe threatened again in the bottom of the sixth inning. Jacoby and Bando chased Seaver from the game with consecutive singles. Sammy Steward replaced Seaver. He walked the first batter he faced to load the bases. Julio Franco hit into a 6-4-3 double play to end the inning.

Candiotti gave up a double to Marty Barrett and a walk to Jim Rice in the top of the eighth inning. Pat Corrales made the call to the bullpen for closer Ernie Camacho. Camacho walked Don Baylor, which loaded the bases. Dwight Evans singled to drive in a run. Rice scored on a Bill Buckner groundout to cut the Indians' lead to one run.

Camacho returned to pitch the top of the ninth. Rich Gedman hit a double, and the momentum was starting to shift in the Sox' favor. Mike Greenwell hit a grounder to the shortstop and was put out at first. Gedman advanced to third on the play. Wade Boggs lofted a fly into foul territory in left field. Mel Hall tracked down the fly ball, but Romero tagged up and faced home to tie the game.

Bob Stanley came in to pitch the bottom of the ninth for the Sox and he brought his gas can to the mound. Chris Bando drew a walk. Tony Bernazard singled. Julio Franco hit into a fielder's choice, leaving runners at first and second. Joe Carter singled to load the bases. Tribe Manager Pat Corrales called on Andre "Thunder" Thornton to pinch hit. Andre knocked a game-winning single for a 5-4 final score.

Throughout the 1980's, Thornton was one of the most beloved ballplayers in Cleveland. He was a prolific home run hitter and run producer on a team that was often mediocre at best. Thornton played 11 seasons for the Indians, mostly as a DH. During his tenure, the Tribe finished above .500 just three times.

Game 125
August 23, 2011 (First Game)
Shin-Soo Choo Walks It Off After an Earthquake

Game 125 of the 2011 Season was the first game of a day-night doubleheader. The doubleheader was the result of a rainout in an earlier series against the Mariners in May. Justin Masterson was matched up with Blake Beavan for the afternoon contest.

Indians center fielder Kosuke Fukudome started off the scoring in the bottom of the first when he drove in Ezequiel Carrera with an RBI double. The M's evened the score at 1-1 in the second via a Miguel Olivo RBI single.

In the bottom of the third, Shin-Soo Choo was at the plate with two outs when the stadium began to lightly shake and sway. Tom Hamilton remarked, "Boy, the press box here is really shaking. What in the world is going on?" Choo drove a fly ball into the right field gap, which went for a double.

The shaking turned out to be a magnitude 5.9 earthquake centered near Richmond, Virginia. Earthquakes occurring in the eastern United States can generally be felt over a broader distance than those in the west due differences in bedrock geology. Several downtown Cleveland office buildings were evacuated, but the game continued. Choo was left on base when Carlos Santana flied out to end the inning.

After Masterson retired the Mariners in order in the top of the fourth, Fukudome doubled to lead off the Indians' half of the inning. Lonnie Chisenhall gave the Tribe the lead once again when he drove in Fukudome with a single through the left side of the infield.

The Mariners retook the lead in the top of the fifth with a two-out rally. Trayvon Robinson lined a double into left field. Ichiro knocked a single into right, and Robinson came around to score. Always hustling, Ichiro advanced to second on the throw to home. Franklin Gutierrez drove in Ichiro for the go-ahead run.

Fukudome came through again with a single in the bottom of the sixth inning. Lonnie Chisenhall drove one down the right field line.

239

Lonnie was in safely with a double, while Fukudome held at third. Matt LaPorta tied the game with a sacrifice fly.

An inning later, Dan Cortes came on to pitch for Seattle. He issued a leadoff walk to Luis Valbuena. Ezequiel Carrera and Asdrubal Cabrera both flied out. Choo drew a two-out walk to keep the inning alive. Carlos Santana stepped in, and poked a single through the right side of the infield. Valbuena sped home and scored the go-ahead run.

Justin Masterson had pitched a strong 8⅓ innings. When he gave up consecutive singles to Miguel Olivo and Kyle Seager, it was clear his day was done. Closer Chris Perez entered the game.

Instead, of getting the final two outs, Perez allowed Trayvon Robinson to drive a double down the right field line. This scored the runners on first and third, and gave Seattle a 5-4 lead.

Brandon League came on to pitch for the M's in the bottom of the ninth. Ezequiel Carrera lofted a double into the right field gap. Asdrubal Cabrera hit into a fielder's choice, but ended up on second due to a throwing error. Choo stepped in with Carrera and Cabrera at the corners. Choo smashed one over the left field wall to give the Indians their sixth walk-off homer of the year.

The earthquake caused localized damage near its epicenter in Virginia. The most notable damage was found in Washington D.C., where cracks appeared near the top of the Washington Monument. The obelisk was closed for three years while repairs were made.

Choo had returned to the ballpark only two hours before game time on Tuesday. His daughter had been born at Fairview Hospital the prior afternoon. He had not planned to play in the double-header, but with Hafner, Kipnis, Sizemore, and Brantley out for the game the Indians asked if he would be willing to play. "It was up to my wife," Choo said. "She understands the baseball life and told me to go.'

Game 126
August 24, 2017
The Win Streak Begins

Indians were 5.5 games ahead of Minnesota in the Division. Cleveland's 70-56 record was 6.5 games back of Houston for the best in the League. However, they had just suffered two tough losses in which the bats could not get going.

This evening, Trevor Bauer was matched up with Sox' ace Chris Sale. The Tribe got to Sale early and often. Jay Bruce and Brandon Guyer led off the bottom of the second inning with consecutive singles. Yandy Diaz drew a walk to load the bases. Roberto Perez scored Bruce on a line-drive single. Gio Urshela broke his bat on a grounder to shortstop. Sale made a matrix-like move to avoid the biggest shard of bat as it whizzed by his head. Guyer scored and Diaz reached third. Perez was forced out at second while Urshela hustled to first to avoid the double-play.

Francisco Lindor drove in Yandy with a line drive to left. Then, Austin Jackson stepped in and grounded one into the hole between second and third. Rafael Devers ranged over to catch it, but could not complete the throw to first. Jackson reached on the throwing error and Urshela scored the unearned run to put the Tribe up 4-0.

Mitch Moreland took Bauer deep to lead off the top of the third inning, but a greater Red Sox threat did not materialize.

Now up 4-1, Edwin Encarnacion drew a walk to lead off the bottom of the third inning. Sale struck out Jay Bruce on three nasty pitches, then issued another walk to Brandon Guyer. Yandy Diaz smashed a double to deep right field that scored Encarnacion. After Roberto Perez grounded out, Gio Urshela drove in two runs with a timely single into center field. Although Sale struck out Lindor to end the inning, his day was done.

Bauer gave up three runs in the bottom of the fourth. Xander Bogaerts drove in two runs with a triple into the left field corner. A Mitch Moreland single sent Bogaerts in to score. The Sox closed the gap and the score sat at 7 to 4.

The bottom of the order combination struck again in the bottom of the fifth inning. Yandy Diaz singled, Roberto Perez walked, and Gio Urshela dropped a single into left to extend the Indians lead to 8-4.

Jay Bruce uncorked the game's first home run in the bottom of the sixth inning. Yandy Diaz lofted a long fly ball into the right field corner. By the time the Sox tracked it down, Yandy was safe on third. Roberto Perez drove a double into right-center to score Diaz.

Blaine Boyer began the seventh inning pitching for the Red Sox. After a leadoff home run by Francisco Lindor, Boyer loaded the bases. Fernando Abad came in from the bullpen. During the pitching change, Boston made some changes in the field including bringing Rajai Davis off the bench and into left field.

Davis, who had just been acquired by Boston, received a standing ovation from the Progressive Field crowd in recognition of his legendary home run in the 2016 World Series. Later in the inning, Yandy Diaz scored Jose Ramirez on a line drive to right field, but was thrown out to end the inning trying to stretch the hit into another triple.

Despite an eighth inning Sox home run by Mitch Moreland, the Indians cruised to a 13-6 victory. This was the first game in the record-setting win streak of late 2017. Several games within the streak will be featured going forward. This win turned the momentum from those bad beats at the hands of the Red Sox and gave the team renewed energy, especially the bottom of the batting order.

Yandy Diaz finished the game with two doubles, a triple, and four runs scored. Gio Urshela had four RBI on two hits. Roberto Perez went 3 for 4 with two RBI.

On beating up the MLB strikeout-leader Francona said, "I guarantee you our guys aren't like, 'Oh, good, Sale is pitching.' He's had his way with us as all good pitchers do. We have probably done better than most teams against him, but boy, he's good. We've just done a fairly good job against him."

Game 127
August 26, 2016
Guyer Turns Two Hit-by-Pitches into Runs Scored

Nearly 32,000 packed the Ballpark in Arlington to watch the first-place Indians take on the Rangers on this summer Friday night. Corey Kluber was matched up with Martin Perez. Jason Kipnis kicked off the scoring in the top of the third when he punched a grounder into right field that scored Roberto Perez from first.

In the top of the sixth inning, with Mike Napoli on third, Brandon Guyer was struck by Martin Perez' 0-1 pitch. Abe Almonte doubled into deep left center to clear the bases and put the Tribe up 5-0. Roberto Perez singled in Almonte. Dario Alvarez replaced Perez and retired Rajai Davis for the final out of the inning.

Alvarez hit Guyer to lead off the top of the eighth inning. After consecutive singles by Almonte and Perez, Alvarez was replaced by Rangers reliever Keone Kela. Kela hit Rajai Davis with his fourth pitch to drive in Guyer. After a Jason Kipnis pop-fly, Almonte scored on a wild pitch.

In the top of the ninth, Guyer finally got on base by making bat-on-ball contact. He dropped a single into short right field, and later scored on a Roberto Perez single. The Tribe routed the Rangers 12-1 and drew within two games of Texas for the best record in the American League.

The two hit-by-pitches brought Guyer's total on the season to 27. Guyer's plate-crowding stance and high-step with his lead foot resulted in a lot of lower-body bruises. Guyer said, "When it's upper—head or upper body—I'll move. I'll throw my arms up or get out of the way. But lower body, I've always been that way with getting hit. That's how it's been the last three years in the big leagues, and college and the Minor Leagues. It's just instinctual."

August Fragerstrom of Fangraphs ran the numbers and found that Guyer was hit by pitch at a higher rate, in nearly 6% of his at-bats, than any player in modern baseball history.

Game 128
September 13, 1995
Charlie Nagy Out-Duels David Cone

Over 41,000 packed Jacobs Field to see the first-place Tribe take on the hated Yankees on this Wednesday night. Rain delayed the start of the game until nearly 9:00 p.m. Charlie Nagy was matched up with reigning Cy Young-winner David Cone in the final game of the series.

Nagy got out to a slow start, walking both Bernie Williams and catcher Mike Stanley in the first inning. However, he got Darryl Strawberry to strike out swinging and bring the inning to a close.

The powerful Indians offense picked him up almost immediately. Kenny Lofton walked to lead off the Cleveland half of the first inning. With Omar Vizquel at the plate, Lofton stole second. He stole third two pitches later. Omar drove him home with a ground ball double into right field. Manny Ramirez eventually scored Vizquel with a two-out RBI single. Cleveland was on top 2-0 after the first inning.

Lofton was dialed in on the basepaths this evening. After knocking a single to short in the bottom of the second, Lofton swiped second base again. However, he was stranded as Cone struck out Vizquel and Thome.

Nagy retired the next seven batters he faced. His sinker was working beautifully. Eight of the first nine outs were either ground ball outs or strikeouts.

In the bottom of the fifth inning, Albert Belle smashed Cone's 1-1 pitch deep into the Cleveland night. This was the first in a flurry of home runs for Belle. Over the next week, he hit eight home runs, and totaled seventeen dingers in September. This tied the mark for home runs in a calendar month set by Babe Ruth in 1927.

Tony Peña started the two-out rally in the bottom of the sixth inning with a single over the second base bag. Kenny Lofton smashed a double into right field, putting Peña on third. Then, Omar Vizquel punched a grounder through the left side of the infield. Omar's single plated the Indians final two runs of the night.

Nagy continued to cruise through the sixth, seventh, and eighth innings. He gave up only one hit, a double to Don Mattingly in the top of the seventh, that was quickly erased.

Although his pitch count was already at 101 after eight innings, Mike Hargrove sent Nagy back to the mound to pitch the ninth. Bernie Williams grounded out for the fourteenth ground ball out of the game. Paul O'Neill gave Nagy a bit of a scare with a long fly ball to center, but Albert Belle was able to track it down on the warning track for the putout. Mike Stanley worked Nagy into a 2-2 count, but eventually struck out swinging to end the game.

Nagy's final stat line for the complete game shutout was three hits, two walks, and five strikeouts on 115 pitches. After one more win in the final days of the strike-shortened season Charlie finished the regular season 16-6.

Game 129
August 26, 2005
Grady Sizemore Straight-Steals Home

The Indians were north of the border and CC Sabathia was on the mound against the Blue Jays and rookie starter Dustin McGowan.

Grady Sizemore led off the game with a line drive single to center. Coco Crisp tapped one back to the mound and was put out at first, but Sizemore was safe at second. Sizemore advanced to third on a wild pitch before Jhonny Peralta struck out swinging.

Sizemore noticed that McGowan was barely looking at him, let alone checking him back to the base. Pitch by pitch, he took a larger and larger lead as Travis Hafner worked against McGowan.

"Throughout the at-bat, I just kept going farther and farther," Sizemore said. "I wanted to see how much they would let me have before they stopped me. They never did, and I told Skins [Third Base Coach Joel Skinner], 'I can take this.' "

Despite the two-strike count, Sizemore took a broad walking lead and turned it into a sprint to the plate. McGowan finally saw Grady out of the corner of his eye. He rushed his pitch, which ended up coming in high. Catcher Guillermo Quiroz did not even attempt to apply a tag as Sizemore slid into home.

Travis Hafner was as surprised as anyone that Grady would attempt the steal on a two-strike count, "If I had swung and hit Grady in the face, I would have had every woman in America mad at me."

Two pitches later, Hafner sent a home run over the Roger's Center wall. He later joked with Sizemore, "If I end up with 99 RBIs this year, you're off my Christmas list.'"

Later in the inning, Ben Broussard notched an RBI with a line drive to left that scored Victor Martinez. The first inning came to a close with the Tribe up 3-0.

Victor Martinez homered off McGowan in the top of the third.

In the top of the ninth, Travis Hafner cracked his second home run of the game, a two-run shot off Justin Speier that drove in Coco Crisp. Victor Martinez followed with a single to right and then Ronnie Belliard took Speier deep as well.

Sabathia went six innings giving up three runs on six hits. It was not his best outing, but the Indians offense more than covered for any mistakes. Bob Howry faced only seven batters in his two innings of work out of the bullpen. David Riske closed things out by pitching a scoreless ninth inning to preserve the 9-3 victory.

The Indians were on a roll, with an 18-6 record since the end of July. However, they would eventually miss the playoffs after getting swept by the White Sox in the final weekend of the season.

Game 130
August 29, 1977
Duane Kuiper's Only Home Run in 3,379 At-Bats

Tribe pitcher Rick Waits was facing future Cy Young winner and South Euclid native Steve Stone and the White Sox. Just over 6,000 fans were present in Municipal Stadium for this Monday night contest. The White Sox were still battling for the division lead, so ABC had decided to show the game regionally as their Monday Night Baseball feature. The telecast was blacked out in Cleveland due to the poor gate attendance. The start time was moved from 7:30 p.m. to 8:40, and then up to 8:30.

Indians second baseman Duane Kuiper was in his third year in the majors. Kuiper was a solid second baseman, with a .281 batting average. However, he did *not* hit for power.

Waits retired the Sox in order to start the game. Stone struck out the leadoff hitter Paul Dade to start the Indians' half of the inning. Kuiper stepped in and sent Stone's pitch into the empty Municipal Stadium seats in right field.

Kuiper later remembered, "I hit it, and I saw Wayne Nordhagen, the right fielder, running after it, and I saw his number. And I never saw a right fielder's number. I saw him running back, and I said, 'You know what? This is going to go out.'"

The ball bounced off an empty seat and back into the outfield. Nordhagen picked it up and fired it back to the Indians dugout. This was Kuiper's first home run in 1,381 at-bats.

Two batters later, Andre Thornton laced a ball into left field which bounced past the charging left fielder Ritchie Zisk. By the time Zisk tracked it down, Thornton had an inside-the-park home run. Bruce Bochte followed with a powerful homer to deep left field to put the Tribe up 3-0.

Stone complained, "I was told the game was going to start at 8:40 local time, and it started 10 minutes early. I couldn't believe it. I need about 25 minutes to warm up...I wasn't ready to pitch. I had nothing in the first inning."

248

Frank Kendall led off the bottom of the fourth inning by dropping a single into left field. Stone struck out Frank Duffy. Paul Dade grounded one to third. Kendall was forced out at second, but Dade beat the throw to first to avoid the double play. With Kuiper at bat, Dade broke to steal second. Sox catcher Brian Downing sailed the pickoff throw into center field. Chet Lemon could not track down the errant throw. Dade came around to score on the two errors. Kuiper flied out, but not before the score was 5-0, Cleveland.

Eric Soderholm touched up Waits for a solo home run in the top of the fifth inning, but a greater threat did not materialize.

The Tribe added further insurance runs through the middle innings. Paul Dade drove in Ron Pruitt when he dropped a single into left field in the sixth. Andre Thornton crushed a solo homer to deep left field in the seventh. Kuiper drove in Kendall once again with another RBI single to left field. Buddy Bell took advantage of another Chicago error. Frank Duffy came around to score and give the Tribe a 9-1 advantage.

Waits went on to pitch a complete game. Chet Lemon led off the Chicago half of the ninth with a double into left field. Eric Solderholm drove him in with a single, but the Sox came up far short. Waits gave up only two runs on six hits while striking out eight White Sox.

Kuiper ended his night 2 for 5 with his 45th RBI of the season. He went on to play twelve seasons in the majors. The home run in Game 130 of 1977 is his only major league homer in 3,379 at-bats.

Since World War II (post-deadball era), no one is within 1,000 at-bats of Kuiper with only one recorded home run. Woody Woodward had only one in 2,187 at-bats for the Braves and Reds. Al Newman had one homer in 2,107 at-bats for the Expos, Twins, and Rangers. Which leaves Duane Kuiper as the undisputed king of *not* hitting home runs.

Game 131
August 31, 1999
10-Run Eighth Inning Comeback

The Indians were 20 games up on the White Sox and absolutely running away with the Central Division. Cleveland had an 80-51 record. The visiting Angels were playing less than .400 baseball.

Despite the disparity in their season records, the Angels got out ahead of the Tribe early. Orlando Palmiero doubled off Indians starter Dwight Gooden to lead off the game. After a sac bunt moved him to third, Garret Anderson knocked a single through the right side of the infield to put the Angels up 1-0.

Jim Thome tied things up in the bottom of the second with a solo home run off Angels starter (and future Tribe ace) Chuck Finley. An inning later, Manny Ramirez plated two runs with a single into center field. The Indians led 3-1, but soon would face a big deficit.

Troy Glaus tied things up with a 2-run homer off Gooden in the top of the fourth inning. Glaus went yard again in the top of the sixth, this time off reliever Steve Reed. The Angels added some more runs in the top of the seventh by way of a two-run blast by Jim Edmunds. The top of the eighth inning saw another five runs from the Halos. Going into the bottom of the eighth the score was 12-4 Anaheim.

Mark Petkovsek replaced Finley on the mound in the bottom of the eighth inning. Alex Ramirez knocked a single through the left side of the infield to lead things off. Jim Thome followed with a line drive double that put Ramirez on third. Richie Sexson cleared the bases with another single up the middle. David Justice and Enrique Wilson also singled to load the bases for catcher Einar Diaz.

Petkovsek was pulled from the game in favor of Shigetoshi Hasegawa. Petkovsek allowed two runs on five hits and did not record an out. Hasegawa recorded two quick outs on pop flies by Diaz and Dave Roberts. Omar Vizquel stepped in with the bases loaded and two out. He singled to left to score Sexson and cut the Angels lead to 12-6. Troy Perceval came on to replace Hasegawa. Robbie Alomar followed with a line drive into short right field which plated two runs. Robbie stole second with Harold Baines at the plate. Harold Baines plated two more runs with a single into right field. Jim Thome drew a walk and moved Baines over into scoring position. With the tying run now at second, Manager Mike Hargrove called on Carlos Baerga to pinch run for the aging Baines who was in his 20th season.

Percival's third pitch to Richie Sexson skipped away from Angels catcher Benjie Molina. Baerga and Thome moved up 90 feet on the wild pitch. Sexson rocked Percival's 1-2 pitch deep into the bleachers in left-center. The three-run homer put the Tribe up 14-12.

Percival plunked David Justice in the side. Justice threw his helmet as he charged the mound. The helmet hit Percival, triggering a bench-clearing altercation. Troy Glaus tackled Justice to the infield, while Molina held back Percival.

After the fight and the resulting ejections, the Indians' lineup was a bit unorthodox. Pitcher Charles Nagy came in to pinch run for David Justice. He was forced out at second on an Enrique Wilson grounder to end the inning.

In the top of the ninth, Paul Shuey came on to pitch and Omar Vizquel moved to right field. He never had the opportunity to record a right field put-out as Shuey retired Troy Glaus and Jeff Huson with consecutive strikeouts. Jim Edmonds and Orlando Palmero hit back-to-back singles to put the tying run aboard, but Shuey got Todd Green to ground out to end the game.

This was the third time in 1999 that the Indians rallied from an 8-run or greater deficit to win. This season of comebacks is unmatched in MLB history.

Game 132

August 29, 2007

Indians Beat Reigning Cy Young Winner Four Times in a Season

This Wednesday night matchup was billed as a faceoff between two pitching titans. Although it became a classic, the path was not exactly straight. Johan Santana was the 2006 Cy Young winner and had mowed down major league lineups for years. However, the Indians had beat him three times already in 2007, mostly with home runs.

Santana came into Progressive Field with a 14-10 record. Sabathia entered the game with a 15-7 record. Both were on the American League All-Star squad earlier in the summer.

Sabathia struggled a bit in the early going. He faced six Twins in the first inning, but managed to get out of the jam without giving up a run.

Grady Sizemore led off the Indians' half of the first with a single. Hitting second, the rookie Asdrubal Cabrera deposited Santana's 3-1 pitch just over the 19-foot wall in left for his second major league homer. After a Travis Hafner groundout, Victor Martinez put one on the home run porch in left field. Ryan Garko grounded out to third. Franklin Gutierrez scorched a ground ball double into left field. He was driven in by a Kenny Lofton single. Casey Blake grounded out to end the inning, but it was quickly 4-0 Tribe.

Although Santana struggled with his velocity, he did not allow more than one hit per inning until he was pulled in the sixth after 104 pitches. He did record his 200th strikeout of the season.

Sabathia held the Twins scoreless until the top of the fifth inning, when Torii Hunter drove in Jason Tyner to end the shutout. Sabathia went six innings giving up two runs on seven hits and two walks. Jensen Lewis came on to pitch the seventh and retired the Twins in order.

Rafael Betancourt pitched the eighth inning for the Tribe. Mike Redmond touched him up for one run, driving in Rondell white who had previously doubled.

Closer Joe Borowski put the tying run on base when Jason Tyner knocked a single through the right side of the infield, but a pop-foul and a game-ending double play took care of the Twins.

This was the fourth time in the season that the Tribe had handed Santana a loss. The following Monday in Minnesota, Sabathia and Santana would face off again. The Indians had Johan's number again with a 5-0 victory in Game 137. Overall on the season, the Tribe were 14-4 against the Twins and 5-0 against the reigning Cy Young winner.

Game 133
August 31, 2004
Omar Notches Six Hits in Historic 22-0 Rout of the Yankees

A sellout crowd of over 51,000 packed Yankee Stadium for this Tuesday night tilt between Jake Westbrook and Javier Vazquez. The Indians were just above .500 and were trailing the Twins by seven games in the Central. The Yankees were leading the AL East, but their record had suffered throughout the month of August and doubt was starting to creep into the clubhouse and owner's suite.

Coco Crisp flied out to center to start the game. Omar Vizquel dropped a single into the right field gap. Matt Lawton got aboard, and Victor Martinez drew a walk to load the bases. Travis Hafner hit a bases-clearing triple to put the Tribe up 3-0.

In the top of the second, Ronnie Belliard bounced one over the wall for a ground rule double. After Jody Gerut drew a walk, Vizquel singled for his second hit of the game. Belliard came around to score and make it 4-0 Tribe. After Matt Lawton drove in another run with a single to right, Vazquez left the mound to a chorus of boos. This 1⅓ inning was the shortest outing of his career as a starter.

In the top of the third, the Indians scored another three runs including two by way of a Vizquel double. This was his third hit of the game, and perhaps should have been an out. Kenny Lofton, at this point with the Yankees, misplayed the ball, which hit off the top of the center field wall.

Westbrook retired the first eleven Yankee batters, including strikeouts of Bernie Williams, Jorge Posada, and John Olerud, on his first trip through the lineup. The Yankees were looking at a nine-run deficit before Gary Sheffield doubled into left field for New York's first hit.

Yankee reliever Tanyon Sturtz found his command in the fourth inning and retired the Indians side in order. However; the Indians offense broke out again in the top of the fifth. Broussard and Belliard hit consecutive doubles to lead off the inning. Coco Crisp jacked a two-run homer off Sturtz. Omar lobbed a single into the left field gap (4 for 4 at this point). Sturtz was pulled in favor of C.J. Nitkowski.

Nitkowski gave up another three runs, and the Indians were ahead 15-0.

Jody Gerut drew a walk to lead off the top of the sixth inning. Coco Crisp grounded one sharply to the shortstop who put Gerut out at third. The speedy Crisp beat the throw to first to avoid the double play. Nitkowski's first pitch to Omar skipped away from the catcher, and Crisp advanced on the wild pitch. Omar added his fifth hit of the game with a double into left field. Crisp came around to score and give the Tribe the sixteen-run lead.

Esteban Loaiza came on to pitch the top of the seventh and would stay on for the final three innings of the game. He held the Tribe scoreless in the seventh. In the top of the eighth, Omar slapped a single through Loaiza's legs and into center field. This was his record-tying sixth hit in a nine-inning game.

After John McDonald grounded out to lead off the top of the ninth inning, Josh Phelps and Ronnie Belliard hit consecutive singles. Jody Gerut stepped in and launched Loaiza's 2-0 pitch into the seats. After Coco Crisp walked, Omar had an opportunity to claim his sole place in the record-books. He hit a liner sharply down the right-field line, but his old teammate Kenny Lofton was there to track it down. Since 1901, one hundred and two players have collected six hits in a nine-inning game. No one has ever recorded the seventh.

Ryan Ludwick knocked a two-out single into center to advance Crisp to third, and Victor Martinez stepped in. Victor smashed Loaiza's first pitch over the wall for the sixth run of the inning. Travis Hafner struck out to end the inning with the score 22-0.

Jeremy Guthrie retired the Yankees in order to put a finish to the most lopsided shutout since 1900, and the most runs allowed by the Yankees at home *ever*. The loss far overshadowed the franchise's two past 18-run defeats: June 17, 1925 against the Tigers and against the Indians in League Park in Game 101 of the 1928 Season (see page 191). With this win, the Indians were back above .500 with a 67-66 record.

Yankees owner George Steinbrenner watched the record-breaking beatdown. He then refused to answer questions before leaving the ballpark.

The New York fans and media were in full panic mode, as the Red Sox were surging in the standings while the Yankees suffered an August collapse. This loss brought the Sox within 3 ½ games of the AL East lead. However, Alex Rodriguez quipped, "The way Cleveland played tonight, we'd better worry about Cleveland, not about Boston."

In the end, the Indians finished 80-82 for the year. They ended up third in the Central Division. The Yankees finished 101-61 and won the Eastern Division. Of course, the Yankees eventually lost to the Red Sox in the ALCS. The Sox went on to win their first World Series in 86 years. So, it was Boston everyone had to worry about all along.

Game 134
September 2, 2006
Kevin Kouzmanoff Hits Grand Slam on First Pitch in the Majors

Both the Indians and Rangers were playing out the string by September of 2006. Cliff Lee was matched up with Edison Volquez for this Saturday night contest. Despite the lack of playoff implications, the 40,000+ at Ameriquest Field in Arlington were treated to something that had never happened before in MLB history.

Grady Sizemore led off the game with a home run. Left fielder Jason Michaels singled to left. After a fly-out by Victor Martinez and a Ryan Garko strikeout, Michaels stole second with Casey Blake at the plate. Blake eventually walked. Volquez then walked Jhonny Peralta to load the bases.

This brought up Kevin Kouzmanoff. He had been hitting nearly .380 at AA Akron and AAA Buffalo throughout 2006. The Indians' top prospect had been called up to the big-league team at approximately 10:00 p.m. the night before. Kouzmanoff's family had scrambled to make it to Texas from his hometown in Colorado.

Kouzmanoff stepped in against Volquez and crushed the first pitch he faced to center field into the batter's eye lawn. He was the first player ever to hit a grand slam on his first major league swing. Only two players had hit grand slams in their first at-bat: Bill Duggleby for the Phillies in 1898, and Jeremy Hermida for the Marlins in 2005. Second baseman Hector Luna popped out to end the frame with the Indians up 5-0.

In the top of the second, Grady Sizemore poked a ground ball single into center field. Jason Michaels sent one into left, which advanced Sizemore to third. Victor Martinez lofted a fly ball to left field. Grady tagged up and scored on the sacrifice fly. From this point on, the game would be in the hands of the Tribe pitching staff.

Cliff Lee gave up two runs on two hits in the bottom of the second, and another two runs on three hits in the bottom of the sixth. Overall, Lee pitched seven strong innings, giving up four runs on seven hits and striking out four Rangers.

The Rangers threatened to spoil Kouzmanoff's record-setting night in the bottom of the ninth. Gerald Laird got aboard with a bunt single against reliever Tom Mastny. Mastny gave up a double to Ian Kinsler that put Laird on third. Nelson Cruz grounded out for the first out of the inning. Gary Matthews hit a line drive single into the right field that scored Laird easily. Kinsler attempted to score from second to tie the game, but was gunned down by a great throw from Casey Blake to Victor Martinez at the plate. Michael Young lined one back to Mastny who caught it for the final out.

Three Indians have hit a home run in their first Major League at-bat. Earl Averill did it on April 16, 1929. He ended his career with 238 homers, which places him fourth in franchise history. Like Kouzmanoff, Jay Bell's debut homer on September 29, 1986 was on the first pitch he saw. It happened to come from Hall of Famer Bert Blyleven.

Kouzmanoff played 16 games for the Indians before being traded to San Diego after the 2006 season. In 2010, Daniel Nava joined Kouz in the first-pitch grand slam record book.

Game 135
September 5, 1992
Matchup with the Mariners Prefigures Some of the Greatest Matchups of the 90's

The 1992 Indians were 62-73 and dead last in the American League East. The only team with a worse record were the Mariners at 56-80. Both teams were in the midst of decades-long rebuilding programs. The Indians had not made the playoffs since 1954, and the Mariners had their first winning season in franchise history in 1991, with a record of 83-79.

However, both teams had some rising stars who would later become some of the biggest figures in baseball. This late-season series between two basement dwellers prefigured some of the highest-profile matchups of the mid-1990's.

Charlie Nagy was matched up with Randy Johnson for the Saturday afternoon matchup on the lakefront. Randy Johnson was tall, and he could throw a fastball, but he was not yet "The Big Unit." In fact, he led the league in walks in 1990, 1991, and 1992.

Ken Griffey Junior blasted Nagy's 2-1 pitch deep to right-center to lead off the top of the second inning with a home run. Nagy issued a four-pitch walk to Tino Martinez, but Tino was cut down attempting to steal second. Jay Buhner poked a single into center field, but Henry Cotto grounded into an inning-ending double play. Nagy had his sinker working. He got out of both the second and fourth innings on ground ball double-plays.

In the top of the fifth, Mariner's catcher David Valle sent a line drive over the wall in left to make it 2-0 Mariners.

The Indians jumped ahead in the bottom of the fifth inning. Brook Jacoby drew a leadoff walk. Junior Ortiz smashed a ground ball through the left side of the infield for a single. Kenny Lofton laid down a bunt, but Seattle catcher Dave Valle tracked it down and fired to third to force out Jacoby. Felix Fermin worked Johnson into a full count, and then drew a walk.

With the bases loaded, Carlos Baerga lined one past the second baseman. Ortiz and Lofton came around to score the tying runs. Then, Albert Belle dropped one in over the third baseman's head. Albert raced into second base as Fermin and Baerga scored to give the Tribe a 4-2 lead.

After consecutive walks in the sixth inning, Mike Hargrove called for reliever Kevin Wickander to face the young All-Star Ken Griffey, Jr. Wickander walked Griffey to load the bases, and then walked Tino Martinez on four pitches to cut the Indians lead to one run. Jay Buhner tied the game at four runs apiece with a sacrifice fly.

Randy Johnson pitched 7⅔ innings, struck out eight Indians and walked seven. Jeff Nelson came in to match up with Paul Sorrento. He recorded the final out of the eighth inning.

The Indians then faced Russ Swan in the bottom of the ninth. After a Kenny Lofton groundout, Swan walked Felix Fermin. Carlos Baerga slapped a single through the left side of the infield that put the speedy Fermin on third.

Wayne Kirby came on to pinch run for Fermin and Albert Belle came to the plate. Belle punched one past the shortstop and into the outfield. Kirby came home to score the winning run.

Albert was 3 for 5 on the day with 3 RBI and a stolen base. He was coming into his own as one of the AL's premier hitters. He would go on to lead the league in RBIs in 1993, 1995 (when he was robbed of the MVP), and 1996.

Late in the 1992 season, Randy Johnson met Nolan Ryan during a series against the Rangers. Ryan suggested a slight change to Randy's delivery that he credits with giving him greater control. For the next four years, Johnson led the league in strikeouts. He became a fixture in big matchups with the Indians. He was the Mariners Opening Day starter in 1994 when the Tribe opened up Jacobs Field. He also started Game Three of the 1995 ALCS, which the Mariners took 5-2.

Game 136
September 3, 2017
Jose Ramirez Five Extra-Base Hits

The Indians entered this game riding a ten-game win streak. The Tribe had a nine-game lead in the division and were wrapping up a weekend series in Detroit against the lowly Tigers. Josh Tomlin was set to pitch against recent call-up Chad Bell.

In the top of the first, Jose Ramirez stepped in against Bell with two outs. He lined the 3-1 pitch to deep left field where it hit the yellow line at the top of the wall. Mikie Matouk jumped and attempted to catch the live ball, but ended up tipping it over the wall and out for a home run.

Yandy Diaz and Brandon Guyer hit consecutive singles in the top of the second to set up Roberto Perez. Perez sent a ground ball single past third base which allowed Yandy to score. Bell walked Greg Allen on six pitches. Francisco Lindor hit a sharp grounder to second base. Ian Kinsler flipped it to Jose Iglesias for the force out at second, but Guyer was able to score. The Indians had a 3-0 lead in the early going.

After recording the first two outs in the bottom of the second, Tomlin gave up three consecutive singles to Candelario, McCann, and Jacoby Jones. Jones' single plated Candelario to cut the Indians lead to 3-1.

Ramirez lined another double into the left field gap to lead off the top of the third inning. He advanced to third on an Encarnacion groundout and then scored on a fielder's choice off the bat of Carlos Santana.

Austin Jackson led off the top of the fifth inning with a ground ball single back up the middle. Ramirez doubled down the left field line. Bell walked Edwin Encarnacion while Zac Reininger was warming up in the bullpen. Reininger took the mound and got Carlos Santana to line out to second base. With the bases still loaded, Yandy Diaz hit a liner through the middle of the infield. Jackson came around to score and made the game 5-1, Cleveland.

In the top of the sixth, after a Greg Allen strikeout, Lindor sent a solo homer to deep right field. Austin Jackson followed with a single to left. Jose Ramirez stepped to the plate and sent a laser shot toward the right field corner. Again, it just cleared the wall and bounced off the railing for Jose's second home run of the game.

Nick Goody replaced Tomlin to get the final out of the sixth inning and then pitched a 1-2-3 seventh. Tomlin gave up only one run on six hits over his 5⅔ innings.

Jose led off the top of the eighth with his third double of the game. It was a well hit ball that bounced behind Jacoby Jones and off the wall in dead center field. Only nine other players have recorded five extra-base hits in a nine-inning game. The list includes two other Indians. Lou Boudreau in Game 81 of 1946, when he hit a homer and slapped four doubles in a loss at Fenway. Kelly Shoppach hit two homers and three triples in a 14-12 loss to the Tigers in Game 106 of 2008.

Gio Urshela came in to pinch run for Ramirez. He never had the opportunity to try for a sixth extra base hit and sole possession of the record. Encarnacion doubled to drive in Urshela and make it a 9-1 game.

The Indians added another two runs and cruised to an 11-1 victory. Jose had 14 total bases. He was just one short of Lonnie Chisenhall's club record set in Game 64 of 2014 (see page 125). This win was the eleventh of the streak that began with Game 126 (see page 241).

Honorable Mention
September 24, 1903 - Bill Bradley Hits for the Cycle

In a 12-2 victory over the Washington Senators, third baseman Bill Bradley hit for the cycle with an extra double. One of the finest hitters of the deadball era, Bradley's accomplishments are largely lost to history but he is remembered as one of the luminaries of early Cleveland baseball along with Nap Lajoie, Addie Joss, and Elmer Flick.

Game 137
September 5, 1969 (First Game)
Rare Walk-off Win for One of the All-Time Worst Teams

The 1969 Cleveland Indians are regarded by many as the worst Indians team of all time. At this point in September, they were 39 games off the pace behind division-leading Baltimore. They were not re-building, so much as they were just bad. The last time the Tribe had finished within striking distance of a playoff spot was a second-place finish in 1959 and the next time they would finish in second was 1994. Although other teams lost more games, the 1969 team was almost entirely forgettable.

The Yankees came to town for a weekend series. It included a Friday double-header to make up for an earlier game that was cancelled by rain. The pitching matchup for game one was quite promising for two bad teams. Sam McDowell would face Mel Stottlemyre of the Yankees.

Indians catcher Duke Sims drove in centerfielder Russ Snyder for an RBI single in the bottom of the first. He gave the Tribe the early lead.

Horace Clark led off the sixth inning for the Yankees with a double into left field. Gene Michael grounded out to second and Clark had to stay put. Roy White added a single that moved Clark to third base. Frank Fernandez lofted a fly ball to deep left field. Clark tagged and scored to tie things up 1-1.

McDowell scattered nine hits, almost evenly throughout the game. He got out of a bases-loaded jam in the top of the eighth by getting a key groundout from Joe Pepitone. He struck out five and walked only two. Likewise, Stottlemyre gave up eight hits and three walks through the first eight innings, but the Indians were not able to take advantage of most of those opportunities.

That changed in the bottom of the ninth when first baseman Russ Nagelson singled to center to lead off the inning. Steve Hargan came in to pinch run for Nagelson. Eddie Leon laid down a solid sacrifice bunt to move Hargan over to second. Third baseman Lou

Camilli grounded out to first, and Hargan was safe on third with two outs.

So far, the Indians were two for seven with runners in scoring position, and the few fans scattered throughout Muni Stadium probably thought that Hargan would be stranded like the nine Indians baserunners before him.

Ken Harrelson came on to pinch hit for McDowell. He was intentionally walked by Stottlemyre. That brought up Jose Cardenal who had replaced Snyder in center field. Cardenal slapped a single into left field to bring home Hargan and win the game.

They would go on to lose the second half of the double-header and 99 games on the season, but this walk-off win was a bright spot for the Tribe. However miserable the 1969 team may have been, they don't touch the Cleveland Spiders, who went 20-138 in their final year in the National League in 1899.

Game 138
September 6, 1986
Joe Carter 5 Hits, 5 Runs Scored

Greg Swindell was matched up with Juan Nieves of the Brewers for this Saturday game in a weekend series in Milwaukee. The Brewers were a mess in the early going.

The Indians scored seven runs on seven hits and three errors in the top half of the first inning. The parade of hits included a double by Joe Carter, and RBI singles by Julio Franco, Pat Tabler, Brook Jacoby, and Andy Allanson. After Allanson's single, the Brewers had seen enough, and Nieves was removed from the mound after only ⅓ of an inning. Mark Knudsen got the final two outs of the inning.

Swindell retired the Brewers in order in the bottom of the first, and reliever Mark Knudson was back on the mound before he could catch his breath. He gave up a leadoff single to Julio Franco, and then Joe Carter drove one over the wall in right center. Carter's homer extended the Indians lead to 9-0.

Carter led off the top of the fourth with a single to left. Pat Snyder moved him over with his double down the right field line. Knudson intentionally walked Brook Jacoby to load the bases and set up a possible double play. Carmelo Castillo grounded one to second base. Jim Gantner fielded it and flipped to Ernie Riles for the force out at second. Carter came in to score as Castillo beat the throw to first. Andy Allanson lined out to end the inning, but not before the Tribe were up 10 runs to none.

In the top of the fifth, Knudson retired Tony Bernazard and Brett Butler quickly. Julio Franco reached on a line drive single to left. Joe Carter stepped in and once again cranked a two-run home run that put the Indians up by a dozen runs.

The Brewers finally got to Swindell in the bottom of the fifth inning. They scored two runs on three hits, cutting the Indians lead to 12-2.

The Tribe notched another four runs on four hits in the top of the sixth inning including homers by Jacoby and Bernazard. After

Bernazard's homer, Mark Knudson's day was finished. Tim Leary came on in relief for Milwaukee.

Swindell gave up a home run to Dale Sveum to lead off the bottom of the sixth inning, and was soon replaced on the mound by Don Schulze. The Indians bullpen was less effective than Swindell had been. Schulze, Bryan Oelkers, and Rich Yett combined to give up four runs on five hits over the final four innings including a three-run home run by Jim Gantner in the bottom of the sixth.

Joe Carter led off the top of the seventh with his second double of the day. He came around to score on a Cory Snyder single. Milwaukee reliever Tim Leary got Carter to strike out, looking to end the Indians half of the eighth. The Tribe went on to win 17 to 9 in a sloppy game that featured 34 hits and seven errors.

Carter's four RBIs put him at 100 for the year. He would go on to lead the MLB with 121 RBIs for the season. This was the third time in 1986 he collected five hits in a game.

Game 139
September 4, 1996
Chad Ogea Complete Game on 104 Pitches

The dominant Indians were visiting County Stadium in Milwaukee for a midweek series. The first-place Indians were 15 games ahead of the Brewers in the AL Central standings at this point, but the Tribe were looking for redemption.

Cleveland lost the opening game of the series in walk-off fashion. Jose Mesa gave up the tying run on a wild pitch and then gave up a game-winning single to Jose Valentin. The night before, Orel Hershiser had a rare klunker of an outing and the Indians lost 8-2. Chad Ogea was matched up with Jeff D'Amico for the final contest of the series.

Albert Belle staked Ogea to an early lead with a two-run double in the bottom of the first that scored Kevin Seitzer and Jim Thome. Sandy Alomar led off the bottom of the second inning with a single into right field. After two quick outs, Kenny Lofton made it a 4-0 game when he took D'Amico deep to right field for his thirteenth home run of the year.

Ogea did not allow a baserunner until the bottom of the fourth when Dave Nilsson poked a single into right field. John Jaha grounded out to end the inning.

Brewers reliever Ramon Garcia gave up a single to Kenny Lofton to lead off the top of the seventh inning. Then, he hit Kevin Seitzer with the 0-1 pitch. Ron Villone replaced Garcia on the mound. Jim Thome stepped in and launched Villone's very first pitch out of the park into deep left center. Thome's homer put the Indians up 7-0.

Ogea had worked very efficiently. Coming into the bottom of the ninth he had given up only four hits and one walk on 97 pitches. He got Dave Nelson to fly out on the 0-1 pitch. John Jaha grounded out on Ogea's 100th pitch of the night. It took him four pitches to retire Jose Valentin on a fly ball to right and complete the shutout. Although he missed the Maddux by a few pitches, it was probably Ogea's finest pitching performance of his six-year career.

Game 140
September 8, 2017
The Streak Reaches 15 Games, Local Promotion Pays Out Big

Local business promotions have been a part of baseball since the dawn of the game. Marketing agencies and the teams themselves constantly look for ways to integrate advertising into the game, the stadium, and the broadcast. In 2017, Universal Windows Direct, a local home remodeling company, was getting set to celebrate its 15th anniversary. In 2016, on the way to the division win and eventually the World Series, the Tribe rattled off 14 wins in a row from Game 66 to Game 79.

Universal Windows Direct concocted a promotion such that any work purchased during the month of July would be refunded in full if the Indians went on a 15-game win streak between August 1st and the end of the season.

SCA Promotions is a Dallas-based company that underwrites promotional contests and sweepstakes. They constructed an actuarial model to calculate the likelihood of a 15-game win streak and accounted for Universal's July sales totals. Universal paid approximately $75,000 to insure themselves against the possible payout.

Beginning with Game 126 on August 24th, the Tribe got on a roll and stayed red hot. Corey Kluber was matched up with White Sox starter Mike Pelfrey for a Thursday night contest on the south side of Chicago that would make or break the summer for over 220 Universal Windows Direct customers.

Francisco Lindor led off the game with a triple. Austin Jackson drove him in with a double to center. Yandy Diaz walked, and then Edwin Encarnacion gave the parrot a ride after a 3-run bomb over the left field wall. The Indians stranded runners on first and third but still closed out the inning with a 4-0 lead.

Kluber was not sharp early. In the bottom of the first, he gave up home runs to Yolmer Sanchez and Jose Abreu which cut the Indians' lead in half.

268

Lindor led off the top of the second with another home run blast and Erik Gonzales took Pelfrey deep for a two-run shot in the top of the third.

Kluber settled in and went seven innings in total, striking out 13 and giving up only two runs on three hits. Greg Allen added to the Tribe lead in the top of the seventh with his own home run.

Kluber handed the game off to Shawn Armstrong who pitched a 1-2-3 eighth inning.

Erik Gonzales hit his second home run of the evening in the top of the ninth off reliever Rob Brantley,

Craig Breslow walked Yoan Moncada to lead off the bottom of the ninth, but then Jose Abreu hit into a 6-4-3 double play. Breslow struck out Nicky Delmonico to end the game.

The Indians 11-2 victory kicked off quite a party back at Progressive Field where a group of Universal Windows customers had gathered for a watch party. SCA was set to pay out rebates totaling over $1.7 Million to over 200 customers.

The Tribe broke their own year-old franchise record for consecutive wins and finished the day 5½ games up on the White Sox in the Central Division. They had their sights set on the 20-game win streak set by the Moneyball A's in 2002.

Game 141
September 28, 1995
Dennis Martinez Breaks Kirby Puckett's Jaw

Dennis Martinez signed with the Indians prior to the 1994 season. He had eighteen years of major league experience under his belt. Martinez was the first native Nicaraguan to play in Major League Baseball. Prior to 1994, he had found lasting success with both the Orioles and Expos, pitched a perfect game, and overcome alcoholism. "El Presidente" was already among the seven pitchers to record 100 wins in both the American and National Leagues.

He had taken the mound for the Tribe on Opening Day both in 1994 against Randy Johnson in Game One at Jacobs Field and again on Opening Day 1995.

The Indians had clinched their first playoff berth in a generation in Game 123 of 1995 (see page 235), and were tuning up for the ALDS as the strike-shortened season was coming to a close.

Martinez took the mound for a getaway Thursday game in Minneapolis against Frankie Rodriguez. The start of the game was rocky for El Presidente. He hit Chuck Knoblauch with the game's second pitch.

Two batters later, Martinez lost his grip on another one. The second wild pitch struck future Hall of Famer Kirby Puckett square in the jaw. Chuck Knoblauch later said, "He did his leg kick and then he just froze. It's almost like he didn't see it or something. He didn't really turn his head."

After Puckett was taken off the field, Marty Cordova drove in Knoblauch to give the Twins a 1-0 lead.

Rodriguez plunked Albert Belle with the first pitch of the second inning. Eddie Murray dropped a single into left field to put runners at the corners for Jim Thome. Thome doubled in Belle, and Murray advanced to third. Manny Ramirez followed with a line drive single into the gap that plated another two runs. That gave Cleveland a 3-1 advantage.

A two-run home run by Matt Lawton tied things up at 3-3 for a time, but the Indians would pull ahead in the top of the fifth inning and not look back. Tony Peña and Kenny Lofton hit consecutive singles to lead off the fifth. Alvaro Espinoza moved them over with an effective sacrifice bunt. Carlos Baerga smashed a grounder to the shortstop. Pat Meares botched the throw to first, and allowed two runs to score.

The Tribe sent ten men to the plate in the top of the seventh inning. They scored five runs on five hits, including homers by Espinoza and Murray.

Ruben Amaro added two more in the top of the ninth inning when he drove in Brian Giles and Herbert Perry with a double into the left field gap. The team's joy in the 12-4 victory was tempered by concern for Puckett.

After the game, Martinez remarked that he had considered asking Manager Mike Hargrove to take him out of the game. "It's the worst I've ever felt in my life. Because when I knocked him down, it did not hit him in the helmet, it hit him right in the face. I felt like the lowest man in baseball when I was on the mound."

Puckett had played 12 seasons for the Twins without ever spending time on the disabled list. His jawbone was broken, and he missed the remainder of the 1995 season. In the off-season he was diagnosed with glaucoma. The rapid degradation of his eyesight ended his major league career. Although the hit-by-pitch injury was unrelated, this episode was a somewhat unfitting end for one of the most beloved figures of 1990's baseball.

Despite the drama of the first inning, Martinez had quite a year. At age 40, he recorded a 3.08 ERA. That figure has not been matched by any Indians starting pitcher save for Cliff Lee's Cy Young season in 2008. His 245 career wins held the mark for most by a Latin-born pitcher until he was surpassed by Bartolo Colon in 2018.

Game 142
September 20, 1929
Joe Sewell's Consecutive Strikeout-less Streak Ends

Joe Sewell was signed to the Indians in 1920 to replace Ray Chapman at shortstop after he died as the result of a hit by pitch. On arrival in Cleveland, first baseman George Burns gave him a black forty-ounce bat. Sewell cared for that bat, never broke it, and used "Black Betsy" for his entire major league career. He quickly got up to speed and helped the Tribe win the 1920 World Series.

On this Friday afternoon in 1929, the Indians were visiting Fenway Park. Ken Halloway took the bump for the Indians against Danny MacFayden. Sewell, who had a legendary eye at the plate had last struck out in Game 27 back on May 19th.

Holloway and MacFayden dueled through four scoreless innings. In the top of the fifth Sewell flied out to lead off the inning. Johnny Hodapp singled to center. Joe's brother, catcher Luke Sewell, singled into right and advanced to second on a throwing error. Ken Halloway walked to load the bases and Dick Porter drove in Hodapp with a sacrifice fly.

Earl Averill walked to lead off the Indians' half of the sixth inning. Lew Fonseca singled into right to advance Averill to second base. Left fielder Ed Morgan popped one foul and was put out by the Sox catcher. Joe Sewell stepped in against MacFayden, and struck out.

It was the first time that Sewell had gone down on strikes in 115 games, or 516 plate appearances. Sewell benefitted from incredible vision and quick processing. He claimed that he was able to see his bat strike the ball.

The Tribe recovered from the shock of Sewell's strike-out, as Johnny Hodapp drove in two with a double down the left field line to put the Tribe up 3-0.

Holloway allowed a single by Phil Todt in the bottom of the sixth, but quickly erased it with a 6-4-3 double play.

Indians right fielder Dick Porter hit one into the right field corner and stretched it into a triple in the top of the seventh inning. Jackie

272

Tavener plated Porter with a single into right field. The Indians had a 4-0 lead.

The Sox would score in the bottom of the seventh and eighth innings, but the Indians' four runs stood up. Wes Ferrell took over for Holloway with one out in the bottom of the eighth and carried the Tribe to an eventual 4-2 victory.

Sewell's strikeout-less streak is one of baseball's hallowed records that seem unlikely ever to be broken. Mookie Betts made news when his strikeout-less streak ended at 129 plate appearances in 2017.

Sewell was so talented at making contact that he averaged just ten strike-outs per season for his career. From 1925 to 1930 he struck out only 33 times while playing every game of the season. While still 1,000 games behind Cal Ripken and Lou Gehrig, Sewell's consecutive games played streak of 1,103 is good for seventh in MLB history. In his fourteen-year career with the Indians and Yankees, no pitcher ever struck out Joe Sewell more than four times.

Game 143
September 30, 1995
Albert Belle Has First Ever 50/50 Season

The strike-shortened 1995 season was quickly coming to a close. The Royals were in town for the final weekend of the regular season. Mark Clark took the hill against Dave Fleming on a beautiful fall Saturday afternoon in front of a sellout crowd.

Clark and Fleming carried their teams through the early innings until Tony Peña hit a comebacker to the mound with one out in the top of the third. Fleming left the game and Melvin Bunch took the mound for Kansas City.

In the top of the sixth inning, the Royals finally broke through when Brent Mayne smacked a line drive double into center field on Clark's first pitch. Two batters later, Tom Goodwin deposited a home run into the bullpen giving Kansas City a 2-0 lead.

Kenny Lofton led off the bottom of the sixth inning with a perfectly placed bunt single and then stole second base. Omar Vizquel flied out to deep right field, allowing Lofton to tag and advance to third. Carlos Baerga grounded to short. He was put out at first while Lofton came around to score.

Next up was Albert Belle. Albert was one of the most fearsome power hitters of the mid-1990's and had risen to legend status in Cleveland for both his prodigious power hitting and his fiery temper. Belle smashed Bunch's 2-2 pitch over the left-field home run porch and through the stadium gates onto Eagle Avenue.

Belle's homer was his 50th of the season, and marked the first and only time a player recorded 50 homers and 50 doubles in the same year. The solo blast tied the game at 2-2.

Mike Hargrove turned the game over to the bullpen to start the seventh inning. Chad Ogea pitched a 1-2-3 seventh. Erik Plunk retired the Royals in order in the eighth. Jose Mesa walked Tom Goodwin in the ninth, but escaped with the tie intact. Alan Embree allowed a single by Juan Samuel to lead off the tenth, but promptly squashed the threat.

274

Backup catcher Jesse Levins led off the bottom of the tenth inning by slapping a double into center field. Jeromy Burnitz came in to pinch run for Levins. The Royals intentionally walked Kenny Lofton. Omar Vizquel laid down a sacrifice bunt that advanced Burnitz to third. Carlos Baerga dropped the game-winning single into center for the Tribe's twelfth and final walk-off win of the regular season.

I remember this game playing on a small black and white TV in our walk-out basement. I was helping my father with fall yard work and we ran inside each time Albert came to bat to wait for history to be made on Channel 43. After Albert hit the home run, dad and I toasted with a 50/50 soda.

Todd Helton had a 54 double 49 home run season in 2001. This is the closest that any player has come to completing the feat. It is important to note that Helton played in 159 games that year, versus Belle's 143 appearances in strike-shortened 1995.

Belle was known to feud with the media. It was a clear rebuke from the baseball writers when Mo Vaughn won the 1995 MVP award. Vaughn had a strong season, but did not approach the historic stat line that Belle generated in 1995. Belle later said, "Actually I'm surprised I got as many votes as I did [from the writers]." He received 11 first-place votes to Vaughn's 12.

Game 144
October 1, 1995
Indians Wrap-Up the Strike-Shortened Season with a .694
Winning Percentage

On the final day of the strike-shortened 1995 campaign the Indians' historic offense was on full display. Their opponent was the second-place Royals, but this was hardly a pennant race as the Tribe had clinched the division crown back in Game 123 (see page 235). Mathematically, KC was 30 games back coming into this final game.

After Chuck Nagy got out of a runners-at-the-corners jam in the top of the first, the lineup went to work against Tom Gordon of the Royals. Kenny Lofton led off the game with a single up the middle. He stole second with Omar Vizquel at bat. Omar drew a walk, and then he and Lofton executed a double-steal with Carlos Baerga at the plate. Carlos lined a single into center to score Lofton.

Alvero Espinoza came on to run for Baerga, and Albert Belle drew a walk. With the bases loaded, Eddie Murray, Jim Thome, and Manny Ramirez hit consecutive singles and the score was quickly 5-0.

Paul Sorrento drew a walk to load the bases once again. Gordon finally got the Royals first out when he retired Sandy Alomar on a fly out to center. Kenny Lofton struck out before Omar punched a two-out single through the left side of the infield to score one more. The first inning came to a close with the Tribe up 6-0.

The bottom of the second inning was just as rough for Gordon. Belle, Murray, and Thome hit three quick singles. The Royals sent Gordon to the showers. Mike Magnante came on to pitch for KC and struck out Paul Sorrento. Next up, Sandy Alomar slapped a single into short right field. Pinch-running Brian Giles scored and Thome dug for home. An error by Royals catcher Brent Mayne allowed Ramirez to score and put Alomar on third. Kenny Lofton drove in Sandy with a grounder to first base, making the score 11-0 after two innings.

Kansas City got to Nagy in the top of the third inning. Tommy Goodwin and Michael Tucker hit back to back singles. Keith

Lockhart lofted a fly ball deep into left field that allowed Goodwin to tag and score. Jon Nunnally drove in Tucker with a line drive double, and Gary Gaetti sent a two-run homer over the wall in right field. The Royals scored four runs on five hits, but Nagy eventually found his footing.

At this point, many of the All-Stars and veterans got the afternoon off. Billy Ripken sent a homer into the left field bleachers to lead off the bottom of the fifth inning. Brian Giles had an RBI single. Paul Sorrento rocked a three-run homer off KC reliever Rusty Meacham. Kenny Lofton drove one into the right field corner and stretched it into an RBI triple. The score was 17-4 in favor of the Indians after five innings.

The bullpen scattered a few more runs, but the Tribe's cruised to an eventual 17-7 victory in this playoff tune-up game.

The 1995 season is often described as "magical." The nucleus of players that had been building since the final years of Municipal Stadium all hit their peak. With the Browns now in Baltimore, the team had the City's full attention–even on a Sunday afternoon in early October.

The team delivered a dozen walk-off wins, including the nine-run comeback over the Jays in Game 34 (page 67), Manny's "WOW" homer in Game 71 (page 139), and Albert Belle's game-winning grand slam in Game 73 (page 142). It was truly a magical time and an offensive lineup that may never be surpassed.

Game 145
September 19, 1917
Stan Coveleski, Ace of the WWI Era, Throws a One-Hitter

The Indians were visiting the Yankees at the Polo grounds as the end of the 1917 campaign was approaching. Sophomore spitballer Stan Coveleski took the hill against Slim Love and the Yankees.

The play-by-play details of this game have been lost to history, but Coveleski mowed through the Yankee lineup. The pinstripes managed only one hit. It was a single by third baseman Fritz Maisel. He walked two and struck out five on the way to a league-leading ninth shutout of the season.

Tris Speaker drove in Ray Chapman with a double and catcher Steve O'Neill drove in Bill Wambsganss to score the only two runs that the Indians would need.

Coveleski once explained, "I wouldn't throw all spitballs. I'd go maybe two or three innings without throwing a spitter, but I always had them looking for it." Sounds familiar to a another doctored-ball Indians great, Gaylord Perry (see page 304).

Coveleski was an anchor of the Indians rotation throughout the late teens and twenties. In 1917, the Indians improve their record to 88 wins, and finished third in the American League. Coveleski won nineteen games and finished third in the league with a 1.81 ERA

His biggest moment came in the 1920 World Series. He recorded three wins in the best-of-nine format, including a complete game shutout in Game 7 that earned the Indians the title. His ERA for the World Series was 0.67.

After a long wait, Coveleski was elected to the Baseball Hall of Fame in 1969. Coveleski poked at the Baseball writers a bit in his induction comments, "It makes me feel just swell." I figured I'd make it sooner or later, and I just kept hoping each year would be the one."

Game 146
September 18, 2000
Bartolo Colon has a Career Night

The Yankees were leading the chase for the American League pennant, while the Indians were scrapping to stay in the wildcard race during this late-season visit to the Bronx. In a prime-time pitching matchup, Bartolo Colon was to face off with Roger Clemens. Clemens had not suffered a loss in his last 15 starts.

Kenny Lofton drew a 10-pitch walk to lead off the game. Then Omar Vizquel bounced a single off the second base bag. After a Robbie Alomar strikeout, Manny Ramirez poked a ground ball single into short right field. Lofton raced around from second base to score. Jim Thome grounded into a double play, but not before the Indians were up 1-0.

Derek Jeter lined one back to the mound and struck Colon sharply in the side. Bartolo was able to recover and flip the ball to first. After a lengthy visit from the training staff, Colon stayed in the game. With two outs, David Justice reached on an error by Tribe left fielder Russel Branyan. However, Justice was quickly left on base as Bartolo struck out Tito Martinez on three pitches.

In the bottom of the second, Kenny Lofton made a play reminiscent of the one featured in Game 111 (page 212). Jorge Posada lofted a fly ball to center that looked like it would surely be a home run. Lofton once again showed off the vertical leap from his past life as a college basketball star. A perfectly timed jump allowed him to bring Posada's homer back over the wall. Back on the warning track, Lofton gingerly flipped the ball from his glove as Posada rounded second and headed back to the dugout.

In the top of the third inning, Clemens struck out Omar and then retired Robbie Alomar on a groundout. Clemens lost his command and composure for a bit. Manny Ramierez started the two-out rally by drawing a walk. Jim Thome's double to right put Manny on third base. Manny was able to scamper home on a passed ball with David Segui at the plate. Segui eventually walked, as did Travis Fryman. However, Russell Branyan left the bases loaded when he struck out.

Colon blew through the Yankees lineup in the middle innings with great force. In the bottom of the sixth inning he struck out the pinstripe side. All three Yankees went down looking. In a post-game interview, Derek Jeter admitted "He's one of the few pitchers who can overpower you. He basically dominated the game."

The Yankees got their second baserunner of the night in the bottom of the seventh when David Justice drew a seven-pitch walk. Colon quickly retired Tito Martinez and Jorge Posada to strand Justice at second.

Bartolo struck out Glenallen Hill to start off the bottom of the eighth inning. His Dominican countryman and long-time friend Luis Polonia stepped to the plate. Polonia knocked Colon's first pitch cleanly into center field. Polonia said, "He'd been throwing me fastballs all night and I was looking for one." Scott Brosius ended the inning when he hit into a 6-4-3 double-play.

Colon returned to pitch the bottom of the ninth. He struck out Jose Vizcaino on six pitches. Chuck Knoblauch whiffed on Colon's 2-2 pitch. Derek Jeter was up with the Yankees down to their final out. When Jeter struck out looking, it ended his streak of getting on base in 41 straight games.

Unfortunately, Polonia's single kept Colon from ending another Yankee streak. The Yankees had not been no-hit for 6,637 games. Hoyt Wilhelm and the Orioles no-hit the Pinstripes on September 20th, 1958. That streak would stand until 2003, when the Astros threw a combined no-hitter in Yankee stadium using six different pitchers.

Bartolo's line of 1 hit, 1 walk, and 13 strikeouts was the best of his career so far. Of course, he would go on to become "Big Sexy", the winningest Latin-American pitcher with 247 wins and the oldest player to hit his first career home run.

Game 147
September 14, 2017
Lindor Keeps the Streak Alive

The Indians entered this Thursday night game riding a twenty-one-game winning streak. Sports talk radio was abuzz with debate about whether a win would place the Tribe in sole possession of the longest winning streak. Either they would pass up the 21-win streak of the 1935 Cubs. Or they would still be chasing the 1916 Giants, who went 26 games *without losing*. The Giant's streak included a tie.

Josh Tomlin was matched up with Jacob Junis for this run at history. The Tribe got behind early as the Royals got to Tomlin in the top of the second inning. He walked Eric Hosmer to lead things off. Then Salvador Perez lined a single into right field that advanced Hosmer to third. Mike Moustakis grounded into a 4-6-3 double play, but Hosmer came home to score.

Abe Almonte lead off the Indians' half of the third with a line drive double down the right field line. With two outs, Lonnie Chisenhall looped a double into right. Almonte dug for home and came around to score the tying run. Chisenhall attempted to stretch the play into a double, but was thrown out at second to end the inning.

In the top of the sixth inning, Tomlin gave up a leadoff double to Whit Merrifield. Lorenzo Cain hit into a fielder's choice that put Merrifield out at third. Melky Cabrera grounded one weakly down the first base line. Carlos Santana charged the ball and flipped it to second to get Cain at second. Eric Hosmer slapped a double down the left field line. The speedy Cabrera came around to score from first and put the Royals ahead 2-1.

Andrew Miller returned from the injured list to pitch the top of the seventh. He allowed two hits, but got Alex Gordon to hit into an inning-ending double play to get out of trouble. One of the more incredible facts about the 2017 winning streak is that the Tribe won 21 games in a row *without* their best relief pitcher.

The Indians offense could not get anything going against Royals reliever Mike Minor in the seventh inning. They loaded the bases against Ryan Butcher in the bottom of the eighth, but consecutive pop-foul outs by Jay Bruce and Carlos Santana ended the threat.

Down one run and facing the imminent end of the streak, Yandy Diaz grounded out to lead off the bottom of the ninth. Tyler Naquin slapped a single through the left side of the infield. Francisco Mejia grounded to second and Naquin was forced out. Erik Gonzalez came on to pinch run for Mejia. The Indians were down to their final out, and Francisco Lindor was hitless on the day so far. Lindor came to the plate looking to keep the Indians' hopes—and the streak—alive.

Lindor worked Herrera into a 2-2 count. Down to his final strike, Lindor laced one into deep left field. Alex Gordon raced to the base of the 19-foot wall and made a leaping attempt, but was unable to make the catch. Gonzalez raced around to score the tying run, and Lindor ended up on second. Austin Jackson grounded out to end the inning and send the game to extra innings tied at 2-2.

Cody Allen needed only eighteen pitches to retire the Royals in the top of the tenth inning. Over the course of the streak Cody Allen did not allow a single run. His ERA was perfect from August 12th through this game.

Jose Ramirez lined Brandon Maurer's 1-1 pitch into right-center and never hesitated in pushing for second. He narrowly beat the throw, and was safe with a double to lead off the bottom of the tenth inning. Maurer had Edwin Encarnacion behind in the count 0-2, but EE hung in and drew a seven-pitch walk.

Jay Bruce stepped to the plate and smacked one into the right field corner. Ramirez raced around from second to score the winning run and give the 2017 Indians a place in history.

During the streak, the Tribe outscored their opponents by a combined score of 140–36 in an unprecedented run of dominance.

Game 148
September 17, 2016
Most Pitchers Used in a Shutout

The *Plain Dealer's* Sunday Sports Headline the next day read, "Sept. 17: The day Cleveland Indians' postseason dreams ended before they began." Of course, that turned out to be false. Although 2016 ended in heartbreak, the heartbreak happened in Game 7 of the World Series and was hardly a foregone conclusion.

The Tribe had an eight-game lead over Detroit in the Central and was poised to clinch the Division, but had been wracked with injuries, most recently to Danny Salazar and Yan Gomes. A strong regular season including a then franchise-record fourteen-game win streak had the Indians in a strong position, but fans and writers were doubting their staying power. Carlos Carrasco was set to square off with Justin Verlander in the premier matchup of the weekend.

Ian Kinsler lined Carlos Carrasco's first pitch right back to the mound that struck Carlos in the hand. Carrasco left the game and was later diagnosed with a broken bone in the little finger of his throwing hand. It was immediately apparent that he was done for the season.

A day that started as an opportunity for a workhorse starter to eat innings and prepare for the post-season became a bullpen day in an instant.

Terry Francona called bullpen coach Jason Bere on the dugout phone, "Tell them to put their seat belts on, because they're all going to pitch, and we're going to win." First up was Jeff Manship, who attempted to right the ship. Manship erased Kinsler by getting Cameron Maybin to ground into a double play. He went on to pitch a scoreless 1⅓ innings.

Kyle Crockett retired the remaining two batters in the top of the second with no damage done.

Cody Anderson was untouched in the top of the third inning. He returned to pitch in the fourth inning. Miguel Cabrera got aboard with a line drive single to left, but Victor Martinez squibbed one in front of the mound. Cody fielded it flipped back to Lindor who stepped on second. Lindor turned and fired to first for a 1-6-3 double-play.

Zach McAllister needed only ten pitches to retire the Tigers side in the top of the fifth inning on three fly ball outs.

Perci Gardner got into a bit of a jam when he hit Jose Iglesias with his fifth pitch. Iglesias stole second with Ian Kinsler at the plate. The play was close, and Terry Francona elected to challenge the call. Upon video review, the safe at second call was confirmed. Kinsler grounded out to short, but advanced Iglesias to third. Cameron Maybin popped out to the edge of the infield grass. Garner intentionally walked the dangerous Miguel Cabrera, which put runners at the corners. He struck out Victor Martinez to end the sixth inning with the scoreless tie intact.

Bryan Shaw walked J.D. Martinez to lead off the Detroit half of the seventh inning, but retired the next three Tigers with no damage done.

Cody Allen dispatched with Detroit in order in the top of the eighth.

Through all of the Indians pitching changes, Justin Verlander worked through the Indians lineup. He pitched seven scoreless innings, giving up only one hit and four walks. Alex Wilson replaced him on the mound for the bottom of the eighth and held on to the scoreless tie.

Andrew Miller came on to pitch the top of the ninth for the Indians. He battled Miguel Cabrera through an 8 pitch at-bat and eventually set Miggy down on a swinging strikeout. J.D. Martinez came up with a two-out single, but was left on base when Justin Upton lined out to right.

Jose Ramirez and Coco Crisp both lined out to begin the bottom of the ninth. Tyler Naquin blooped a single into center field. Rajai Davis came off the bench to pinch run for Naquin and promptly stole second base. The Tigers intentionally walked Abe Almonte to set up a force-out. With Brandon Guyer facing an 0-2 count, Rajai and Almonte executed a double steal. The Indians were gaining momentum, but the rally was squandered when Guyer grounded out to third base.

Andrew Miller returned to pitch the top half of the tenth inning. Miller struck out the first two Tigers, and then got Jose Iglesias to ground out weakly back to the mound.

Justin Wilson stayed on to pitch the bottom of the tenth for Detroit. Carlos Santana drew a walk to lead off the inning. Jason Kipnis laid down a bunt, but Jarrod Saltalamacchia scooped it up in front of the plate and forced Santana out at second. With Francisco Lindor at the plate, Kipnis advanced to second on a wild pitch, and then stole third. Lindor drew a seven-pitch walk, putting runners at the corners. Detroit issued Mike Napoli an intentional walk to load the bases and set up a double play.

Jose Ramirez stepped in and knocked Wilson's 2-2 pitch into center field scoring Kipnis easily. Jose's walk-off single was the club's tenth walk-off win of the season. Miller was credited with the win and later remarked, "We have no other choice ... we have to find a way to win - no matter who is starting." There could not have been a better tagline for the six weeks that were about to come between Game 148 and Game 7 of the World Series.

The Indians used nine pitchers in the 1-0 victory. They combined for a four hit, ten strikeout win. The bullpen crew gave up only three walks throughout the whole game.

Game 149
September 20, 2000 (Second Game)
Omar Vizquel Straight Steals Home

The Indians were fighting for the Wild Card spot and Boston was trying to keep their fading playoff hopes alive as the Indians visited Fenway to play back-to-back doubleheaders in the middle of the week. In the first game of the series, the Indians defeated Pedro Martinez for the first time in ten attempts. In the second game, Dave Burba was matched up with Paxton Crawford.

Troy O'Leary doubled to left field to lead off the bottom of the second for the Sox. After a Trot Nixon strikeout, Lou Merloni drove in O'Leary with a line drive to deep left field.

In the bottom of the fourth inning, the Red Sox extended their lead to 3-0 when Scott Hatteberg doubled with two outs. Lou Merloni followed with an RBI double, and then Brian Daubach drove in Merloni with a liner into center field.

The Indians came up with their own two-out rally in the top half of the fifth inning. Bill Selby was hit by Crawford's pitch to get on base. Kenny Lofton moved him over to second with a single into center field. Omar Vizquel drew a five-pitch walk to load the bases. Robbie Alomar poked a single into left-center that scored Selby and Lofton. Robbie and Omar executed a double-steal with Manny Ramirez at the plate.

Manny drew a walk to load the bases again. Boston called on Rheal Cormier to relieve Crawford. Cormier entered the game facing Jim Thome with the bases loaded. Cormier was focused on the matchup with Thome and took his time moving into the stretch for every pitch. He neglected the crafty Vizquel on third.

Jim Riggelman took two steps out of the third base coach's box and appeared to just say "Go." Vizquel broke for home, and barely had to slide as he came in to score the tying run. Cormier never even attempted a throw to the plate as Omar tied the game 3-3 in bold fashion.

Trot Nixon smashed a home run over the wall in left-center to lead off the bottom of the fifth inning and put the Sox back on top 4-3. In the bottom of the sixth inning, Ricardo Rincon gave up a line drive single into center field. Steve Karsay came in from the bullpen to pitch against Lou Merloni. Merloni already had two doubles in the game. Merloni grounded into a 4-6-3 double play to end the inning.

Chan Perry grounded out to begin the Indians' half of the seventh inning. Kenny Lofton singled to right and then Omar drew a walk. With runners on first and second, Rich Garces came on in relief for the Sox. Robbie Alomar flied out to center, but Manny Ramirez and Jim Thome plated two runs with back-to-back singles. The Tribe was up 5-4 in the middle of the seventh.

Steve Karsay and Paul Shuey held things down through the late innings, before closer Bob Wickman came in to face Merloni with the bases loaded in the bottom of the eighth. Wickman got Merloni to ground into a 5-4-3 double play to end the eighth.

Despite walking Trot Nixon to put the tying run on base, Wickman was able to close the door in the bottom of the ninth to seal the 5-4 victory.

In June 2008, Omar was 41 years old and playing for the Giants in an interleague matchup against the A's. He straight stole home to score the first run of the game in a very similar situation. Statistics are somewhat unreliable, because of the many factors that go into stealing home; however, this likely makes Omar the oldest player to straight-steal home.

Game 150
September 24, 1950
Bob Lemon Helps Out His Own Cause

Bob Lemon led a very solid Indians rotation in 1950 along with Bob Feller, Early Wynn, and Mike Garcia. Despite outstanding pitching, the Indians were in the middle of the pack in the standings. They were sitting in fourth place in the American League when Detroit came to town in the waning days of the 1950 season. Lemon was matched up with Ted Grey on this Sunday afternoon at Municipal Stadium.

Johnny Lipon grounded out to third to lead of the game for the Tigers. Lemon walked the next three batters. Johnny Groth popped one straight up and was put out by catcher Jim Hegan. Lemon got out of the bases-loaded jam in when he got Jerry Priddy to ground out to the shortstop.

The Indians also loaded the bases against Ted Grey with a single and two walks in the bottom of the first. Grey escaped this situation when Tribe shortstop Ray Boone popped out to left field.

Lemon came up to bat for the second time in the bottom of the fourth inning. He helped out his own cause by smashing a two-out homer which put the Indians up 1-0.

Tigers shortstop Johnny Lipon tied things up in the top of the seventh. He led off the inning with a solo home run off Lemon. Lemon retired the next eight Tigers he faced.

After Lemon issued a walk to Lipon in the bottom of the ninth, George Kell grounded out back to the mound to end the inning.

Gray struck out Joe Gordon and Jim Hegan in the bottom of the ninth to send the game to extra innings tied 1-1.

Pat Mullin knocked a single into center field to start off the extra frame for Detroit. Vic Wertz laid down a sacrifice bunt that moved Mullin over to second. The Indians intentionally walked Johnny Groth to set up a force-out on an infield hit. Jerry Priddy grounded one to second. Tribe second baseman Joe Gordon flipped it to Ray

Boone for the out at second. Priddy beat the throw to first, and Detroit had runners on the corners with two outs. Lemon cut down Don Kolloway for his fifth strikeout in ten innings.

Lemon himself was up to lead off the bottom of the tenth. He slapped a hit into the massive outfield at Municipal Stadium. Lemon dashed around the basepaths and stretched it into a triple. Gray intentionally walked both Dale Mitchell and Bobby Kennedy to load the bases. Larry Doby was put out on a pop foul. Next up, Luke Easter grounded one sharply to first. Kolloway got to the bag for the out, but had no play on Lemon coming home to score the winning run.

Lemon threw a 10-inning complete game giving up only one run on five hits. He notched two of the Tribe's six hits on the day and scored the Indians only two runs. Lemon recorded his 22nd win (of an eventual 23) on the season. It was also his league-leading 22nd complete game. In addition to his starting duties, he appeared seven times out of the bullpen in 1950 and went 6 for 26 as a pinch hitter.

Lemon was selected to the All-Star team in seven consecutive seasons. He was elected to the Hall of Fame in 1976, and his number 21 is one of the retired numbers hanging in the Progressive Field stands.

Game 151
September 27, 1914 (First Game)
Nap Lajoie Notches His 3,000th Hit

Napoleon "Nap" Lajoie's star power helped to make the early American League a success. When he signed with the Cleveland club in 1902, his former team disputed the validity of the contract. As a result, Lajoie did not travel to Pennsylvania for two years (missing all away games against the Athletics). The A's won 34% more at home than they did on the road in 1902, a variance which is largely explained by not having to face the best hitter in the game in their own park.

In 1902, Nap's .378 average led the American League. To start the 1903 season, local media held a poll to rename the team that had been the Blues and the Bronchos in its first two campaigns. "Naps" was the runaway favorite.

1902 was the first of 10 years LaJoie would hit above .300 for Cleveland. He led the league in hits in 1904 (208 hits), 1906 (214), and 1910 (227 hits). All of those hits piled up into quite a career.

The Yankees were visiting League Park on the second-to-last weekend of the baseball year. In the first game of the day, Guy Morton and his abysmal 1 and 13 win-loss record was on the mound for Cleveland. He was facing off with Marty McHale.

The play-by-play account of this game has been lost to history, but we know that one of Cleveland's seven hits on the day was Lajoie's 3000th. The *Cleveland Press* reported, "Lajoie, of Cleveland, made his three-thousandth big league hit in the first game. It being a two-base hit, the ball being taken out of play and presented to Lajoie as soon as he reached second."

The Cleveland club went on to win 5-3. However, they would finish the season with only 51 wins–dead last in the American League.

Honus Wagner was the first player in modern baseball history to record 3,000 hits on June 9, 1914 for the Pittsburgh Pirates. Some historians also recognize Cap Anson of the Chicago Colts as a member of the 3,000-hit club, but all of his hits came in the nineteenth century under significantly different rules.

Twenty-nine players have joined the 3,000-hit club since Wagner and Lajoie reached the milestone in 1914. However, none have been so dominant or so beloved that the team was re-named in their honor.

Lajoie finished his career with 3,243 hits, 2,052 of those came with the Naps. He remains the all-time franchise hits leader, 87 ahead of Tris Speaker. Long-tenured modern-day stars like Omar Vizquel and Kenny Lofton are more than 400 hits behind Lajoie. As of 2019, the active franchise hits leader is Carlos Santana with 1,143.

Game 152
October 2, 1908
Addie Joss Throws a Perfect Game in a Pennant Race

The Naps, White Sox, and Tigers were in a three-way pennant race going into the last week of the season. Cleveland was one game behind Detroit, and Chicago was half a game behind Cleveland.

On Friday October 2, the White Sox traveled to Cleveland to kick off a weekend series at League Park. "Big Ed" Walsh took the mound for Chicago with an incredible 39 and 14 record for the season so far. However, Walsh had yet to win at League Park that season. Two of his three loses in Cleveland had come against Addie Joss, the "Human Hairpin" with the corkscrew delivery.

Joss took the mound with a 23-11 record and an incredible strikeout to walk ratio of 4.20. During the team warmups, Joss spotted Walsh on the White Sox bench. A local reporter snapped a photo of the two ace pitchers having a quiet conversation before one of the biggest matchups of the season.

Both pitchers came out dealing. Joss sat down the first nine White Sox he faced.

In the bottom of the third, Naps centerfielder Joe Birmingham led off with a single into right. Birmingham took a wide lead off first and Walsh made his pickoff move. Birmingham broke for second. The throw to second struck Birmingham in the back and bounced into center field. He reached third without a slide.

After Freddy Parent grounded out to short and Joss struck out attempting to bunt, leadoff hitter Wilbur Good came to the plate. Walsh got Good to strike out swinging, but the third strike sailed out of catcher Osee Schrecongost's reach. Birmingham came home on the wild pitch and gave the Naps a 1-0 lead.

In the middle innings, both pitchers mowed through the opposing lineup. Ed Walsh was striking out two or more Naps an inning, but Joss was also getting the White Sox out with ruthless efficiency.

292

Around the bottom of the seventh, the crowd began to sense that history was on the line. The horns, cowbells, and other noisemakers that were customary at League Park fell silent as the tension was building.

Joss faced three pinch hitters in the bottom of the ninth. Doc White grounded out to second. Lee Tannehill whiffed for Joss' third strikeout of the day. John Anderson came in to pinch hit for Ed Walsh with two outs. He smacked a line drive down the left field line that fell just foul. It was the nearest that Chicago came to a hit all day. Following the foul, Anderson grounded to the third baseman for the 27th out.

Joss had pitched just the second Perfect Game in baseball history, and he had done it using only 74 pitches.

Among pitchers with over 1,000 innings in the books, Addie Joss and Ed Walsh have the lowest ERAs in baseball history. Walsh's 1.82 over fourteen seasons edges out Joss' 1.89 over nine years. Joss remains the *all-time* leader in WHIP with a mark of 0.968.

Joss is the only player ever to be inducted into the Baseball Hall of Fame with less than 10 years of play in MLB. Joss died of tuberculosis just before the 1911 season began. In 1978 the 10-year tenure rule was waived to include Cleveland's original pitching ace in Cooperstown.

Game 153

September 19, 2008

Gary Sheffield Charges Fausto Carmona

Both the Indians and Tigers were well out of the playoff picture behind the Division-leading White Sox. It was only 70 degrees and the breeze was blowing in off the lake, but balls were jumping out of Progressive Field as though it were mid-August.

Fausto Carmona retired the first nine Tigers he faced. Meanwhile, Shin-Soo Choo put the Tribe up 1-0 with a solo home run off Armando Galarraga in the bottom of the first.

Curtis Granderson doubled down the left field line to lead off the bottom of the fourth inning. After two outs, Miguel Cabrera took Fausto deep with a two-run homer to left center. Miggy's blast gave Detroit the 2-1 advantage.

Carmona returned to form and pitched 1-2-3 innings in both the fifth and sixth. Then Grady Sizemore tied things up with a solo home run to right-center in the bottom of the sixth inning.

Maglio Ordonez led off the Detroit half of the seventh with a single. Miguel Cabrera stepped in and launched his second homer of the night off Carmona. Matthew Joyce grounded out, and Gary Sheffield stepped in with the 4-2 lead.

Carmona's second pitch hit Sheffield square in the elbow. Sheffield walked all the way to first carrying his bat and maintaining a staredown on Fausto. Brandon Inge stepped up to the plate as the crowd buzzed. Every eye in the building was fixed on the tension between Fausto and Sheffield.

While Inge stood in for Fausto's first pitch, Carmona spun and made a pickoff move to first. Sheffield took exception to the pickoff move. He motioned toward Inge and told Fausto, "Throw to the Plate."

Helmets and gloves came off as Sheffield charged the mound. 6-foot-4, 270-pound Carmona caught him in a headlock and landed three or four solid punches before the benches arrived to push and shove the two apart. Victor Martinez in his catching gear went down after a block in the back and got up looking to knock a Tiger out.

294

Brandon Inge was able to pull Victor away from the Fray while fellow Venezuelan Miguel Cabrera got between Victor and the rest of the Tigers.

Once things settled down and ejections were sorted out, Edward Mujica struck out Brandon Inge. Victor Martinez gunned down Jeff Larish (who had replaced Sheffield on first) at second for a strike-out throw-out double play to end the frame.

Ramon Santiago tripled to lead off the eighth inning for the Tigers, He was driven in by Dusty Ryan's sacrifice fly to give Detroit a 5-2 lead.

Jamey Carrol pinch hit for Andy Marte to lead off the Indians' half of the eighth and grounded out to second. Asdrubal Cabrera popped out to short. Grady Sizemore blooped a two-out double into short left field which chased Galarraga from the game.

Casey Fossum emerged from Detroit's bullpen and threw five straight balls. He issued a walk to Ben Francisco, and then Shin-Soo Choo hit a prodigious three-run blast to right center on Fossum's first strike. Choo's homer tied the game at 5-5.

Rafael Betancourt and Rafael Perez combined to retire the side in the ninth inning.

Freddy Dolsi hit Kelly Shoppach with his second pitch in the bottom of the ninth to put Shoppach on first. Dolsi replaced by Bobby Seay on the mound. During the pitching change, Josh Barfield came on to pinch run for Shoppach. Travis Hafner struck out swinging, and then Ryan Garko singled down the left field line to put the winning run at third. Utility infielder Jamey Carroll lofted a fly ball to deep right field. It dropped in for a Walk-off single, sending Tribe fans home vindicated and victorious.

Game 154
September 23, 2005
Bob Wickman Converts His 45th Save of the Season

Most closers live and die by the fastball. Bob Wickman relied on his sinker. Wickman lost part of his right index finger in a farm accident as a child. He credited the motion of his sinker to the unusual grip he adapted. A wily and strategic closer, Wickman walked batters he did not want to face rather than overpower them. His sinker was his out pitch and so the difference between a game-ending double-play and a blown save could be a bad hop in the infield.

The Indians were a game and a half back of the White Sox in the division race. They were visiting the abysmal Royals for the second-to-last weekend of the season. CC Sabathia was matched up with Jose Lima for the Friday night contest.

Lima retired the Tribe in order in the first inning. Chip Ambres led off the Royals' half of the first by sending CC's 2-2 pitch into the fountains at Kauffman Stadium to give Kansas City an early 1-0 lead.

Travis Hafner drew a five-pitch walk to lead off the second inning. Victor Martinez hit a grounder to the second baseman, and Hafner was forced out while Victor reached first safely. Martinez advanced to second when Lima sent in a wild pitch that KC catcher John Buck could not track down. Ronnie Belliard went down on strikes, but first baseman Jose Hernandez tied things up for the Tribe with an RBI single into center field.

The Indians broke things open in the top of the third inning. Grady Sizemore was hit by Lima's second pitch. Grady stole second and then scored on a ground ball that Jhonny Peralta scorched past the shortstop. Travis Hafner teed off on Lima, sending a two-run homer over the wall in straightaway center. Victor Martinez scorched a double down the right field line. Ronnie Belliard drove in Victor with a single into left field. The inning came to a close with the Tribe up 5-1.

The Royals would chip away at the Indians lead as Chip Ambres came into score for the Royals on a wild pitch in the third.

Victor Martinez restored the four-run lead with an RBI double in the top of the fifth inning.

Sabathia continued to have control issues in the bottom of the fifth. He gave up a single to Andres Blanco, threw another wild pitch to Ambres, and hit Matt Diaz with a pitch to put runners at the corners. The Royals manufactured three runs in the inning to bring the score to 6-5 and send CC into the clubhouse early.

Indians reliever Bob Howry blew his save opportunity when he gave up a home run to Mark Teahen. Teahen's solo homer tied the game in the bottom of the eighth inning.

The Royals kicked it around a bit in the ninth. Grady Sizemore reached on an error and then advanced to third on a throwing error as Coco Crisp tried to beat out a grounder. Sizemore scored on a ground ball single into left off the bat of Jhonny Peralta. This put the Tribe up 7-6 and set up a tense save situation for Bob Wickman.

Wickman entered the game looking for his 45th save of the season. He struck out Denny Hocking swinging. Pinch hitter Aaron Guiel fell victim to Wickman's sinker and grounded out to first. Terrance Long flied out to left on the first pitch to give the Indians the win.

This was one of the few instances where Wickman did not put at least one runner on base. It was a rare respite for fans from the heartburn-inducing situations Wickman would build up and eventually overcome.

Jose Mesa is the Indians leader for saves in a season. He converted 46 saves in 48 opportunities. Wickman is tied for second on the list with Joe Borowski, who also saved 45 in 2007.

Wickman chalked up 139 total saves with the Indians. That made him the all-time franchise leader, until he was surpassed by Cody Allen in 2018.

Game 155

September 23, 1997

Comeback Win Against the Yankees Clinches the Central

The Indians began the day 7½ games up on the White Sox with seven games left to play. They had departed Kansas City with a bad taste in their mouths after a walk-off single by Rod Myers. The Yankees were four games back, but still alive in the East as Kenny Rogers took the mound against Charles Nagy.

Nagy threw a 1-2-3 first inning, but things went downhill from there. He walked Bernie Williams to lead off the second. Cecil Fielder touched him up for an RBI double, and then Homer Bush dropped a two-run single into left field to put the pinstripes up by three runs.

Sandy Alomar closed the gap momentarily with a two-run homer in the bottom of the second inning, but New York answered with a two-run shot by Tino Martinez in the next frame.

Nagy gave up two runs on four singles in the top of the fifth inning and left the game with the Yankees up 7-2. Reliever David Weathers did not fare much better. He gave up RBI singles to Rey Sanchez and Bernie Williams that put New York up 9-2.

Manny Ramirez kicked off the comeback with a leadoff single to right. Matt Williams doubled into center, scoring Manny from first. David Justice grounded out, but moved Williams over to third. Sandy Alomar likewise grounded out, but Williams scored on the play. Kevin Seitzer got aboard with a single before Tony Fernandez put a line drive home run into the left field bleachers. It was 9-6 Indians after six innings.

Hideki Irabu set the Tribe down in order in the bottom of the seventh inning.

David Justice took Irabu's first pitch over the left field wall in the eighth. After Sandy Alomar doubled to left, Mike Stanton took over for Irabu on the mound. Then, Tony Fernandez singled in Alomar. The Tribe had closed the gap and were down just one run headed into the ninth inning.

Jeff Nelson came out to pitch for the Yankees in the ninth. He walked Bip Roberts on six pitches to lead off the inning. Omar Vizquel laid down a sacrifice bunt that put Roberts in scoring position. After Manny Ramirez struck out, Matt Williams drew a five-pitch walk. David Justice singled in Bip Roberts to tie the game 9-9.

Sandy Alomar smacked a line drive single into center that pushed Williams across the plate for the biggest comeback win of the 1997 season.

After the walk-off celebration, the team's attention turned to scoreboard watching. Just ten minutes after Alomar's single, the White Sox fell to the Twins and gave the Indians the Central Division crown for the third straight year, kicking off another celebration in the clubhouse.

Game 156
September 22, 1967
Tony Horton Ends a Marathon with a Walk-off Homer

The Indians were playing out the string in 1967, having long been eliminated from the playoffs. Luis Tiant was matched up with Gary Peters of the White Sox this Friday evening in front of only about 5,000 of the Cleveland faithful. The White Sox were locked in a four-way battle for the American League pennant. Boston and Minnesota were tied at the top of the standings with Chicago one game behind. The Tigers were just one and a half games off the pace.

However, a mid-season arrival was giving Cleveland fans hope for a better team in the future. In June, the Indians dealt Gary Bell to the Red Sox for Don Demeter and 22-year old first baseman Tony Horton. With the opportunity to play every day, Horton had blossomed and was quickly becoming a star.

Second baseman Vern Fuller drew a walk to lead off the bottom of the second. Larry Brown knocked an RBI double into left to score Fuller and put the Tribe up 1-0.

Tiant pitched brilliantly, giving up only three hits through the first eight innings. Peters also pitched well, but the Indians offense squandered some opportunities.

Tiant let the 1-0 lead slip away in the top of the ninth when Don Buford doubled to right and then Smoky Burgess hit a pinch-hit RBI single into right to tie the game at 1-1.

The Indians stranded runners at first and second in the bottom of the ninth to send the game to extra frames.

Stan Williams was nearly perfect in relief for the Indians. The only baserunners he allowed were when Don Buford reached on an error in the top of the eleventh and a walk that he issued to Wayne Causey in the top of the thirteenth.

Tony Horton stepped in against Chicago reliever Roger Nelson to start the Indians half of the thirteenth. He launched the game-winning home run into the Cleveland night.

300

Horton was one of the Indians most promising young players through the late 1960's. Terry Pluto later called him "the most tragic Indian."

Throughout the 1969 and 1970 seasons, Horton struggled through slumps and was particularly affected by heckling from the small Cleveland crowds related to his salary negotiations with the team. After being benched in the fifth inning of a game against the Yankees in August 1970, Horton returned to his apartment and attempted suicide.

He survived, and recovered, but never played professional baseball again. He returned to his native California, went into business, and never looked back. In 1997, the New York Daily News reported the story for the first time with quotes from teammates and others involved. The Daily News approached Horton for an interview, but he declined.

Sam McDowell said of Horton, "From what I understand, the doctors told him he had to completely divorce himself from baseball. Baseball was what drove him to his state. He was so high-strung, with such a drive to succeed, and when he wasn't succeeding it set him off."

As fans, we make heroes and villains out of the players on the field based on their statistics and accomplishments. It sometimes takes a story like Tony Horton's to remember that athletes are humans with their own lives outside the lines.

Game 157
September 24, 2013
Jason Giambi Walk-off Keeps the Tribe's Playoff Hopes Alive

Back in Game 16 of 2013, a 5-RBI game likely kept Jason Giambi on the roster (see page 30). In Game 105 he became the oldest player to hit a walk-off home run (see page 200).

The Indians entered this Tuesday night contest barely hanging on to the second wildcard spot in the new playoff format. The White Sox sent Hector Santiago to the hill to face Ubaldo Jiminez. After two rough years, Ubaldo had been carrying the Indians rotation since Justin Masterson's early-season injury.

Santiago hit Ryan Raburn with his fourth pitch. Raburn took first to lead off the inning. Asdrubal Cabrera grounded a ball to the shortstop, and Raburn was forced out at second. Yan Gomes shot a line drive down the left field line that sent Cabrera to second base. Michael Brantley put the Tribe out in front with an RBI single into center field.

Ubaldo walked Connor Gillespie to lead off the top of the fourth inning. Paul Konerko knocked a single into right field to advance Gillispie to third. After Ubaldo struck out Adam Dunn, Avasail Garcia hit a long fly to left. Gillespie scampered home and tied the game on the sacrifice fly.

Jiminez gave up five hits and struck out seven over 6⅓ innings of work. In the top of the seventh inning, he gave up a single to Gordan Beckham and walked Josh Phegley. Cody Allen entered the game looking to put the Indians back in control. Instead, Alejandro De Aza singled to left, scoring Beckham and putting the Sox up 2-1.

Hector Santiago came into the game to pitch for the Sox in the bottom of the seventh inning. Michael Brantley took Santiago's first pitch deep into right field to tie things up at two runs apiece. Mike Aviles lined one into left that dropped for a single. Michael Bourn laid down a sacrifice bunt that moved Aviles over to second. Nate Jones came on to pitch and got Nick Swisher to fly out to center. Jason Kipnis stepped in and lined Jones' 1-1 pitch into left to put the Tribe on top 3 runs to 2.

Joe Smith retired Paul Konerko, Adam Dunn, and Avisail Garcia in order in the top of the eighth. Nate Jones returned the favor, setting down the Indians' side in order in the bottom half of the inning.

Chris Perez came on looking for the save in the top of the ninth. Dayan Viciedo smashed Perez' third pitch over the right field wall to tie the game. Perez struck out the next two White Sox before he hung his first pitch to Alejandro De Aza. De Aza's homer to right-center put the Sox up 4 to 3. After Alexei Ramirez poked a single through the left side of the infield, Perez left the mound to a chorus of boos.

Marc Rzepczynski hit the only batter he faced before Bryan Shaw got the final out in the top half of the ninth.

Yan Gomes struck out swinging to lead off the Indians' half of the ninth. Michael Brantley poked a seeing-eye single through the right side of the infield and was safely aboard. Mike Aviles struck out, and things were looking bleak. With two outs, Michael Brantley took a gamble and stole second to get into scoring position with Jason Giambi at the plate.

Giambi crushed Addison Reed's 1-1 pitch deep into right field. This was his third pinch-hit Walk-off for the Indians. "Yeah I ran into it, I hit it," Giambi said. "There's nothing more special, that's what keeps me coming back every year." With that he bested his own record as the oldest player to hit a walk-off homer.

This was the Indians 11th walk-off win of the season, and fifth win in a row. Most importantly, it kept them one game ahead of the Rangers in the Wild Card race.

Game 158
September 26, 1973
Gaylord Perry Complete Game Shutout

Gaylord Perry spitballed his way to the 1972 Cy Young Award by posting a 24-16 record for the worst team in the American League. In fact, Perry accounted for 39% of the Indians wins during his tenure with the team.

His success stemmed mainly from his talent as a pitcher, but also from the performance of being Gaylord Perry. Although the spitball had been outlawed in 1920, Perry admitted to doctoring balls with saliva, KY jelly, sweat, and virtually any viscous substance at hand. He even occasionally threw a "puffball" where he would rosin his hands so thoroughly the ball would leave his hand in a distracting plume of dust.

Perry had an elaborate setup that included touching his cap, belt, glove, and other parts of his uniform. Whether the ball was doctored or not, hitters were so focused on catching him in the act that they whiffed on entirely legal pitches. He once boasted, "I don't even have to throw it [the spitball] anymore, because the batters are set up to believe it's there, waiting for 'em."

In 1973, he continued to baffle hitters both with legal sliders and forkballs along with the occasional illicit greaseball. Gaylord came into this game with an 18-19 record. As things turned out in 1973, he was the hard-luck loser more often than not. The Tribe had long been mathematically eliminated from the playoffs. Their 69-89 record had them 26½ games off the pace in the AL East, but Gaylord Perry never stopped trying to fool the opposition.

He retired the Red Sox side in the top of the first inning. Bill Lee likewise threw a 1-2-3 inning for the Sox in the bottom of the frame.

Perry gave up a hit to Carl Yastrzemski to lead off the top of the second, but Yaz was quickly erased by a 6-4-3 double play ball off the bat of Orlando Cepeda.

Tribe DH John Ellis smashed a homer to lead off the bottom of the second inning, thrilling the 1,453 fans on hand at Municipal Stadium.

304

Boston proved a challenge in the middle innings. Cecil Cooper dropped a single into center field. Perry issued a walk to Doug Griffin that put the tying run on second base. Mario Guerrero grounded out to first to end the inning.

In the top of the sixth, Tommy Harper got aboard with a single into right field. He stole second, then Rick Miller lined out to left. Reggie Smith grounded one to the right side of the infield. Cecil Cooper ranged to his left, fielded the ball and flipped to Perry at first base for the out. Harper advanced to third on the play. Gaylord pitched around the dangerous Carl Yastrzemski. After taking first base, Yaz stole second. The Sox had runners at second and third when Orlando Cepeda came to the plate. Perry struck Cepeda out looking to end the inning. It was the last time a Red Sox hitter would reach base this evening.

Red Sox starter Bill Lee did his part as well. He gave up only one run on seven hits and no walks.

In the top of the ninth, Perry faced the heart of the Sox order. He got Reggie Smith to fly out. Yastrzemski grounded out to second. He struck out Orlando Cepeda again to end the game.

It was Perry's fourth win in a row, and brought his record to 19-19 for the season. For the second year in a row, Perry had a league-leading 29 complete games.

The rise of pitch counts and bullpen specialists has certainly affected the game and the way it is played. For comparison, The Tribe's stellar starting rotation combined for five complete games in 2016. Shane Bieber shared the league lead in complete games for the 2019 season with two.

Game 159
September 29, 2005
CC Sabathia Throws a Three-Pitch Inning

Since August 1st, the Indians had gone 37-15. They closed the gap in the division standings to three games with four to play. The Central-leading White Sox were in Detroit looking to avoid a historic late-season collapse. The Indians had Tampa Bay in town and CC Sabathia on the hill against Casey Fossum.

The Rays put runners at first and third early on. CC got himself out of the jam by getting Aubrey Huff to ground out to second.

The Tribe got an early lead with some timely two-out hitting in the bottom of the first inning. Jhonny Peralta drew a walk and was driven in by Travis Hafner's home run. Victor Martinez poked a single into center before Ronnie Belliard belted one out of the park to make it 4-0 Indians.

In the bottom of the second inning, Grady Sizemore grounded into a double play that allowed Aaron Boone to hustle home from third. Jhonny Peralta led off the Indians' half of the third with a homer that chased Fossum from the game.

The top of the fifth inning witnessed one of the most uncommon occurrences in baseball. Jonny Gomes grounded CC's first pitch to third base and was easily put out at first. Alex Gonzales stepped in and hit a nearly identical grounder to third on the first pitch. To the dismay of hitting coaches everywhere, Toby Hall swung at CC's first pitch and grounded out to short.

According to *Baseball Almanac* there have been 187 three-pitch innings in MLB history. Based purely on rarity, this feat is more unlikely than a no-hitter. There have been 260 modern-era no-hitters to date.

Sabathia worked through the later innings confidently with a 6-0 lead. Overall, he scattered five hits while striking out nine Rays over eight innings of work.

Rafael Betancourt came on to close the game and faced only three Rays. He got Jonny Gomes to strike out swinging to end the game and preserve the shutout.

Sabathia closed out a strong 2005 season with a 15-10 record and 7.4 strikeouts per nine innings. Fangraphs credited him with the highest fastball velocity in the American League in 2005.

Despite the strong outing, the playoff math was not on the Tribe's side. The White Sox defeated the Tigers later in the day to clinch the division. The next day, Chicago arrived in Cleveland for the final weekend series of the year. The Indians were still very much alive in the Wild Card chase before being swept by the Sox in front of sellout crowds. They handed the wildcard berth to Boston on the final day of the season in their own sort of collapse.

Other Indians who have thrown three-pitch innings include Addie Joss in 1903, Fritz Coumbe in 1915, Ed Klepfer in 1917, Johnny Allen in 1937, Charles Nagy in 1997, and Bob Wickman twice in 2005.

Game 160
September 29, 2017
Ramirez Knocks 90th Extra-Base Hit

Chicago was in town to start off the final series of the regular season. While the Tribe had long clinched the Central Division crown, they were locked in a fight with the Astros for home-field advantage and looking for their 101st win of the season.

Trevor Bauer took the hill for the Tribe with 189 strikeouts on the year. He would have to have a career night to join Corey Kluber and Carlos Carrasco with over 200 Ks for the season. Mike Pelfrey was slated to pitch for the White Sox.

Bauer got right to work, striking out Yolmer Sanchez to lead off the game and Jose Abreu to end the top of the first. The Tribe loaded the bases against Pelfrey, including a double by Jose Ramirez before Carlos Santana's line out to deep left ended the threat.

Bauer pitched another 1-2-3 inning in the second, but all of the outs came on batted balls.

Jason Kipnis was aboard with a walk to lead off the Indians' half of the second inning. After a Yandy Diaz strikeout, Kipnis stole second with catcher Roberto Perez at the plate. Perez eventually drew a walk, and then Francisco Lindor lined out to left for the second out.

Austin Jackson poked a two-out RBI single over the second base bag and into center field. Jose Ramirez drove a double down the left field line that scored Perez and Jackson. Edwin Encarnacion reached on an error and Jose was able to come around and score during the confusion. Jay Bruce blasted a homer into deep left-center to cap off the 6-run inning.

Bauer collected two more strikeouts in the top of the third inning. The Indians scored four more in the bottom of the frame, including a bases-clearing double by Encarnacion.

Yolmer Sanchez was the first White Sox to reach base, and he did so in a big way. He led off the top of the fourth inning with a homer. This turned out to be the Sox only run of the day. Bauer notched three more strikeouts before being relieved by Joe Smith in the top of the seventh.

With a 9-0 lead, the Tribe relievers cruised to a Friday-night victory and held on to home-field advantage heading into the playoffs.

The Indians narrowly missed being the fourth team in MLB history to have three starters with 200 strikeouts for the season. Kluber (265) and Carrasco (226) far surpassed the mark, with Bauer falling just short at 196.

Jose Ramirez' two doubles (55 on the year) gave him 90 Extra-base hits for the season. That put him 4th in Indians history for Extra-Base Hits. He trailed only Albert Belle (103 in 1995), Hal Trosky (96 in 1936) and George Burns (94 in 1926).

Game 161
October 9, 1910
St. Louis Attempts to Hand the Batting Title to Nap Lajoie

At the beginning of the 1910 season, Hugh Chalmers of the Chalmers Automobile Company pledged to give a Model 30 car to the player with the best batting average in either league.

Going into the last day of the season, Ty Cobb was leading the batting race by a healthy, but not insurmountable margin of .385 to Nap Lajoie's .376. Cobb was sitting out the final game of the season for Detroit claiming an eye ailment. The Naps and Lajoie would play a double-header at Sportsman's Park against the Browns.

Prior to the first game, St. Louis manager Jack O'Connor told third baseman Red Corriden to play back on the outfield grass. He reportedly told the rookie Corriden, "one of Lajoie's line drives might kill you."

During the first game of the day, Lajoie bunted three times up the third base line, reaching safely each time. He also hit a triple, but it was not enough as the Browns broke the 4-4 tie with a Walk-off hit in the bottom of the ninth.

In the second game, Corriden returned to his spot behind the cut of the infield grass. Knowing a good thing when he saw it, Lajoie laid down three more bunts up the line to go along with another infield single. In his fifth at-bat of the second game, Browns shortstop Bobby Wallace misplayed the ball. Lajoie beat his throw to first, but the play was scored as an error on Wallace.

Coach Harry Howell then sent a bat boy with a note to the official scorer, a woman named E.V. Parrish, with an offer of a bribe. Howell offered up a new suit of clothes if she would change her call and give Lajoie a 9 for 9 stat line for the double-header. Miss Parrish declined.

The Naps won the second game of the doubleheader to finish the season 71-81 in fifth place in the American League.

The next day, newspapers posted a wide variety of unofficial batting averages and declared Lajoie the winner. Critics of the cruel and impersonal Cobb rejoiced.

However, once *The Sporting News* crunched all of the numbers for the season, they put Cobb ahead .3850687 to Lajoie's .3840947. Commissioner Ban Johnson conducted an investigation and confirmed the result. Cobb was the batting champion. Ban Johnson insisted that both O'Connor and Howell be fired from the Browns. They were both effectively blacklisted from professional baseball for their tampering in the batting race.

Chalmers delivered Model 30's to both players, effectively calling the batting race a tie. However, even Chalmers may have had a preference for the more affable Lajoie. "I've always understood," Nap later said, "that the automobile I got ran a lot better than the one they gave to Ty."

Game 162
September 30, 2018
Four Starters have 200+ Strikeouts

The 2017 Indians set an MLB season record with 1,614 strikeouts by the entire pitching staff. They were the first team to maintain a strikeout rate of greater than ten per nine innings. The 2018 Indians picked up the strikeout mantle and ended up with another unique achievement.

Carlos Carrasco took the mound on the last day of the season against Eric Skoglund of the Royals.

Francisco Lindor reached on a fielding error by Skoglund when he dribbled the 3-1 pitch down the first base line. Lindor then stole second with Michael Brantley at the plate. Brantley struck out looking, but Lindor broke for third on the 1-1 pitch to Jose Ramirez. Royals catcher Eric Haas sailed the pickoff throw into left field. Lindor picked himself up and scampered home to give the Tribe a 1-0 lead.

Lindor led off the top of the third by golfing a strike low in the zone over the wall in left-center. His 38th homer of the season put the Indians up 2-0.

In the bottom of the fifth, Brian Goodwin got aboard with a single to left. He stole second and advanced to third on an Alcides Escobar groundout. Carrasco walked Brett Phillips and the Royals had runners at the corners. Meibrys Viloria hit a sharp ground ball back up the middle. It skipped over Carrasco's glove and into center field scoring Goodwin and cutting the Indians lead to 2-1.

To stay stretched out and set up the playoff rotation, Trevor Bauer came on to pitch in the bottom of the sixth. Carrasco's final line was one run on three hits and six strikeouts. This brought his season strikeout total to 231.

Bauer faced only fourteen Royals in four innings of work. His defense of the one run lead through the final four innings earned him his first (and still only) save. He added two strikeouts bringing his season sum to 221.

This game's pitchers along with Corey Kluber (222 strikeouts) and Mike Clevinger (207) comprised the first pitching staff to have four 200+ strikeout pitchers in the same year. Only three teams had previously had three 200+ K pitchers: the 1967 Twins, 1969 Astros, and 2013 Tigers. The 2017 Indians narrowly missed joining this club.

The overall pitching staff was 4th in the league in strikeouts with 1,544.

Reflection

Baseball is particularly suited to the long arc of history. We often read about records broken after 100 years or more. Unlikely streaks and seemingly impossible outcomes that occur despite the odds are played out for our enjoyment on grass and dirt. Baseball invites comparison, debate, and is best enjoyed across generations.

While this book takes in 120 years of baseball history, it will surely be out of date some day soon. As the games and years roll on, new records will be set, unlikely things will happen, and new stars will emerge. Some of these stories will be surpassed by even greater new ones. Maybe we will even see a World Series parade in Cleveland in this century.

It is my hope that these stories spark your own memories and encourage you to create new ones with the ones your love. If nothing else, you can always borrow the conversation starter that helped me to collect these stories:

"What is the most unique thing you ever saw at an Indians game?

Acknowledgements

First, I would like to thank my father Alex D. Harnocz for the initial concept for this book. This was supposed to be the Cavalier's Perfect Season—82 games would have been half as much work! I am thankful for the folks at Baseball-Reference.com, without the amazing resource they have built this would not be possible. To Millie Harnocz for her exceptional copy editing. Thanks to those who shared their personal anecdotes and connections to these games both in person and through the /r/clevelandindians community. Finally, to my wife Julie in appreciation for all her encouragement and patience.

Made in the USA
Monee, IL
27 February 2022

91971594R00177